# DATE DUE

| | | | |
|---|---|---|---|
| | | | |
| | | | |
| | | | |
| | | | |
| | | | |
| | | | |
| | | | |
| | | | |
| | | | |
| | | | |
| | | | |
| | | | |
| | | | |
| | | | |
| | | | |
| | | | |
| | | | |

DEMCO 38-296

*The Language of Banking*

# THE LANGUAGE
## OF
# BANKING

*Terms and Phrases Used
in the Financial Industry*

*by*
MICHAEL GORDON HALES

McFarland & Company, Inc., Publishers
*Jefferson, North Carolina, and London*

British Library Cataloguing-in-Publication data are available


Library of Congress Cataloguing-in-Publication Data

Hales, Michael G., 1946–
    The language of banking : terms and phrases used in the financial
industry / by Michael Gordon Hales.
        p.   cm.
    ISBN 0-89950-919-3 (lib. bdg. : 50# alk. paper) ∞
    1. Finance—Dictionaries.   I. Title.
HG151.H345   1994
332′.03 — dc20                                                    94-3646
                                                                      CIP

*McFarland & Company, Inc., Publishers*
  *Box 611, Jefferson, North Carolina 28640*

To my beloved wife,
my pride and joy,
DIANE,
with all my love


And a special dedication to
Caitlin Michelle Dozack
and
Nicholas David Camarda

# Introduction

On a recent sun-drenched afternoon in Santa Monica, California, an audience of several hundred bankers were preparing to listen to a luncheon keynote address by Lawrence Lindsey, distinguished member of the Board of Governors of the Federal Reserve. The forum was a conference on community reinvestment, and its participants came from throughout the United States to learn how to better serve the needs of their respective communities.

The general mood of the conference was that of pride in the efforts undertaken by lending institutions to increase the availability of credit to all sectors of the community. Certain banks, thrifts and credit unions were applauded for their individual programs designed to reach out to small businesses and low- and moderate-income consumers. The participants were basking in a warm combination of Southern California sunshine and a sense of accomplishment. Discrimination in lending was hailed as a thing of the past, the nightmare of a bygone era.

Not, however, according to the Federal Reserve. Not according to the scores of consumers and small business owners who are regularly denied access to credit and other financial services simply because they do not understand the language in which those products and services are described and offered. Governor Lindsey cited one embarrassing illustration after another of the confusion and frustration endured by even highly educated consumers in their effort to obtain credit.

Even the United States' best universities do not prepare their graduates with a working knowledge of terms such as "adjustment period," "APR," "ARM," "index rate," "margin," "caps," "buy-downs," "conversion clauses," "negative amortization" and "points." And the understanding of these terms is crucial just to exercise the American Dream — to buy a house!

The financial services industry is guilty of *unconscious discrimination* and the problem is getting more serious. Only the military and aerospace industries employ more acronyms than bankers and only the computer industry has coined more phrases and invented more definitions. The paradox is clear: In a concentrated effort to better serve the public, bankers have more thoroughly confused us.

*The Language of Banking* was prepared as an antidote for unconscious discrimination. It is a guidebook for unwary consumers and business owners who find themselves immersed in a foreign land where everyone to whom they must reach out for help speaks a foreign language. It is also designed as a working reference tool for students of finance, accounting and economics.

Banking and finance "dictionaries" of several hundred pages in length and several thousand entries are readily available to the inquiring consumer and student. *The Language of Banking,* however, was compiled with a different objective in mind: to provide understandable explanations of those terms and phrases which are most commonly found in practical financial transactions such as deposits and withdrawals, savings and investments, borrowing money, trust department services,

1

and foreign exchange. Terms and phrases which are outside of this scope of banking functions have been intentionally omitted.

Finally, the term "banking" itself has changed over recent years. To the consumer, the distinction between commercial banks, savings and loan associations, credit unions, mutual savings banks and trust companies has vanished. In the 1990s, just about any institution that accepts deposits, cashes checks and lends money is a "bank." "Banking" is a broad function, and *The Language of Banking* is designed to better define the components of that function.

Michael Gordon Hales
Laguna Hills, California
1994

# THE LANGUAGE
OF
# BANKING

# A

**ABA**   SEE AMERICAN BANKERS ASSOCIATION.

**ABA NUMBER**   SEE AMERICAN BANKERS ASSOCIATION (ABA) NUMBER.

**ABILITY TO PAY**   The general determination by a lender of the borrower's financial capability to pay back the amount borrowed. Used frequently as a criterion in approving or denying consumer installment loans. A common formula for calculating the borrower's ability to pay is:

| | |
|---|---|
| Net monthly income: | $_____ |
| less: rent or mortgage | _____ |
| other loan payments | _____ |
| revolving charge payments | _____ |
| utilities | _____ |
| food | _____ |
| miscellaneous other | _____ |
| Net income less expenses | _____ |
| Requested monthly loan payment | _____ |
| Balance or excess | _____ |

**ABSOLUTE PRIORITY**   A concept favoring the rights of creditors by requiring that they be satisfied prior to the rights of stockholders in corporate reorganizations or liquidations.

**ABSTRACT OF TITLE**   A document which traces the history of ownership of real property from the first recorded ownership through successive transfers to present ownership.

**ACADEMIC CONSULTANTS**   An advisory group initiated by the Board of Governors of the Federal Reserve System in the 1960s to provide a forum for the exchange of views between the Board and members of the academic community in economics and banking.

**ACCELERATED DEPRECIATION**   Depreciation at a higher than normal rate making the tax allowance sooner and more beneficial to the owner.

**ACCELERATION**   If an installment obligation goes into default, all remaining payments of principal and interest can become immediately due and payable. If certain covenants or conditions of any loan are breached prior to maturity, the entire unpaid balance may become due and payable. For example, the provisions of a loan may include an acceleration clause stating that, among other things, the borrower must maintain adequate fire insurance coverage protecting the collateral and naming the lender as loss payee. Failure to renew fire insurance protection during the term of the loan may be a breach of that condition. Relying on the acceleration clause, the lender may sue on the entire unpaid balance even though the loan has not yet matured.

**ACCELERATION CLAUSE**   A clause in a loan agreement that permits a creditor to demand principal payment ahead of schedule if the borrower violates other promises or fails to perform.

**ACCEPTANCE**   As defined by Article 3-310 of the Uniform Commercial Code, the drawee's signed engagement to honor the draft as presented. It must be written on the draft, and may consist of his signature alone. It becomes operative when completed by delivery and notification. A draft may be accepted although it has not been signed by the drawer or is otherwise incomplete or is overdue or has been dishonored. Where the draft is payable at a fixed period after sight and the acceptor fails to date his acceptance the holder may complete it by supplying a date in good faith. Where the drawee's proffered acceptance in any manner carries the draft as presented the holder may refuse the acceptance and treat the draft as dishonored in which case the drawee is entitled to have his acceptance cancelled. The terms of the draft are not carried by an acceptance to pay at any particular bank or place in the United States, unless the acceptance states that the draft is to be paid only at such bank or place. Where the holder assents to an acceptance varying the terms of the draft each drawer and endorser who does not affirmatively assent is discharged (UCC Sec. 3-412).

**ACCOMMODATION ENDORSEMENT**   A specific guarantee to induce a lender to make a loan to another party who may not qualify for the loan on his or her own merits. The accommodation endorser guarantees the fulfillment of the contract and becomes liable to the lender should the borrower default. A promissory note which has received an accommodation endorsement is commonly referred to as an accommodation note. The accommodation party is the person who signs the note as maker, drawer, acceptor or endorser, thus guaranteeing performance of the borrower under the terms of the note.

**ACCOUNT**   Used in a variety of ways, "account" generally refers to the credit established against which debits may be made. Types of accounts may include checking, savings, NOW, money market, IRA, and so forth. For example, the Electronic Fund Transfer Act defines "account" as a "demand deposit (checking), savings, or other consumer asset account (other than an occasional or incidental credit balance in a credit plan) held either directly or indirectly by a financial institution and established primarily for personal, family or household purposes. "The Equal Credit Opportunity Act defines "account" as an extension of credit.

**ACCOUNT ANALYSIS**   The determination of the profitability or expense of maintaining an account during a certain period. An account analysis may calculate the bank's earnings on the collected average daily balance, then subtract therefrom certain activity charges such as costs related to processing deposits, returns, night depository fees or other component charges in order to determine profit or loss of maintaining the account for a certain period. For example:

ABC WHOOPIT MANUFACTURING, INC.          ACCT. 1234567890
150 MOUNTAIN INCLINE                                NOVEMBER 1990
SHADOW VILLAGE, NV.

*Balance Information*

| | |
|---|---|
| Average Daily Balance | $10,961 |
| less avg. daily float | 1,032 |
| less 12% reserve requirement | 1,192 |
| Adjusted Average Daily Balance | 8,738 |

## 6 • Account

*Account Activity*

| ACTIVITY | VOLUME | @ | TOTAL |
|---|---|---|---|
| Monthly Charge | 1 | 10.00 | 10.00 |
| FDIC per $1000 | 10 | 5.787% | 0.58 |
| Deposits | 40 | 1.100 | 44.00 |
| Cash deposited per $1000 | 11 | 1.000 | 11.00 |
| Proofed: on-us | 18 | 0.075 | 1.35 |
| Proofed: ACH | 728 | 0.080 | 58.24 |
| Proofed: other | 857 | 0.090 | 77.13 |
| Proofed: other | 77 | 0.120 | 9.24 |
| Returns | 7 | 3.000 | 21.00 |
| Debits posted | 170 | 0.120 | 20.40 |
| Night depository | 1 | 2.000 | 2.00 |
| Error correction | 2 | 1.000 | 2.00 |
| TOTAL SERVICES PROVIDED | | | 256.94 |

*Analysis Summary*

| | |
|---|---|
| Account earnings | $ |
| Less total price of services | 256.94 |
| Profit/Loss | |

**ACCOUNT RECONCILIATION**   The utilization of the auxiliary "on-us" field in the check MICR line to produce a list which includes the number and sum of paid and outstanding checks in numerical sequence. This assists high volume accounts in the reconcilement of customer and bank records.

**ACCOUNT SERVICING BANK**   A bank that services an account for the account owner bank. Also known as the "due from" bank.

**ACCOUNTS PAYABLE**   The amount owed creditors for goods or services, normal recurring bills such as utilities, other bills such as attorney's fees or insurance premiums, education, travel, entertainment, conferences and other obligations generally due in less than one year. A current liability, accounts payable represents the amount owed to a creditor or creditors for services rendered or merchandise purchased on open-end or short term credit.

**ACCOUNTS RECEIVABLE**   Generally, money due from sales or services rendered to customers. Accounts receivable may be used to secure a commercial loan ("accounts receivable financing") or sold to a third party for working capital ("factoring"). Accounts receivable are deemed current assets if collectable within one year and generally provide a company with its primary source of working capital. During financial analysis, accounts receivable are used to determine the acid test or "quick" ratio and the "sales to receivables" ratio which represents the average collection period the company must wait after making a sale before receiving cash. To calculate the sales to receivables ratio, annual sales are divided by 360 to determine the average daily sales. The average daily sales are then divided into accounts receivable to determine the average collection period. For example, the ABC Company has annual sales of $1.3 million. The average daily sales ($1.3 million divided by 360) are $3,611. ABC Company's accounts receivable as of January 1 total $325,000. By dividing accounts receivable ($325,000) by the average daily sales ($3,611) we see that ABC Company's average collection period (the average number of days it takes for ABC Company to receive payment after a sale) is 90 days.

**ACCRUAL BASIS**   An accounting principle by which revenue is recorded at the time it is earned and expenses are recorded as soon as they result in a liability, regardless of the date of actual payment or collection. For example, accrued expenses are those which are known and enforceable, even if not yet due and payable; such as when goods have been delivered and used prior to payment for them. Accrued income, however, is income earned but not yet received.

**ACH**   SEE AUTOMATED CLEARINGHOUSE.

**ACID TEST RATIO**   Cash plus receivables plus marketable securities divided by current liabilities. A measure of financial health, the ratio asks: "how would this borrower repay the loan if sales stopped completely?" Also commonly referred to as the "quick ratio," the acid test ratio is used by credit analysts to determine a borrowing company's ability to meet its current and short term obligations. The acid test ratio groups liquid current assets by adding together cash on hand, qualified accounts receivable and marketable securities and dividing the total by current liabilities. For example: ABC Company has cash on hand totaling $15,450; accounts receivable are $235,700 and marketable securities have a present value of $95,825. The company's current liabilities, consisting of a completely drawn down line of credit in the amount of $100,000 and other liabilities due in less than one year in the amount of $65,750. Cash, receivables and marketable securities divided by current debt ($346,975 / $165,750 = 2.0933) equals a ratio of 2.09 : 1. This means that ABC Company's liquid assets could be used to satisfy its current debt obligations if necessary.

**ACKNOWLEDGMENT**   A written or wired notification that an item has been received and, generally, that it is available for immediate payment.

**ACQUITTANCE**   A written evidence or notification of the discharge of a debt.

**ACTION TO QUIET TITLE**   A legal process whereby any person who claims an interest in real property which is not in the possession of another may bring a suit in equity against another person who claims a similar interest in the property to determine the right, title and interest of the parties.

**ACTIVITY CHARGE**   A charge imposed by banks against depositors for checks or deposits (debit or credit activity). SEE ALSO ACCOUNT ANALYSIS.

**ADD-ON INTEREST RATE**   An installment lending technique where the finance charges are computed by adding the interest payable to the full amount of loan principal. Ten percent add-on means $10 interest per $100 per year. The add-on rate method gives artificially low interest rate figures, but may be quite accurate in determining the dollar cost of the loan. The add-on rate may be calculated using the following formula which is generally accurate for loan terms of three years or less:

$$\text{add-on rate} = APR \times \frac{\text{(the number of months of the loan} + 1)}{\text{twice the number of months of the loan}}$$

or

$$\text{add-on rate} = \frac{\text{APR } (n + 1)}{2n}$$

Thus, a one-year loan at 19.5 APR would convert to an add-on rate of 10.6% as follows:

$$\text{add-on rate} = \frac{19.5 \ (12 + 1)}{2 \times 12} = \frac{19.5 \ (13)}{24} = 10.6\%$$

Borrowers could easily calculate that a $2000 loan at 10.6% add-on for 12 months could cost $212 in interest and monthly payments would be approximately $184.33.

**ADJUSTABLE RATE MORTGAGE (ARM)** Any loan made to finance or refinance the purchase of, and secured by a lien on, a 1 to 4 family dwelling, including a condominium unit, cooperative housing unit, or a mobile home where such loan is made pursuant to an agreement intended to enable the lender to adjust the rate of interest from time to time. ARM loans include (1) loan agreements where the note and/or other loan documents expressly provide for adjusting the interest rate at periodic intervals, and (2) fixed rate mortgage loan agreements that implicitly permit rate adjustment by having the note mature on demand or at the end of an interval shorter than the term of the amortization schedule unless there has clearly been made no promise to refinance the loan (when demand is made or at maturity) and all disclosure requirements have been met.

**ADJUSTMENT PERIOD** The period between one rate change and the next. With most adjustable rate mortgages, the interest rate and monthly payment change every year, every 3 years, or every 5 years. However, some ARMs have more frequent interest and payment changes. Therefore, a loan with an adjustment period of 3 years is referred to as a "3-year ARM" and the interest rate can change once every 3 years.

**ADMINISTRATOR** A person or a bank appointed by an appropriate court to manage and distribute the estate of a person who either died without leaving a will or whose will did not name an executor. Generally, then, when an executor has not been named by the deceased, an administrator will be appointed by the court. An *administrator ad colligendum* is one appointed to collect foreign assets. An *administrator de bonis non* refers to the individual or bank appointed to complete the settlement of an estate when the administrator originally named in the will has failed to complete the duties. An *administrator durante absentia* is appointed by the court to serve as a substitute for the administrator or executor who for some reason is temporarily absent. An *administrator pendente lite* is one appointed to protect the assets of an estate during legal contest of the will or legal disagreement over the appointment of an administrator or executor.

**ADVERSE ACTION** The refusal to grant credit in substantially the amount or on substantially the terms requested in an application unless the creditor makes a counteroffer (to grant credit in a different amount or on other terms) and the applicant uses or expressly accepts the credit offered. It can also refer to the termination of an account or an unfavorable change in the terms of an account that does not affect all or a substantial portion of a class of the creditor's accounts; or a refusal to increase the amount of credit available to an applicant who has made an application for an increase. The term does not include a change in the terms of an account expressly agreed to by an applicant; any action or forbearance relating to an account taken in connection with inactivity, default, or delinquency as to that account; a refusal or failure to authorize an account transaction at a point of sale or loan, except when the refusal is a termination or an unfavorable change in the terms of an account that does not affect all or a substantial portion of a class of the creditor's accounts, or when the refusal is a denial of an application for an increase in the amount of credit available under the account; a refusal to extend credit because applicable law prohibits the creditor from extending the credit requested; or (5) a refusal to extend credit because the creditor does not offer the type of credit or credit plan requested.

**ADVERSE ACTION LETTER**  Once adverse action has been taken by a lender, the Equal Credit Opportunity Act, as implemented by federal Regulation B, requires written notification to the borrower. This written notification is commonly referred to as an "adverse action letter" and its content is prescribed by federal Regulation B. SEE ALSO REGULATION B.

**ADVICE**  Generally, a written memorandum of activity affecting a loan or deposit account such as a credit advice, debit advice, or advice of payment.

**ADVISORY COMMITTEES**  A committee of the Federal Reserve Board. To help it deal with its complex and varied responsibilities, the Federal Reserve System makes use of advisory and working committees. The Federal Reserve Act provides for a Federal Advisory Council consisting of one member from each Federal Reserve District. The board of directors of each Reserve Bank annually selects one council member, usually a prominent banker in the District. The council is required by law to meet in Washington, DC, at least four times a year. It confers with the Board of Governors on economic and banking developments and makes recommendations regarding the activities of the Federal Reserve System.

Another statutory advisory group is the Consumer Advisory Council, which usually meets with the Board of Governors four times each year. The council has thirty members. Some represent the interests of the financial industry and consumers, and some are academic and legal specialists in consumer matters.

After passage of the Depository Institutions Deregulation and Monetary Control Act of 1980, the Board of Governors established the Thrift Institutions Advisory Council, whose purpose is to provide information and views on the special needs and problems of thrift institutions. This advisory group comprises representatives of savings banks, savings and loan associations, and credit unions.

**AFGHANI**  Monetary unit of Afghanistan.

**AFRICAN DEVELOPMENT BANK**  The Abidjan, Ivory Coast headquartered bank which was formed in 1964 to help provide development capital for Africa.

**AFTERNOON**  As defined by the Uniform Commercial Code, Section 4-104, the period of a day between noon and midnight.

**AGENT**  An individual or corporation authorized to act on behalf of another person who is the principal. A bank may also be appointed as an agent.

**AGREEMENT CORPORATION**  A federally or state-chartered corporation that has entered into an agreement or understanding with the Board of Governors of the Federal Reserve System that it will not exercise any power that is impermissible for an Edge Act corporation.

**AGRIBUSINESS**  The business of agriculture. This relatively modern term is used to encompass businesses directly involved in or related to farming and ranching, recognizing agriculture as a major force of the economy.

**ALL-SAVERS CERTIFICATES**  A now defunct certificate of deposit which offered high yield while exempting from federal income taxation the first $1,000 of interest income ($2,000 on a joint return). All-Savers certificates were created under the Economic Recovery Tax Act of 1981.

**ALTERATION**  A change by rewriting, erasing, or otherwise modifying the terms of a check or other negotiable instrument. An altered check is one in which the date, payee or amount has been modified. According to Uniform Commercial Code Article 3-407, "(1) Any alteration of an instrument is material which changes the contract of any party thereto in any respect, including such change in (a) the number or relations of the parties; or (b) an incomplete instrument, by completing it otherwise than as authorized; or (c) the writing as signed, by adding to it or by removing any part of it. (2) As against any person other than a subsequent holder in due course: (a) alteration by the holder which is both fraudulent and material discharges any party whose contract is thereby changed unless that party assents or is precluded from asserting the defense; (b) no other alteration discharges any party and the instrument may be enforced according to its original tenor, or as to incomplete instruments according to the authority given. (3) A subsequent holder in due course may in all cases enforce the instrument according to its original tenor, and when an incomplete instrument has been completed, he may enforce it as completed." A material alteration does not discharge any party unless it is made by the holder. Spoilation by any meddling stranger does not affect the rights of the holder. It is, of course, intended that the acts of the holder's authorized agent or employee, or of his confederates, are to be attributed to him. A material alteration does not discharge any party unless it is made for a fraudulent purpose. There is no discharge where a blank is filled in the honest belief that it is as authorized; or where a change is made with a benevolent motive such as a desire to give the obligor the benefit of a lower interest rate. Changes favorable to the obligor are unlikely to be made with any fraudulent intent; but, if such an intent is found, the alteration may operate as a discharge.

**ALTERNATIVE PRICING**  A choice given to a borrower between paying interest "tied to prime," that is, at a fixed percentage point spread over the bank's prime lending rate, or at a fixed percentage point spread over the rate the bank is paying on selected certificates of deposit.

**AMERICAN BANKERS ASSOCIATION**  The national banking trade association. The American Bankers Association was formed in 1875 to "promote the general welfare and usefulness of banks and financial institutions" and seeks to keep its members aware of developments affecting the industry, to help educate bank personnel, to pursue improvements in bank management and services, and to represent the interests of commercial banks to government.

**AMERICAN BANKERS ASSOCIATION**  The national banking trade association. The American Bankers Association was formed in 1875 to "promote the general welfare and usefulness of banks and financial institutions" and seeks to keep its members aware of developments affecting the industry, to help educate bank personnel, to pursue improvements in bank management and services, and to represent the interests of commercial banks to government.

**AMERICAN BANKERS ASSOCIATION NUMBER** The 9-digit number located in the MICR line of every check and the fractional number found in the upper right hand corner. In the MICR line, the first two digits designate the Federal Reserve district on which the check is drawn; the third and fourth digits designate the paying bank's reserve bank and classify the bank into "city," "regional" or "country" Federal Reserve Clearing categories. The following four digits, the bank's ABA suffix, identify the specific bank or branch. The final digit is the check digit, a suffix digit by which a computer, through a programmed mathematical formula, can test the validity of an account number. In the upper right-hand corner, the first group of hyphenated digits designates the location of the bank, the second designates the bank's name and the third (below the line) designates the Federal Reserve district and area within the district.

**AMORTIZATION**  The gradual and systematic reduction of debt by application of equal periodic payments. Such payments generally must be sufficient to recompense current interest due during the repayment period and to repay the entire principal by the time the loan reaches maturity. An amortization schedule is a table which shows the amounts of principal and interest due at regular intervals and the corresponding unpaid principal balance at the time each installment payment is made.

**AMOUNT FINANCED**  The amount financed is the net amount of credit extended and, since it must be used to calculate the annual percentage rate accurately, its correct value must be obtained and disclosed. To calculate the amount financed, all amounts and charges connected with the transaction either paid separately or included in the contractual obligation must be determined. For example: a consumer signs a note secured by real property in the amount of $5,435. The note amount includes $5,000 proceeds disbursed to the consumer, $400 in precomputed interest, $25 paid to a credit reporting agency for a credit report, and a $10 service charge. Additionally, the consumer pays a $50 loan fee separately in cash at consummation. The consumer has no other debt with the bank. The amount financed is $4,975. The amount financed may be calculated by first subtracting all finance charges included in the note amount ($5,435 less $400 less $10 = $5,025). The $25 credit report is not a finance charge because the loan is secured by real property. The $5,025 is further reduced by the amount of prepaid finance charges paid separately, for an amount financed of $5,025 less $50 = $4,975. When the amount financed is itemized, all prepaid finance charges must be shown as a total amount (although they may be further itemized and described at the option of the lender) even if portions of the total are also reflected elsewhere in the documentation. For example, prepaid credit guarantee insurance premiums paid to third parties are prepaid finance charges that must be included in the prepaid finance charge total, even if shown elsewhere.

**ANNUAL PERCENTAGE RATE (APR)**    The annual percentage rate is the cost of consumer credit expressed in simple annual interest percentage terms. There are two acceptable methods for calculating annual percentage rate: the "actuarial" method and the "U.S. Rule." Either will produce virtually the same results and understanding the difference in mathematical computations is not important. Note, however, that these methods establish the approved standard. For example, any disclosed APR on a closed end credit that deviates by more than 1/8 or 1 percent above or below the standard is inaccurate and constitutes a violation of disclosure under federal Regulation Z. The Federal Reserve Board rate tables are the more practical method of computing annual percentage rate. An APR determined in accordance with the Federal Reserve Rate table instructions will comply with the requirements of Regulation Z. Volume I of the tables applies to single-advance transactions involving up to 480 monthly payments or 104 weekly payments. It may be used for regular transactions and for any of the following irregularities: irregular first period, irregular first payment, irregular final payment.

Volume II applies to transactions involving multiple advances and any type of payment or period irregularity. An estimated annual percentage rate may be made in accordance with the following example: A multi-advance construction loan with a commitment amount of $110,000 is made on May 19. There are two points and a $1000 loan origination fee that are both prepaid finance charges. The construction period is eight months and the contract interest rate is 13.5 percent. Interest is payable on the amount actually advanced for the time it is outstanding. The amount advanced is $55,000. The estimated finance charge is:

$4950 (interest on $55,000 at 13.5% for 8 months)
+ $3200 (2 points plus $1000 loan origination fee)
$8150 estimated finance charge. Regulation Z requires that the borrower be provided with the estimated annual percentage rate and provides the following formula:

$$\text{estimated APR} = \frac{\text{estimated finance charge} \times 100}{\text{amount financed} - \text{prepaid finance chg}} \div \text{term} \times 12$$

or

$$\text{estimated APR} = \frac{\$8150 \times 100}{\$55,000 - 3200} \div 8 \times 12 = 23.60 \text{ percent}$$

**ANNUITY**    A fixed dollar amount paid over a specific period of time.

**APPLICANT**    Any person who requests or who has received an extension of credit from a creditor. Included in this definition is any person who is or may become contractually liable for an extension of credit including guarantors, sureties, endorsers and similar parties.

**APPLICATION**    An oral or written request for an extension of credit that is made in accordance with procedures established by a creditor for the type of credit requested. The term does not include the use of an account or line of credit to obtain an amount of credit that is within a previously established credit limit. A "completed application" means an application in connection with which a creditor has received all the information that the creditor regularly receives and considers in evaluating applications for the amount and type of credit requested (including, but not limited to credit reports, any additional information requested from the applicant, and any approvals or reports by government agencies or other persons that are necessary to guarantee, insure, or provide security for the credit or collateral). The creditor shall exercise reasonable diligence in obtaining such information.

**APR**   SEE ANNUAL PERCENTAGE RATE.

**ARM**   SEE ADJUSTABLE RATE MORTGAGE.

**ARTICLES OF INCORPORATION**   A document filed by those persons or that person intending to incorporate with the secretary of state or other appropriate state agency.

**ASSETS**   The resources and property owned by an individual or business including, for example, cash, accounts receivable, inventories, equipment, machinery, stocks and bonds, household furniture, jewelry, objects of art, real estate, patents and other tangible and intangible property, real and personal, that has commercial or exchange value.

**ASSIGNED ACCOUNT**   Generally an account receivable pledged as collateral for a loan. Under usual circumstances, the payor, as a customer of the borrower, is unaware of the assignment which is strictly an agreement between the borrower and the bank. May also be referred to as an "assigned book account."

**ASSIGNED BOOK ACCOUNT**   SEE ASSIGNED ACCOUNT.

**ATM**   SEE AUTOMATED TELLER MACHINE.

**ATS**   SEE AUTOMATIC TRANSFER SERVICE.

**ATTESTATION**   The act of bearing witness for another in order to authenticate a document.

**AUDIT**   The periodic examination of the assets, liabilities, income and expenses of a company.

**AUTHORIZATION CODE**   A numeric code provided, upon request, to a merchant. The code signifies the bank's approval and authorization of a specific charge to a credit card account. Also used to authorize a cash advance on a credit card account, the authorization code is generally issued by an authorization center which, by checking a cardholder account with the card issuing bank, can determine if sufficient credit exists to authorize a particular transaction.

**AUTOMATED CLEARINGHOUSE (ACH)**   An association of banks in a certain geographic area formed to exchange checks and drafts drawn on each other. While automated clearinghouses electronically process interbank credits and debits, they may also handle the direct deposit of Social Security payments, automatic payroll deposits and preauthorized payments. A computer-based clearing and settlement operation often operated by a Federal Reserve Bank, ACHs were established for the exchange of electronic transactions among participating depository institutions. Such electronic transactions can be substituted for paper checks used to make recurring payments such as payroll or preauthorized insurance premiums. The U.S. Treasury uses the ACH extensively to pay certain obligations of the government.

An automated clearinghouse processes and delivers electronic debit and credit payments among participating depository institutions. Electronic debits include preauthorized cash concentration debits, insurance premiums and mortgage payments deducted from a customer's account at a depository institution. Electronic credits include preauthorized corporate trade payments, direct deposit of paychecks and corporate dividends added to a customer's account at a depository institution. Participating institutions are primarily commercial banks, savings banks, savings and loan associations, credit unions, and foreign bank branches and agencies in the United States.

ACHs are similar to check clearing houses. However, at a check clearing house member institutions exchange presorted packages of checks drawn against each other. At an ACH, member institutions deliver magnetic tapes, or other computer-acceptable records, containing payment instructions for sorting and subsequent delivery to other participating institutions. There are 28 automated clearing houses in the United States serving more than 24,000 receiving depository institutions. Since 1978, all ACHs have participated in an interregional network that enables an ACH to exchange electronic payments with others throughout the nation. Previously, an ACH could only receive and exchange payments for institutions located in the area it served.

Annually more than 925 million ACH payments were made through, or by, ACHs. Of those, 407 million payments were originated by the federal government and almost 518 million were originated by the private sector.

There are at least five participants in an ACH transaction. The first is the customer or employee, who authorizes electronic entries to be applied to an account at a depository institution. For example, a customer may authorize a company to withdraw funds electronically from a bank account, on a specified day, to pay recurring bills. Alternatively, an employee may authorize a company to electronically deposit checks into the employee's account on paydays.

The second participant is a company, which introduces the electronic payment data into the "banking system" through its depository institution. The company originates the ACH payments data.

The third participant is the originating depository institution, which receives the electronic payment data from the company. The originating depository institution retains the payments to be applied to accounts of its customers and forwards the remaining electronic payments to ACH.

The fourth component is the ACH, which receives the electronic entries from the originating depository institution and processes and delivers the electronic payments to the appropriate receiving depository institution. Settlement is made on the books of a Reserve Bank. The ACH transmits to electronic entries for institutions served by other ACHs to the appropriate ACH.

The final participant is the receiving depository institution, which receives the electronic entries from the ACH and posts them to the accounts of its customers.

Thus, ACHs enable speedier payments and reductions in costs for participating institutions. The originating and receiving institutions handle payroll and bill payments in electronic form, reducing personnel costs normally associated with handling large amounts of paper. Likewise, companies that pay their employees through direct deposit eliminate the lost time the employees incur in depositing payroll checks during working hours and reduce the costs of distributing paychecks by mail or courier. Consumers also benefit by having paychecks or federal recurring payments deposited directly and safely in their depository institutions, or by having recurring bills paid automatically, without having to write a check or deliver cash.

**AUTOMATED TELLER MACHINE (ATM)**   A machine that provides a variety of banking services, such as accepting deposits, dispensing cash withdrawals, transferring funds between accounts, making cash advances, processing loan payments, providing account balance information, and so forth. ATMs may be located inside the bank lobby, or in exterior walls or remote locations in order to provide 24 hour, 7 days a week service. ATMs are usually accessed by the insertion of an "ATM card" (which is generally an embossed plastic card with a magnetic stripe) and a personal identification number (PIN) which is entered by the user on a key pad. Automated teller machines are differentiated from cash dispensers in that the functions of the latter are limited to account inquiry and funds withdrawal only. Other terms sometimes used to describe such teminals are customer-bank communications terminal (CBCT) and remote service unit (RSU). Groups of banks sometimes share ATM networks located throughout a region of the country that may include portions of several states.

**AUTOMATIC DEPOSIT PLAN**   Funds deposited by payor electronically to payee. Popular among Social Security recipients and employees of companies whose bank provides automated payroll processing, funds in an automatic deposit plan are deposited directly to a prearranged account. Also referred to as "direct deposit," this form of crediting transaction accounts is becoming increasingly preferred. SEE ALSO DIRECT DEPOSIT.

**AUTOMATIC TRANSFER SERVICE (ATS) ACCOUNT**   A depositor's savings account from which funds may be transferred automatically to the same depositor's checking account to cover a check written or to maintain a minimum balance.

**AVAILABILITY DATE**   The date on which deposited funds are deemed collected and available for withdrawal. Under the provisions of the Expedited Funds Availability Act (Federal Reserve Regulation CC), availability schedules which indicate the time that must pass before certain deposited funds may be available for withdrawal, must be made available to bank customers in prescribed format.

**AVERAGE DAILY BALANCE**   The average amount kept on deposit in a customer's account as determined by adding the daily balances for a set period then dividing the total by the number of days in the period. The portion of the average daily balance that is uncollected is referred to as average daily float and is subtracted to determine the average collected balance. SEE ACCOUNT ANALYSIS.

**AVERAGE TAX RATE**   The sum of all the tax rates that are applied to income divided by the number of rates applied.

# *B*

**BAHT**   Monetary unit of Thailand.

**BALANCE SHEET** A statement of financial position that shows the assets, liabilities and net worth of a business.

**BALBOA**   Monetary unit of Panama.

**BALLOON PAYMENT** The final payment on a loan which may be larger than a regular payment because the loan is not fully amortized.

**BANK FOR INTERNATIONAL SETTLEMENTS (BIS)** The BIS, located in Basel, Switzerland, was established in 1930 to administer the post–World War I reparations agreements. Since the 1960s, the BIS has evolved into an important international monetary institution, and has provided a forum in which central bankers meet and consult on a monthly basis. As an independent financial organization, the BIS performs a variety of banking, trustee, and agent functions, primarily with central banks. At present the BIS has 29 members, 28 of which are central banks. The Federal Reserve is represented at BIS meetings, but is not a member. The BIS is the only international financial institution in which most Eastern European countries are members.

**BANK HOLDING COMPANIES** A form of bank ownership which provides an alternative to individuals directly owning bank stock. In general, a bank holding company is any company, corporation, or business entity that owns stock in a bank or controls the operation of a bank through other means. Individual investors then hold stock in the parent holding company instead of directly owning bank stock. Although this bank ownership role broadly defines bank holding companies, other functions are also important in describing these companies. For example, the holding company structure provides a means for acquiring additional banks or for expanding into a wider range of activities. Holding companies further offer a way of consolidating management and operations across these various interests.

Because of such functions, bank holding companies have become the dominant form of bank ownership over the last fifteen years. By 1984, 5619 bank holding companies were in operation and controlled banks that held 89 percent of the total deposits of commercial banks in the United States. Moreover, holding companies have been popular among all sizes of banking organizations. For larger organizations, the principal benefits of holding companies have been in the acquisition of additional banks, expansion into permissible nonbanking activities, better access to funds, and the consolidation of certain functions for more efficient operations. Smaller holding companies, however, are often formed because of consolidated tax benefits, control or estate considerations, or the need to provide additional services to local communities. As a result of widespread holding company growth, such companies greatly influence the structure of U.S. banking, the operation and management of banks, and the types of activities conducted by banking organizations.

The Bank Holding Company Act of 1956 and the 1970 amendments to this act establish the legal framework under which bank holding companies operate. In drafting the 1956 act, Congress had several purposes in mind, some of which were also reflected in the 1970 amendments:

- Control the creation and expansion of bank holding companies
- Separate bank holding companies' business of managing and controlling banks from unrelated nonbanking business
- Promote competition in banking and minimize the danger inherent in concentration of economic power through centralized control of banks
- Subject bank holding companies to examination and regulation.

To accomplish these purposes, the Bank Holding Company Act of 1956 extended Federal Reserve regulation and supervision to companies that owned or controlled two or more banks. One-bank holding companies were brought under Federal Reserve supervision when Congress passed the 1970 amendments. Together, these two pieces of legislation define bank holding companies and set the general standards for holding company formations, acquisition of additional banks, and expansion into nonbanking activities.

The act defines any company that has control over a bank as a bank holding company. A company is judged to control a bank if it: (1) directly or indirectly owns, controls, or has power to vote at least 25 percent of any class of the bank's voting stock; (2) controls in any manner the election of a majority of a bank's directors; or (3) is judged by the Federal Reserve Board to exert a controlling influence over bank management or policies through other means. The term company includes corporations, partnerships, associations, or long-term trusts, but does not extend to bank ownership by individuals. Also, to be termed a bank in the bank holding company definition above, an institution must both accept deposits legally withdrawable on demand and make commercial loans. Thus, a company controlling institutions which do not perform both of these functions would not be treated as a bank holding company. Institutions insured by the Federal Savings and Loan Insurance Corporation or chartered by the Federal Home Loan Bank Board are also excluded from being banks.

Before a company can become a bank holding company or acquire additional banks, it must apply to the Federal Reserve System and receive approval for its proposal. The Federal Reserve, in deciding upon such applications, must evaluate the competitive effects of any proposal. Other factors the Federal Reserve must consider are "the financial and managerial resources and future prospects of the company or companies and the banks concerned, and the convenience and needs of the community to be served."

Bank holding company formations and bank acquisitions must also be consistent with state law. For example, the laws of a particular state will determine whether holding companies in that state may expand statewide and whether limits exist on the number of banks or share of state deposits they can acquire. In addition, the Douglas Amendment to the Bank Holding Company Act prohibits a holding company from acquiring a bank in another state unless the laws of that state specifically authorize such acquisitions. Thus, state laws influence a holding company's expansion both within a state and across state lines.

To separate banking from unrelated nonbanking activities, the Bank Holding Company Act prohibits holding companies from owning or controlling nonbanking interests except under limited circumstances. The most important exception to this prohibition is for activities the Federal Reserve Board determines "to be so closely related to banking or managing or controlling banks as to be a proper incident thereto." In implementing this provision of the act, the Board has constructed a list of permissible nonbanking activities and reviews other activities on a case by case basis. Before a company can engage in such activities, it must first file a notice or application with the Federal Reserve. Examples of nonbanking activities conducted by bank holding companies are found in Section 225.25(b) of Federal Reserve Regulation Y, and include: underwriting credit insurance, mortgage banking, operation of consumer finance companies and industrial banks, limited securities brokerage activities, full-payout leasing, and data processing services of a financial, banking, or economic nature for other parties.

Once a holding company receives approval for formation or expansion, its subsequent operations must comply with certain provisions of the Bank Holding Company Act and other applicable banking laws. In particular, the Bank Holding Company Act gives the Federal Reserve System authority to examine bank holding companies and their subsidiaries and assess whether the provisions of the act are being met and sound banking principles are followed. Under this authority, the Federal Reserve periodically inspects bank holding companies to determine if any company relationships or practices could be detrimental to subsidiary banks. These inspections focus on such aspects as condition of the parent organization and its subsidiaries, intercompany transactions and relationships, holding company debt and the potential demands it places on subsidiary bank earnings, and compliance with applicable laws and regulations. In addition, amendments to the Bank Holding Company Act prohibit holding companies from requiring the customers of a subsidiary bank to purchase additional services from any subsidiary of the company. Other banking laws further limit the amount and type of transactions between a subsidiary bank and certain other holding company affiliates.

**BANK INSURANCE FUND (BIF)** The insurance provided by the Federal Deposit Insurance Corporation for deposits in commercial banks. SEE ALSO FEDERAL DEPOSIT INSURANCE CORPORATION.

**BANK REGULATION** The formulation and issuance by authorized agencies of specific rules or regulations, under governing law, for the conduct and structure of banking.

**BANK SECRECY ACT OF 1970** Federal legislation compelling banks to keep records of all customer transactions and to report any cash financial dealings involving more than $10,000 to the U.S. Treasury Department.

**BANK SUPERVISION** Concern of financial regulators with the safety and soundness of individual banks, involving the general and continuous oversight of the activities of this industry to ensure that banks are operated prudently and in accordance with applicable statutes and regulations.

**BANKERS' ACCEPTANCES** Negotiable instruments (time drafts) drawn to finance the export, import, domestic shipment or storage of goods. They are termed "accepted" when a bank writes on the draft its agreement to pay it at maturity, using the word "accepted." A bank may accept the draft for either the drawer or the holder. These acceptances are drafts or bills of exchange — orders to pay a specified amount of money at a specified time. Drafts may be drawn on individuals, businesses or financial institutions. A bankers' acceptance, however, must be drawn on and accepted by a bank.

Banks accept these drafts on behalf of their customers, who are obligated to pay the bank the amount financed on or before the maturity date. The bank, however, becomes the primary obligor of the draft or bill of exchange drawn on and accepted by it. Unlike a more traditional loan, however, an acceptance doesn't necessarily reduce a bank's lending capacity because the bank can raise funds by selling the acceptance. The acceptance is nevertheless an outstanding liability of the bank and is subject to the reserve requirement, unless it is of a type eligible for discount by a Federal Reserve Bank.

One common type of acceptance results from letters of credit in foreign trade transactions. For example, a U.S. firm importing goods from a foreign firm may ask a U.S. bank to issue a letter of credit on behalf of the importer to the foreign exporter. The letter authorizes the foreign exporter to draw a time draft upon the U.S. importer's bank in payment for the goods. When the goods have been shipped, the foreign exporter may discount the draft with the exporter's bank and receive immediate payment, rather than the importer's bank remitting funds under the draft or waiting until maturity for payment. The foreign exporter's bank forwards the draft and applicable shipping documents to the importer's bank in the United States for acceptance. The U.S. bank stamps the word "accepted" on the face of the draft along with an officer's signature, thus, making the draft a bankers' acceptance. The importer's bank may discount the acceptance for the foreign bank, and the importer's bank will earn the difference between the discounted amount paid to the foreign bank and the face amount of the bill, plus the commission for originating the instrument. The importer's bank may then sell the acceptance it created in the open market to a dealer or investor and, thus, recoup the payment to the foreign bank.

Two significant terms used in reference to bankers' acceptances are third-country acceptances and finance bills.

Third country acceptances are created to finance both the shipment of goods between foreign nations and, to some extent, the storage of goods overseas. They principally reflect use of the U.S. acceptance market by foreign borrowers, especially Asian importers and exporters.

Finance bills, which aren't related to specific transactions, are accepted by some banks as a means of extending short-term credit, presumably to provide working capital to the drawer of the draft. In general, they can't be discounted or purchased by Reserve Banks—for that reason they are also referred to as "ineligible acceptances"—and are not counted in the survey of total outstanding acceptances reported monthly by the Fed, but must be reported in reports of condition (call reports). Member banks and covered United States branches and agencies of foreign banks must maintain reserves against ineligible acceptances.

Maturities on bankers' acceptances that are eligible for purchase at times extend to nine months, but more commonly range from 30 to 180 days. Maturities are usually arranged to cover the time required to ship and dispose of the goods being financed.

Although market rates for acceptances are low in relation to loan rates, they do not fully reflect the cost of acceptance financing to the borrower. The accepting bank charges a fee for the service. Thus, the cost to the borrower is the fee plus the discount on the acceptance.

The dealer market involves 20 to 25 large firms, most of which operate nationwide and also engage in buying and selling U.S. government securities. Most of these dealer firms are headquartered in New York City.

Participants in this over-the-counter market, in addition to the dealers, are domestic and foreign accepting banks, Edge Act corporations, other financial and nonfinancial institutions, governmental units, individuals and central banks, including the Federal Reserve.

In October 1983, Congress enacted the Bank Export Services Act ("BESA"). Section 207 of this legislation liberalized the statutory requirements affecting bankers' acceptances involving the domestic shipment of goods; raised the limits on the aggregate amount of "eligible" bankers' acceptances that may be created by a member bank; and allowed portions of bankers' acceptances that are conveyed to others through participation agreements to be excluded from a bank's limits on bankers' acceptances, provided certain requirements are met.

In April 1984, the Federal Open Market Committee announced that, effective July 2, 1984, the U.S. central bank would discontinue use of repurchase agreements on bankers' acceptances in open market operations to manage reserves. The Federal Reserve will continue to buy and sell acceptances, as agent, for foreign central banks and to take delivery of acceptances as collateral for advances.

The action was taken because the use of repurchase agreements on acceptances for reserves management had declined in relative importance in recent years, and because the market for acceptances reached a scale of activity which did not require or justify continuing Federal Reserve support.

The action continued the disengagement from the market begun in 1977, when the Federal Reserve ceased buying acceptances on an outright basis. (Federal Reserve Bank of New York; Fedpoints 12).

**BANKWIRE**   An electonic communications network owned by an association of banks and used to transfer messages between subscribing banks. Bankwire also offers a clearing service called Cashwire that includes a settlement facility.

**BASE DRIFT**   The Fed has been announcing target ranges for the growth of M1 and other monetary aggregates since 1975. These ranges have been expressed in terms of rates of growth from a base quarter to the quarter four quarters later. The term "base drift" refers to the Fed's practice of using the *actual* dollar level of an aggregate in the base quarter as the base level for the target range, rather than the midpoint of the targeted range set in the preceding targeting period.

A long standing objective of Fed monetary policy has been to reduce the longer run growth of M1 and the other monetary aggregates over time to noninflationary rates in order to restore price stability. To date, however, relatively little progress has been made toward reducing the longer run growth of M1. Most economists believe that the Fed should give greater emphasis to M1 than the other monetary aggregates, because M1 has had the most predictable relationship with nominal GNP over the longer run, and it is more amenable to Fed control than the other aggregates. Perhaps for these reasons, M1 is the monetary aggregate that receives the greatest attention from the general public. The trend growth rate of M1 was 6.7 percent over the nine year period from the beginning of 1976, which was the first full year for which monetary targets were announced, until the end of the fourth quarter of 1984, compared to 5.6 percent in the preceding ten years. Further, there has been little change in the trend rate with the period.

The United States has experienced a sharp reduction in inflation since 1980. For example, annual inflation as measured by the GNP deflator declined from 10.2 percent in 1980 to 4.3 percent in 1982 and has remained below 4 percent since then. The Fed must be given credit for pursuing the restrictive monetary policy that made this reduction in inflation possible. Inflation actually increased sharply during the first five years of monetary targeting. Annual inflation as measured by the GNP deflator rose from 4.7 percent in 1976 to 8.2 percent in 1979 and 10.2 percent in 1980. Effective M1 overshot the upper bound of the Fed's target ranges in 1977 and 1978, and it came within the upper third of the implied range in 1979. This performance created doubts about the Fed's commitment to its money supply targets and tended to encourage the increase in inflation in the late 1970s.

After renewing its commitment to disinflationary policy in October 1979, the Fed again let effective M1 overshoot its target in 1980, and the inflation rate remained high throughout that year. Then, in sharp contrast to the preceding four years, effective M1 actually undershot its range in 1981. . . . By the summer of 1982, the unusual decline in M1 velocity together with the recession and developing strains in financial markets led the Fed to de-emphasize its M1 target. M1 grew over the next four quarters at a very high 12.3 percent rate. In retrospect, the 1982 decision to accommodate the increased demand for M1 appears to have been appropriate in the sense that inflation has remained low.

An argument can be made, however, that the usual decline in velocity in 1982 and some of the strain in financial markets that accompanied it have been due to the substantial deceleration in the growth of effective M1 in 1981 and the sharp reduction in actual inflation that followed. It was reasonable to expect that velocity would decline as falling inflation reduced nominal interest rates and lowered the cost of holding money. But it was extremely difficult to predict either how much or how quickly the public would revise its inflationary anticipations downward in the face of the pronounced monetary shock; hence, it was particularly difficult to forecast the size and timing of the decline in velocity. . . . Net base drift was substantially upward over the 1975–1984 period, although in retrospect some part of the drift that occurred in 1982 and 1983 may have been fortuitous in the sense that inflation remained low through 1984. In any event, since there has been both upward and downward base drift during the period, the cumulative drift tends to understate the quantitative significance of base drift on a year-to-year basis. . . . The allowance of base drift greatly reduces the disciplinary features of monetary targeting and therefore probably reduces its effectiveness and credibility. The modifications of the present procedure would eliminate base drift, give the Fed an incentive to control the growth of the money supply more closely in the short run, and in all likelihood increase the public's confidence in the Fed's commitment to restore and maintain price stability.

**BIF**   SEE BANK INSURANCE FUND.

**BIRR**   Monetary unit of Ethiopia.

**BIS**   SEE BANK FOR INTERNATIONAL SETTLEMENTS.

**BOARD OF GOVERNORS OF THE FEDERAL RESERVE SYSTEM**   The apex of the Federal Reserve's organization is the Board of Governors in Washington, DC. The Board's prime function is the formulation of monetary policy. In addition, the Board has broad supervisory and regulatory responsibilities over the activities of various banking institutions and the operations of the Federal Reserve Banks. The Board also has responsibilities in the area of the nation's payments mechanism and for federal consumer credit regulations.

The Board is an agency of the federal government. It consists of seven members appointed by the President of the United States and confirmed by the Senate. The full term of a Board member is fourteen years, and the seven terms are arranged so that one expires in every even-numbered year. A member may not be reappointed after having served a full term. The Chairman and the Vice Chairman of the Board are named for four year terms by the President from among the Board members, and they may be redesignated as long as their terms as Board members have not expired. These designations are also subject to confirmation by the Senate.

The members of the Board constitute a majority of the Federal Open Market Committee (FOMC), which directs the System's open market operations and thereby the general course of monetary policy. In addition to its FOMC functions, the Board reviews and approves discount rate actions of the Federal Reserve Banks and issues regulations governing the administration of the discount window at those Banks. The Board may also use reserve requirements as a monetary policy instrument by exercising its authority to vary certain reserve ratios of depository institutions within ranges prescribed by law.

The Board exercises broad supervisory authority over the operations of the twelve Federal Reserve Banks. This authority includes oversight of their activities in providing services to depository institutions and of their examination and supervision of certain banking institutions. Each of the Banks must submit its budget to the Board for approval. Certain expenditures—such as those for construction or major alterations of Bank buildings and for the salaries of the Bank's presidents and first vice presidents—are subject to the Board's specific approval. The Board also approves the appointments of the president and the first vice president of each Federal Reserve Bank.

The Board has supervisory and regulatory responsibilities over banks that are members of the Federal Reserve System, bank holding companies, bank mergers, international banking facilities in the United States, Edge Act and agreement corporations, foreign activities of member banks, and activities of the U.S. branches and agencies of foreign banks. The Board also sets margin requirements, which limit the use of credit for purchasing or carrying securities. In addition, the Board plays a key role in assuring the smooth functioning and continued development of the nation's vast payments system. Another area of Board responsibility involves the implementation by regulation of major federal laws governing consumer credit such as the Truth in Lending Act, the Equal Credit Opportunity Act and the Home Mortgage Disclosure Act.

The Board is required to submit a number of reports to the Congress, including an annual report on its operations and special reports twice each year on the state of the economy and the System's objectives for the growth of money and credit. The Board also makes available detailed statistics and other information about the System's activities through a variety of publications such as the monthly *Federal Reserve Bulletin*. Materials relating to the Board's regulatory functions are presented in another publication, the *Federal Reserve Regulatory Service*. The Board pays the expenses of carrying out its duties not out of funds appropriated by the Congress but out of assessments upon the Federal Reserve Banks. Each year a public accounting firm audits the Board's financial accounts. Those accounts are also subject to audit by the General Accounting Office.

**BOLIVAR**   Monetary unit of Venezuela.

**BOLIVIANO**   Monetary unit of Bolivia.

**BOND**   A contract for long-term debt.

**BOND INDENTURE**   A written agreement between the issuer of a bond and the bond holder.

**BOOK-ENTRY**   One form in which Treasury and certain government agency securities are held. Book-entry form consists of an entry on the records of the U.S. Treasury Department, a Federal Reserve Bank, or a financial institution.

**BOOK ENTRY PROCEDURE**   The book-entry procedure of the Federal Reserve, United States Treasury and several federal and international agencies has succeeded in largely replacing paper U.S. government and agency securities with computer entries at Reserve Banks. By eliminating certificates, government and agency securities are better safeguarded and more rapidly transferred by the nation's depository institutions.

Securities in book-entry form are less vulnerable to theft and loss, cannot be counterfeited and do not require counting or recording by certificate number. In addition, owners do not submit coupons to obtain interest payments or present certificates to redeem securities. All Treasury securities held in physical form by depository institutions—whether owned by them or held on behalf of others—are eligible for conversion to book entry and for transfer by wire.

The first steps toward modern securities clearance were taken in the 1920s when Treasury securities became transferable by telegraph among banks in different Reserve districts.

At that time, all transfers required specific approval by the Treasury's Commissioner of the Public Debt. In time, these telegraphic transfers of securities became known as CPDs, drawing from the initials of the office approving the transfers. Under the early CPD system, the sender of a security, usually a commercial bank, delivered certificates to the local Federal Reserve office. That office, as fiscal agent of the United States, retired the securities and sent a telegram to another Reserve office located near the institution receiving the security. The Reserve office receiving the telegram issued identical physical securities to the bank to which they were being transferred or they were deposited in that bank's safekeeping account at the Federal Reserve.

The difficulties involved in making actual deliveries of physical government securities to and from the Federal Reserve Bank in New York City (and among the banks and dealers in the city) led to the establishment of New York's Government Securities Clearing Arrangement (GSCA) in 1965. The GSCA permitted the telegraphic transfer of securities during the day with a net settlement in physical securities at the end of the day.

In 1968, another major step toward automating the government securities market was taken when a Treasury regulation authorized the first book-entry procedures to eliminate paper U.S. government securities. Under these procedures, securities were issued and transferred electronically on the records of a Reserve Bank.

At the end of 1977, it was possible to eliminate the GSCA due to the widespread use of book entry. In addition to the U.S. Treasury, several government sponsored agencies have issued book-entry regulations and many of their securities have been available in book-entry form since the 1970s. Beginning in late 1983, short-term agency discount notes also became eligible for book-entry. Finally, mortgage-backed securities issued by the Federal Home Loan Mortgage Corporation and the Federal National Mortgage Corporation were issued in book-entry form beginning in 1985.

Depository institutions, as well as several agencies, have direct or on-line access, via computer or terminal links, to the securities transfer network in the New York Federal Reserve District. The network, known as Fedwire, allows district depository institutions to transfer securities for their own account or the accounts of customers directly to one another and to depository institutions throughout the United States. Securities transfers compose about 28 percent of the transactions on Fedwire, which also moves funds. SEE FEDWIRE, AND FCRS-80.

As part of the program to expand the use of book-entry, the Treasury began offering new bills exclusively in book-entry form in 1979. In August 1986, with the introduction of a program named Treasury Direct, the Treasury began marketing all new notes and bonds only in book-entry form. Treasury Direct makes principal, interest and redemption payments on notes and bonds bought through the Fed directly into an individual investor's account at a financial institution. These payments are made electronically rather than by check. The Treasury Direct system was expanded to include bills in 1987.

**BREAK-EVEN** To have no profit or loss; the point at which revenues exactly cover expenses.

**BRIDGE LOAN** SEE SWING LOAN.

**BROKER DEALER** Any person, other than a bank, engaged in the business of buying or selling securities on its own behalf or for others.

**BROKERS' LOANS** Money borrowed by brokers from banks for uses such as financing specialists' inventories of stock, financing the underwriting of new issues of corporate and municipal securities, and financing customer margin accounts.

**BUYBACK AGREEMENT** SEE REPURCHASE AGREEMENT.

**BUYDOWN** A lump sum payment made to the creditor by the borrower or by a third party to reduce the amount of some or all or the consumer's periodic payments to repay the indebtedness.

# C

**CALL REPORT** A call report is a report of financial condition required by regulatory agencies of financial institutions and "called" for periodically. It is a sworn statement of financial condition which includes a detailed balance sheet, report of income, and stockholder dividends filed on the last day of each calendar quarter.

**CANCELLATION** Cancellation occurs when either party to a contract puts an end to the contract for breach by the other and its effect is the same as that of "termination" except that the cancelling party also retains any remedy for breach of the whole contract or any unperformed balance. On "termination," all obligations which are still executory on both sides are discharged but any right based on prior breach of performance survives.

**CANCELLED CHECK**   A check which has been presented for payment and charged to the depositor's account.

**CAPITAL ASSET**   A relatively long-lived asset that is generally not purchased for immediate resale.

**CAPITAL STOCK**   All shares that evidence ownership in a corporation.

**CAPITAL STRUCTURE**   The total amount of long-term money used to start and run a company, including stock, long-term debt, and retained earnings.

**CASH BASIS ACCOUNTING**   A system of tracking income and expenses based on when cash is actually exchanged. Income is recognized only when cash is received, and expenses are recognized only when cash is paid.

**CASH BUDGET**   A projected accounting of the cash inflows and outflows for a given period.

**CASH FlOW**   The cash coming into a business from revenues versus the cash going out to pay expenses. Positive cash flow means more came in than went out; negative cash flow means the reverse.

**CASH ITEM**   A check or any other item payable on demand and collectible at par that the Reserve Bank of the District in which the item is payable is willing to accept as a cash item.

**CASH POSITION**   The difference between cash inflows and outflows for any given period; how much cash the business has for the period.

**CD**   SEE CERTIFICATE OF DEPOSIT.

**CEASE-AND-DESIST ORDER**   An order issued after notice and opportunity for hearing, requiring a depository institution, a holding company, or a depository institution official to terminate unlawful, unsafe, or unsound banking practices. Cease-and-desist orders are issued by the appropriate federal regulatory agencies under the Financial Institutions Supervisory Act and can be enforced directly by the courts.

**CEDI**   Monetary unit of Ghana.

**CERTIFICATE OF ACCRUAL ON TREASURY SECURITIES (CATS)**   SEE STRIP.

**CERTIFICATE OF DEPOSIT (CD)**   A form of time deposit at a bank or savings institution; a time deposit cannot be withdrawn before a specified maturity date without being subject to an interest penalty for early withdrawal. Small denomination CDs are often purchased by individuals. Large CDs of $100,000 or more are often in negotiable form, meaning they can be sold or transferred among holders before maturity. An acknowledgment by a bank of receipt of money with an engagement to repay it.

**CERTIFICATION**   Certification of a check is acceptance. Where a holder procures certification the drawer and all prior endorsers are discharged. Unless otherwise agreed, a bank has no obligation to certify a check. A bank may certify a check before returning it for lack of proper endorsement. If it does so, the drawer is discharged.

**CHARITABLE REMAINDER TRUST**  A charitable trust that pays trust income to taxable beneficiaries. Upon termination of the trust, the principal transfers tax free to a designated charity or a number of designated charities. SEE ALSO CHARITABLE TRUST.

**CHARITABLE TRUST**  A trust created for charitable purposes, such as educational, scientific, or artistic, and organized as a legal charity.

**CHECK**  A check is a negotiable instrument drawn on a bank and payable on demand. It is a draft or order upon a bank purporting to be drawn upon a deposit of funds, for the payment of a certain sum of money to a certain person therein named, or to his order, or to bearer, and payable instantly on demand.

**CHECK CLEARING**  The movement of checks from the banks or other depository institutions where they are deposited back to those on which they are written, and funds movement in the opposite direction. This process results in credits to accounts at the institutions of deposit and debits to accounts at the paying institutions. The Federal Reserve participates in check clearing through its nationwide facilities, though many checks are cleared by private sector arrangements.

**CHECKING ACCOUNT**  A demand account subject to withdrawal by preauthorized electronic transfer of funds or by checks drawn against funds on deposit therein.

**C.H.I.P.S.**  SEE CLEARING HOUSE INTERBANK PAYMENT SYSTEM.

**CHRISTMAS CLUB ACCOUNT**  A savings account into which periodic deposits are made either at will or by preauthorized transfer. The accumulated balance is generally withdrawn in full at a predetermined date prior to Christmas and the funds are used by the depositor for Christmas or other holiday expenditures.

**C.I.F.**  SEE CUSTOMER INFORMATION FILE.

**CLEARINGHOUSE**  An institution where mutual claims are settled between accounts of member depository institutions. Clearinghouses among banks have traditionally been organized for check-clearing purposes, but more recently have cleared other types of settlements, including electronic fund transfers.

**CLEARING HOUSE INTERBANK PAYMENTS SYSTEM**  The Clearing House Interbank Payments System is a computerized network for transfer of international dollar payments, linking about 140 depository institutions which have offices or subsidiaries in New York City. About 105,000 interbank transfers valued at $350 billion are made daily through the network. The transfers represent about 90 percent of all interbank transfers relating to international dollar payments. Until late spring 1970, most international dollar payments were made by official bank checks. At that time, the New York Clearing House Association (a group of the largest New York City banks), organized C.H.I.P.S. for eight Federal Reserve member commercial banks that were also members of the Clearing House. The system eventually was expanded to include other commercial banks, Edge corporations, United

States agencies and branches of foreign banks, Article XII investment companies, and private banks.

Initially, in the C.H.I.P.S. arrangement, final settlement, or the actual movement of balances in the Federal Reserve, occurred on the morning after the transfers. Next-day settlement was acceptable until volume rose substantially, and the Clearing House and C.H.I.P.S. participants became increasingly concerned about overnight and over-weekend risks. On October 1, 1981, a major change was made, enabling same-day settlement through a special account at the Federal Reserve Bank of New York.

Under an agreement signed in August 1981, the New York Fed established a settlement account for C.H.I.P.S.-settling participants into which debit settlement payments are sent and from which credit settlement payments are disbursed. Settlement is made at the close of each business day by C.H.I.P.S.-settling participants sending and receiving Fedwire transfers through the settlement account. Fedwire is the U.S. central bank's electronic funds and securities transfer network. (SEE FEDWIRE.) Settlement is completed when all settling participants owing funds have made payments to the special account and funds have been transferred from the special account to C.H.I.P.S.-settling participants due funds.

EXAMPLE

Suppose a London bank wants to transfer $1 million from its account at a New York correspondent bank "A" to an account at a bank outside New York City, through a New York correspondent bank "B." Banks "A" and "B" are both C.H.I.P.S. participants.

Bank "A" receives the London bank's transfer message by telex or through the S.W.I.F.T. system. S.W.I.F.T., the Society for Worldwide Interbank Financial Telecommunications, is a private electronic message transfer system to which some depository institutions and central banks belong. (SEE S.W.I.F.T.)

Bank "A" verifies the London bank's message and enters the message into its C.H.I.P.S. terminal, providing the identifying codes for the sending and receiving banks, and the identity of the account at bank "B" which will receive the funds, and the amount. The message is then stored in the C.H.I.P.S. central computer. As soon as bank "A" approves and releases the "stored" transaction the message is transmitted from the C.H.I.P.S. computer to bank "B." The C.H.I.P.S. computer also makes a permanent record of the transaction and makes appropriate debits and credits in the C.H.I.P.S. account of banks "A" and "B."

When correspondent bank "B" receives its credit message, it notifies the bank outside New York that the funds have been credited to its account. Immediately following the closing of the C.H.I.P.S. network at 4:30 P.M. (eastern time) the C.H.I.P.S. computer produces a settlement report showing the net debit or credit position of each participant.

A separate settlement report shows the net position of each settling participant. The net position of a non-settling participant is netted into the position of its correspondent settling participant. Each settling participant has a set period to determine whether it will settle the net position of its participant respondents. After that time, if no settling participant refuses to settle, the settling participants with net debit positions have until 5:45 P.M. (eastern time) to transfer their debit amounts through Fedwire to the C.H.I.P.S. settlement account on the books with the New York Fed. When this procedure has been accomplished, the clearing house, acting on the New York Fed's behalf, transfers those funds via Fedwire out of the settlement account to those settling participants with net creditor positions. The process usually is completed by 6 P.M. (eastern time). Fedwire transfers of funds are final and irrevocable when the recipient receives or is advised of the transfer. Because of the potential risk on large-dollar transfer networks, the Federal Reserve board introduced a policy in March 1986 to control and reduce "daylight overdrafts." Daylight overdrafts occur when an institution has sent more funds over Fedwire than it has in its reserve or checking account,or has sent more funds over C.H.I.P.S. than it has received. The policy statement encourages each depository institution that incurs daylight overdrafts to adopt a "cross-system sender net debit cap." The cap amount is a multiple of the depository institution's adjusted primary capital and represents the maximum debit a depository institution may incur at any one time on all of the large-dollar wire transfer systems in which it participates. SEE ALSO S.W.I.F.T.

**CLIFFORD TRUST**  A "ten year" trust which allows the transfer of income producing assets from a parent to a child for a minimum period of ten years and one day, after which the assets are returned to the parent. SEE ALSO TRUST.

**CLOSE**  To execute the documents necessary to bind the parties to an agreement; i.e., to "close a loan."

**CLOSED-END CREDIT**  Generally, any loan or credit sale agreement in which the amounts advanced, plus any finance charges, are expected to be repaid in full over a definite time. Most real estate and automobile loans are closed-end agreements.

**CLOSING COSTS**  The expenses or fees related to the sale or transfer of real property such as title fees, appraisal fees, recording fees, and so forth.

**CLOUDED TITLE**  SEE TITLE DEFECT.

**COLLATERAL**  Property that is offered to secure a loan or other form of credit and that becomes subject to seizure on default. (Also called security.)

**COLLECTING BANK**  A collecting bank is any bank handling an item for collection except the payor bank.

**COLON**  Monetary unit of Costa Rica and El Salvador.

**COMMERCIAL CODE**  The Uniform Commercial Code (UCC) relates to certain commercial transactions in or regarding personal property and contracts and other documents concerning them, including sales, commercial paper, bank deposits and collections, letters of credit, bulk transfers, warehouse receipts, bills of lading, other documents of title, investment securities, and secured transactions including certain sales of accounts, chattel paper and contract rights. The UCC provides for public notice to third parties in certain circumstances, regulates procedure, evidence and damages in certain court actions involving such transactions, contracts or documents, and makes uniform the law with respect thereto.

**COMMERCIAL LENDING**  Short or long term loans or lines of credit to businesses generally made for the purchase of equipment, inventory, or for working capital.

**COMMERCIAL PAPER**   Commercial paper is short-term, unsecured debt issued in the form of promissory notes, and sold by financial and nonfinancial organizations as an alternative to borrowing from banks or other institutions. The paper is usually sold to other companies which invest in short-term money market instruments. Because commercial paper maturities do not exceed nine months and proceeds are typically used only for current transactions, the notes are exempt from registration as securities with the United States Securities and Exchange Commission.

Currently, more than 1,300 companies in the United States issue commercial paper. Financial companies comprise the largest group of commercial paper issuers, accounting for more than 70 percent of commercial paper outstanding at the start of 1985.

Financial-company paper is issued by firms in commercial, savings and mortgage banking; sales, personal and mortgage financing; factoring; finance leasing and other business lending; insurance underwriting; and other investment activities. Bank-related paper accounts for about 25 percent of all financial-company paper. Typically, it is issued by bank holding companies, nonbank subsidiaries of the holding company, and nonbank subsidiaries of the bank, but not the bank itself. Such paper is an obligation of the parent company or nonbank subsidiary and is not insured by the FDIC.

The remaining 30 percent of commercial paper outstanding at the start of 1985 was issued by nonfinancial firms such as manufacturers, public utilities, industrial concerns and service industries.

There are two methods of marketing commercial paper. The issuer can sell the paper directly to the buyer or sell the paper to a dealer firm, which re-sells the paper in the market. The dealer market for commercial paper involves large securities firms which operate internationally. Most of these firms are also dealers in U.S. government securities. Direct issuers of commercial paper are usually financial companies which have frequent and sizable borrowing needs, and find it more economical to place paper without the use of an intermediary.

On average, direct issuers save the dealers' fee of 1/8 of a percentage point, or $125,000 on every $100 million placed. This savings compensates for the cost of maintaining a permanent sales staff to market the paper. In addition, direct issuers often have greater flexibility in adjusting the amounts, interest rates, and maturities it issues to suit the needs of investors with whom they have continuing relationships.

Dealer-placed paper is usually issued by nonfinancial companies and smaller financial companies. The size and frequency of the borrowings usually do not warrant maintenance of a sales staff by the issuer. Interest rates on commercial paper often are lower than bank lending rates, and the differential, when large enough, provides an advantage which makes issuing commercial paper an attractive alternative to bank credit.

Commercial paper rates are quoted on a discount basis. When any security is sold at a discount, the purchaser pays less than the face amount of the paper. The yield is the difference between the purchase price and the face amount. Daily interest rates are published weekly by the Federal Reserve Bank of New York covering maturities of 5 days to 180 days for dealer paper, and 30 days to 180 days for directly placed paper. These rates are unweighted arithmetic averages of offering rates — the rates at which dealers or issuers are willing to sell. The rates are reported at 11 A.M. daily by five direct users and five major dealers for paper of industrial firms with "Aa" bond ratings. Before averaging, fractions are rounded to two decimal places.

Commercial paper maturities range from 5 days to 270 days, but most commonly is issued for less than 30 days. Paper is usually issued in denominations of $100,000 or more, although some companies issue smaller denominations.

The most often cited rates on commercial paper are the 30-, 90- and 180-day dealer-placed paper rates, which are published weekly by the Federal Reserve Board of Governors in the "Selected Interest Rates" H.15 statistical release. These rates are generally averages of the five daily figures for a normal business week. A four-day average is used for a holiday week.

Five organizations currently rate commercial paper. These ratings have a strong influence on rates for commercial paper, although the published rates reflect only paper of companies with at least "AA" bond ratings. Standard & Poor's, Inc. and Moody's Investors Services each rate more than 1,300 issuers. McCarthy, Crisanti, Maffei, Inc. rates more than 500 issuers. Fitch Investor Services Corp. rates more than 240 issuers. Duff and Phelps, Inc. rates more than 100 issuers. Standard & Poor's uses ratings of A-1, A-2, or A-3; Moody's uses P-1, P-2 or P-3; McCarthy uses MCM-1 to MCM-6; Fitch uses F-1 to F-4, and Duff uses Duff 1 + , Duff 1-, Duff 2, and Duff 3.

Ratings are reviewed frequently and are determined by the issuer's financial condition, bank lines of credit and timeliness of repayment. Unrated or lower rated paper is not easily sold, and only the paper with the highest ratings from Moody's and Standard & Poor's is widely accepted by investors.

Investors in the commercial paper market include private pensions funds, money market mutual funds, governmental units, bank trust departments, foreign banks and investment companies. There is limited secondary market activity in commercial paper, since issuers can closely match the maturity of the paper to the investor's needs. If the investor needs ready cash, the dealer or issuer usually will buy back the paper prior to maturity.

**COMMUNITY REINVESTMENT ACT OF 1977 (CRA)**   The Community Reinvestment Act of 1977 (CRA) was enacted as Title VIII of the Housing and Community Development Act of 1977 on October 12 of that year. The CRA neither prohibits any activity, nor attempts to allocate credit or encourage unsound lending practices. The purpose of the CRA is to

• encourage banks to help meet the credit needs of their local communities,

• provide guidance to banks on how the regulatory agencies assess their records in satisfying continuing and affirmative obligations to help meet the credit needs of their local communities, including low- and moderate-income neighborhoods, consistent with safe and sound operations, and

• provide for weighing those records when considering certain bank applications.

Many factors determine a bank's local community, including the bank's size, geographic factors, economic forces and local tradition. No single definition or rigidly applied rule would be appropriate to all local communities and banks. As a result, CRA regulations do not provide a definition of "community." They do state broad guidelines for bank use in preparing a delineation. The guidelines are:

• existing boundaries, such as those of Standard Metropolitan Statistical Areas

(SMSAs) or counties in which the bank's office or offices are located. Standard Metropolitan Statistical Area (SMSA) means Metropolitan Statistical Area (MSA) and Primary Metropolitan Service Area (PMSA) as defined by the US Office of Management and Budget. Where appropriate, portions of adjacent areas should be included. The bank may make adjustments for areas divided by state borders or significant geographic barriers, or areas that are extremely large or of unusual configuration. In addition, a small bank may delineate those portions of MSAs or counties it reasonably may be expected to serve.

• The bank's effective lending territory, which is defined as that local area or areas around each office or group of offices where it makes a large portion of its loans and all other areas equidistant from its offices as those areas. Adjustments such as those indicated above may be made.

• Any other reasonably delineated local area that meets the purposes of the Community Reinvestment Act and does not exclude low- and moderate-income neighborhoods.

In delineating the local community or communities that comprise its entire community, a bank must not arbitrarily exclude low- and moderate-income neighborhoods. Maps must be used to portray community delineations and the reasonableness of the delineations must be reviewed by bank examiners. A local community consists of the contiguous areas surrounding each office or group of offices, including low- and moderate-income neighborhoods in those areas. More than one office of the bank may be included in the same local community.

*Community Reinvestment Act Statement*: The board of directors of each bank is required to adopt a CRA Statement for each delineated community. Each statement includes:

• a delineation of the local community
• a list of the specific types of credit within certain categories that the bank is prepared to extend within the local community
• a copy of the standard public notice.

Also, banks are encouraged to include:

• a description of how their current efforts, including special credit-related programs, help meet community credit needs
• a periodic report of their record of helping to meet community credit needs
• a description of their efforts to ascertain the credit needs of their communities, including attempts to communicate with members of their communities about credit services.

Copies of each current CRA Statement must be provided to the public upon request. The bank may charge a fee for reproduction not to exceed actual costs.

*Files of Public Comments and Recent CRA Statements:* Each bank must maintain files that are readily available for public inspection consisting of:

• any signed, written comments received from the public within the last two years that specifically relate to any CRA Statement or to the bank's performance in helping to meet the credit needs of its community or communities
• any responses by the bank to those comments
• any CRA statements in effect during the past two years.

The files must not contain any material specifically prohibited by the regulation. Each bank must maintain its files as follows:

• all materials at the head office

- those materials relating to each local community at a designated office in the community.

*Public Notice:* Each bank must provide, in the public lobby of each of its offices other than off-premises electronic deposit facilities, the standard public notice as prescribed by the regulation. The notice informs interested persons:

- of the availability and location of the bank's current CRA Statement for the community in which the bank operates and copies of current CRA Statements for other communities served by the bank

- that signed, written comments about the bank's CRA Statement(s) or its performance in helping to meet community credit needs may be sent to a designated bank official and to the regulatory agencies

- of the respective addresses of the bank and regulatory agency

- that such letters, or the bank's response, may be made public

- that they may read the bank's files of public comments and all CRA Statements in effect during the past two years, both for the community in which the bank's office is located and when applicable, for the bank's entire community

- of the addresses where such files may be reviewed

- that they may request to read any comments received by regulatory agencies

- that they may request from the appropriate regulatory agency an announcement of applications covered by the CRA filed with the agency.

*Review and retention of records*: Each bank's board of directors must review the CRA Statement at least annually and act upon any material change at its first regular meeting after that change. Such actions must be noted in its minutes. All CRA Statements in effect over the last two years and all written, signed CRA public comments received during that period must be maintained. Each current CRA Statement must be readily available for public inspection at the head office of the bank and at each office of the bank in the local community delineated in the statement, except off-premises electronic deposit facilities.

*Assessing the record of performance:* Bank regulatory agencies must assess the record of the bank's performance in helping to meet the credit needs of its entire community, including low- and moderate-income neighborhoods, consistent with safe and sound operation of the bank. The following factors should be considered:

(1) Bank activities to ascertain the credit needs of its community, including the extent of its efforts to communicate about its credit services.

(2) The extent of the bank's marketing and special credit related programs to inform community members about its credit services.

(3) The extent of participation by the bank's board of directors in formulating policies and reviewing the bank's performance with respect to the purposes of the Community Reinvestment Act.

(4) Any practices intended to discourage applications for types of credit listed in the bank's CRA Statement(s).

(5) The geographic distribution of the bank's credit extensions, applications and denials.

(6) Evidence of prohibited discriminatory or other illegal credit practices.

(7) The bank's record of opening and closing offices and of providing services at offices.

(8) The bank's participation, including investments, in local community development and redevelopment projects or programs.

(9) The bank's origination of loans for residential mortgages, housing rehabilitation, home improvement, and small businesses or small farms within its community, or the purchase of such loans originated in its community.

(10) The bank's participation in governmental insured, guaranteed, or subsidized loan programs for housing, small businesses, or small farms.

(11) The bank's ability to meet various community credit needs based on its financial condition and size, and legal impediments, local economic conditions and other factors.

(12) Other factors that reasonably bear upon the extent to which a bank is helping to meet the credit needs of its entire community.

**COMPTROLLER OF THE CURRENCY (OCC)**   The Office of the Comptroller of the Currency is the oldest of the federal bank regulatory agencies. Established by the Currency Act of 1863 and strengthened by the National Bank Act of 1864, the Comptroller is the primary supervisory agency for national banks. There ware 4906 national banks at the end of 1984. That was more than 34 percent of the commercial banks in the United States. National banks held $1151 billion in deposits, which was nearly 59 percent of all bank deposits nationwide.

The Comptroller is a bureau of the Treasury Department and is headed by a single person appointed by the President to a five-year term. The office includes bank supervision, national operations, policy and planning, industry and public affairs, and law departments. In addition to its headquarters in Washington, the Comptroller has six district offices.

The National Bank Act empowered the Comptroller to exercise control over the operations of national banks through chartering, supervision and bank examinations. Later, these powers were broadened to include review of branch and merger applications. As a result, the comptroller now influences the number of national banks and their expansion through policy decisions on charters, branches, and mergers.

To assure compliance with its supervisory policies, the comptroller can revoke a bank's charter, issue cease and desist orders, and remove or suspend bank officials. For violations of some regulations or rulings, a bank and its officers, directors, employees, or agents can be fined.

**CONFESSION OF JUDGMENT**   An illegal contract provision. SEE CREDIT PRACTICES RULE.

**CONSOLIDATION LOAN**   A loan made to consolidate or group together several existing loans or other outstanding indebtedness for the purpose of reducing interest costs and/or monthly payment obligations.

**CONSTRUCTION LOAN**   An extension of credit for the purpose of erecting or rehabilitating buildings or other structures, including any infrastructure necessary for development.

**CONSUMER**   A consumer is a natural person who seeks or acquires goods, services, or money for personal, family, or household purposes.

**CONSUMER ADVISORY COUNCIL**   A statutory body established by Congress in 1976. The Council, with 30 members who represent a broad range of consumer and creditor interests, advises the Board of governors of the Federal Reserve System on the exercise of its responsibilities under the Consumer Credit Protection Act and on other matters on which the Board seeks its advice.

**CONSUMER CREDIT PROTECTION ACT**   The Consumer Credit Protection Act (CCPA) was enacted by Congress on May 29, 1968, and became effective on July 1, 1969. The law incorporates seven major pieces of legislation, each of which is known separately by its descriptive title. The parts of the Act are:

• Truth-in-Lending Act (TILA), Title 1, Chapters 1 to 3. Truth-in-Lending was the only matter considered when the CCPA was enacted.

• Fair Credit Billing Act (FCBA), Title 1, Chapter 4. The Act became effective on October 28, 1975.

• Consumer Leasing Act of 1976, Title 1, Chapter 5. The Act became effective March 23, 1977.

• Fair Credit Reporting Act (FCRA), Title VI of the CCPA. The Act became effective on April 25, 1971.

• Equal Credit Opportunity Act (ECOA), Title VII of the CCPA. The Act has an effective date of October 28, 1975 and is implemented as Regulation B of the Federal Reserve Board.

• Fair Debt Collection Practices Act (FDCPA), Title VIII of the CCPA. The Act has an effective date of March 20, 1978.

• Electronic Fund Transfer Act (EFTA), Title IX of the CCPA. The Act has two original effective dates, February 8, 1979, for 2 of its provisions and May 10, 1980, for the remainder. The Act is implemented by Regulation E of the Federal Reserve Board.

**CONSUMER CREDIT REGULATORS**   The Board of Governors of the Federal Reserve System is charged with writing most of the consumer credit regulations enforced by 12 different federal agencies. One group of these regulators consists of the 12 Federal Reserve Banks, each having responsibility in its district for the lending practices of state-chartered commercial banks which are members of the Federal Reserve System. The central bank's role as consumer credit "rule-maker" was established in 1968 by the United States Congress in the Consumer Credit Protection Act. Previously, consumer credit regulation was the responsibility of individual states.

Examination of state member commercial banks is the primary enforcement procedure used by the Reserve banks to assure compliance with the consumer protection regulations. Specially trained examiners review accepted and rejected consumer loan files (including mortgages), application forms, savings and checking account operations, and other aspects of consumer business. Reserve banks' internal complaint files are also reviewed to see if problems are indicated in any area of a member banks' operations. After examination, a member bank is judged in compliance or agrees to establish procedures to ensure compliance with regulations. When necessary, follow-up examinations are made.

Reserve banks also investigate potential violations against state member banks reported by consumers. Complaints against other lenders are sent to the appropriate regulatory agency. When a complaint is received by the Reserve bank's consumer affairs staff, it is acknowledged by letter and, in all cases, the state member bank is asked for comments. The bank's response is reviewed by the consumer affairs staff and, if necessary, by legal, examining or Board personnel. The consumer is then advised of the results of the investigation.

The *Comptroller of the Currency* is responsible for enforcing consumer credit laws for commercial banks with national charters. The agency conducts consumer credit compliance examinations and investigates consumer allegations against national banks.

The *Federal Deposit Insurance Corporation* enforces consumer credit laws for insured banks which are not Federal Reserve members. It has a separate compliance examinations program. The FDIC also conducts inquiries to determine the merits of all discrimination complaints.

The *Federal Home Loan Bank Board* enforces regulations for federally chartered savings and loan associations. In addition to regular examinations to determine compliance, it investigates consumer complaints.

The *National Credit Union Administration* is the enforcement agency for federally chartered credit unions. Its enforcement activities, like those of the other financial regulatory agencies, include examiner training, specialized examination procedures, and, if a violation is discovered, follow-up with credit union officials. The NCUA also conducts field investigations of written consumer complaints and institutes corrective action.

The *Federal Trade Commission* enforces requirements of the Consumer Credit Protection Act applicable to retailers, finance companies and other lenders not subject to the jurisdiction of any other agency. Potential violations are identified through several sources, including consumer complaints, consumer and civil rights organizations, and other enforcement agencies. When there is evidence of a violation, an informal inquiry is made and, if necessary, a full investigation.

The *Department of Transportation*, the enforcement agency for domestic and foreign air carriers, monitors industry practices through consumer complaints. Enforcement measures include contacting the carrier or supplying information to the consumer.

The *Interstate Commerce Commission* is the enforcement agency for regulated common carriers.

The *U.S. Department of Agriculture* has within it several agencies with responsibilities under various consumer credit laws. One sub-agency is the Packers and Stockyards Administration. The agency's monitoring is handled on a complaints-received basis. Another sub-agency is the Farmers Home Administration, itself a lender. It operates under the enforcement authority of the FTC, and is primarily concerned with farm loans. Complaints against the Farmers Home Administration itself concerning the denial of loans are handled by the USDA's office of Equal Opportunity.

The *Small Business Administration* is the enforcement agency for small business investment companies for the purposes of the equal credit opportunity regulation and, through a letter of understanding with the FTC, other recipients of SBA assistance. Those businesses subject to SBA review are monitored for compliance, subject to on-site reviews.

The *Farm Credit Administration* enforces the requirements of the consumer credit laws pertaining to federal land banks and federal land bank associations, federal intermediate credit banks, and production credit associations. The FCA's enforcement activities include examinations conducted every 12 to 18 months.

The *banking departments of individual states* continue to play a role in certain aspects of consumer credit regulation, such as the determination of usury ceilings.

They, too, provide consumer assistance within their areas of responsibility. (Federal Reserve Bank of New York; fedpoints 17)

**CONSUMER GOODS**  Goods are "consumer goods" if they are used or bought for use primarily for personal, family or household purposes. As opposed to "consumer goods," goods are (1) "equipment" if they are used or bought for use primarily in business (including farming or a profession) or by a debtor who is a non-profit organization or a governmental subdivision or agency or if the goods are not included in the definitions of inventory, farm products, or consumer goods; (2) "farm products" if they are crops or livestock or supplies used or produced in farming operations or if they are products of crops or livestock in their unmanufactured states (such as ginned cotton, wool-clip, maple syrup, milk and eggs), and if they are in the possession of a debtor engaged in raising, fattening, grazing or other farming operations. If goods are farm products, they are neither equipment nor inventory; (3) "inventory" if they are held by a person who holds them for sale or lease or to be furnished under contracts of service or if he has so furnished them, or if they are raw materials, work in process or materials used or consumed in a business. Inventory of a person is not to be classified as his equipment.

**CONSUMER LEASING ACT**  The Consumer Leasing Act of 1976 is intended to ensure meaningful and accurate disclosure of the terms of personal property leases for personal, family or household use. Those disclosures enable the consumer to (1) compare the various lease terms, (2) be aware of any liabilities the lease imposes on the lessee at the end of the lease, and (3) compare lease terms with credit terms where appropriate. The Act, originally implemented by Regulation Z, and revised as Regulation M (12 CFR 213) applies only to consumer leases. A consumer lease is defined as a contract, in the form of a lease or bailment, which meets all of the following criteria:
- it must have a duration of more than 4 months,
- the total lease obligation must not exceed $25,000,
- the property leased must be used principally for family, personal, or household purposes,
- the lease must be to a natural person, and
- the lease must be for the use of personal property. The Act *does not apply* to leases:
- for commercial or agricultural purposes or to a government, governmental agency, instrumentality or organization,
- of real property,
- of personal property that are incidental to the lease of real property and that provide that the lessee has (1) no liability for the value of the property at the end of the lease, except for normal wear and tear, and (2) no option to purchase the leased property, or
- that meet the definition of a credit sale.

*Required Disclosures:*  Prior to the consummation of the lease, the lessor is required to give the lessee a dated, written statement that identifies both the lessor and lessee and that clearly, conspicuously, and accurately sets forth the following disclosures in a meaningful sequence whenever applicable:
- a brief description that adequately identifies the leased property for all parties to the lease;

- the total amount of the initial payment required of the lessee at consummation, such as refundable security deposits and advance payments;
- the number, amount due dates, or periods of payments under the lease and the total amount of such periodic payments;
- the total amount paid or payable by the lessee over the lease term for official fees, registration, certificate of title, license fees, or taxes;
- the total amount of all other charges, such as disposition and maintenance charges, that are individually itemized and payable by the lessee to the lessor and that are not included in the periodic payments;
- a brief identification of insurance required in connection with the lease, including, (1) if provided or paid for by the lessor, the types and amounts of coverage and cost to the lessee, and (2) if not provided or paid for by the lessor, the types and amounts of coverages required of the lessee;
- a statement identifying any express warranty or guaranty made by the manufacturer or the lessor for the leased property. (The lessor need not list the warranties or guarantees in the disclosure statement. A reference to the standard manufacturer's warranty would suffice.)
- an identification of the party responsible for maintaining or servicing the leased property, together with a brief description of the scope of that responsibility, and a statement of reasonable standards for wear and use, if the lessor sets such standards;
- a description of any security interest held or to be retained by the lessor in connection with the lease and a clear identification of property to which the security interest relates;
- the amount or method of determining the amount of any penalty or other charge for delinquency, default, or late payments;
- a statement of whether or not the lessee has the option to purchase the leased property and (1) if at the end of the lease term, at what price, and (2) if prior to the end of the lease term, at what time, and the price or method of determining the price;
- a statement of the conditions under which either party to the lease may terminate it prior to the end of the lease term, and the amount or method of determining the amount of any penalty or other charge for early termination;
- a statement that the lessee shall be liable for the differential between the estimated value of the property and its realized value at early termination or at the end of the lease term, if such liability exists. Estimated value may be defined as a reasonable approximation of the anticipated value of the property at the end of the lease. Realized value is defined as any of the following: (1) the price received by the lessor for the property at disposition, (2) the highest offer for disposition, or (3) the fair market value of the leased property at the end of the lease term;
- when the lessee's liability at early termination or at the end of the lease is based on the estimated value of the leased property, a statement that the lessee may obtain, at his or her expense, a professional appraisal of the property by an independent third party, agreeable to both the lessee and the lessor, at the end of the lease or upon early termination, and that the appraisal will be binding;
- when the lessee's liability at the end of the lease term is based upon the estimated value of the property, [A] a statement of the value of the property at the consummation of the lease, the itemized total lease obligation at the end of the

lease, and the difference between them. The value of the property at the consummation of the lease is equal to the cost of the lessor of the lease property, including, if applicable, any increase or markup by the lessor prior to consummation. The total lease obligation is equal to the total of: (1) the scheduled periodic payments under the lease, including that portion of the payments attributable to depreciation, cost of money, lessor's profit and taxes, but excluding any refundable security deposits and maintenance and insurance premiums contained in the periodic payments, (2) any nonrefundable cash payment required of the lessee or agreed upon by the lessor and lessee or any trade-in allowance made at consummation, (3) the estimated value of the leased property at the end of the term; [B] a statement that to the extent that the estimated value of the lease property at the end of the lease term exceeds the realized value by more than three times the average monthly pease payment, there is a rebuttable presumption that the estimated value is unreasonable and not in good faith. The lessor must disclose that he or she can only collect the amount of such excess liability by a successful court action in which he or she pays the lessee's attorney's fees, unless the excess is due to unreasonable wear and tear or excessive use; [C] a statement that the requirements of the previous paragraph do not preclude the right of a willing lessee to make any mutually agreeable final adjustment regarding such excess liability,provided such agreement is reached after the end of the lease term.

If information required to be disclosed is unknown or not reasonably available at the time the disclosures are made, a financial institution may estimate the information. Any estimates must be identified as such and must be based on the best information reasonably available.

**CONSUMER PRICE INDEX (CPI)**   Also commonly referred to as the "cost of living index," the CPI is a monthly measurement by the U.S. Department of Labor, of the changes in prices of goods and services.

**CONTRIBUTION MARGIN PERCENTAGE**   The percent of each dollar of sales that is left after variable cost percentage has been deducted; the amount from each dollar of sales that is contributed to cover fixed costs and profits.

**CORDOBA**   Monetary unit of Nicaragua.

**CORRESPONDENT BANK**   A bank that accepts deposits of and performs banking services for other depository institutions.

**COSIGNER**   Any person who assumes personal liability, in *any* capacity, for the obligation of another consumer without receiving goods, services, or money in return for the obligation. This includes any person whose signature is requested to allow a consumer to obtain credit or to prevent collection of a consumer's obligation that is in default. A person who meets this definition is a cosigner whether or not designated as such in the contract. For open-end credit, a cosigner is a person who signs the debt instrument but does not have the contractual right to obtain credit under the account.

A cosigner is not:

• a spouse whose signature is required on a credit obligation to perfect a security interest pursuant to state law;

- a person who does not assume personal liability, but only provides collateral for the obligation of another person;
- a person who has the contractual right to obtain credit under an open-end account, whether exercised or not.

**COST OF FUNDS**   Interest paid on borrowed money; calculated from the respective costs of the several sources of funds available for lending, the net aggregate cost of funds is considered when determining the applicable interest rates to be charged on consumer, commercial and mortgage loans.

**COUNTER TRANSACTION**   A deposit, withdrawal, transfer or other transaction made at the teller counter as opposed to a transaction made at a remote electronic device such as an automated teller machine.

**COVENANTS**   Formal agreed upon terms and conditions which are part of a loan agreement.

**COVER**   After breach of a contract by seller, the buyer may "cover" by making in good faith and without unreasonable delay any reasonable purchase of, or contract to purchase goods in substitution for, those due from the seller.

**CPI**   SEE CONSUMER PRICE INDEX.

**CRA**   SEE COMMUNITY REINVESTMENT ACT OF 1977.

**CREDIT**   The promise to pay in the future in order to buy or borrow in the present. The right to defer payment of debt.

**CREDIT APPLICATION**   SEE APPLICATION.

**CREDIT CARD**   Any card, plate, or coupon book that may be used repeatedly to borrow money or buy goods and services on credit.

**CREDIT HISTORY**   A record of how a person has borrowed and repaid debts.

**CREDIT INSURANCE**   Decreasing term insurance, usually written on the life or health of a borrower and in favor of the lender as beneficiary. Credit insurance is frequently written to cover the outstanding balance on a consumer loan; insurance premiums may be financed over the term of the insured loan.

**CREDIT INVESTIGATION**   An inquiry or series of inquiries made by a lender to determine the creditworthiness of a prospective borrower.

**CREDIT LIMIT**   That amount established as the ceiling, or maximum amount, of credit to be extended. Frequently applicable to open-end credit plans such as revolving lines of credit and credit card accounts.

**CREDIT PRACTICES RULE**   The Federal Home Loan Bank Board and the Federal Reserve Board adopted a credit practices rule under Section 18(f)(1) of the Federal Trade Commission Act (15 USC 45) in response to a similar one adopted by the Federal Trade Commission for creditors other than banks and savings and loan associations. The rule is contained in 12 CFR 535 for savings and loan associations and Subpart B of Regulation AA (12 CFR Part 227) for banks.

The rule prohibits banks from using: (1) certain provisions in their consumer credit contracts; (2) certain late charge accounting practices; and (3) deceptive co-signer practices. The rule also requires that a disclosure notice be given to a cosigner prior to becoming obligated. Finally, the rule prohibits financial institutions from enforcing in purchased contracts the same provisions that they are prohibited from including in their own consumer credit contracts. The rule applies to the consumer credit contracts of all banks and their subsidiaries other than those used for the purchase of real estate. Dwellings such as mobile homes and houseboats are not considered real estate if they are specified as personal property under state law. A consumer is a natural person who seeks or acquires goods, services, or money for personal, family, or household purposes. There is no monetary limitation on the coverage of the rule.

### Prohibited Contract Provisions

1. Confession of judgment. A confession of judgment is a provision (which may also be known as a cognovit or warrant of attorney) in which the borrower waives both the right to notice and the opportunity to be heard in the event of a suit on the obligation. The following are *not* prohibited:

• confessions in Louisiana for the purpose of executory process;

• confessions executed after default or the filing of a suit on the debt;

• powers of attorney contained in a mortgage or deed of trust for foreclosure purposes or given to expedite the repossession or transfer of collateral.

2. Waiver of exemption. A waiver of exemption is a provision in which the consumer relinquishes the statutory right to protect his or her home (known as the homestead exemption), possessions, or wages from seizure to satisfy a judgment unless the waiver is given for property that will serve as security for the obligation. Any other types of waivers (for example, waiver of demand, presentment, protest, notice of dishonor, and notice of protest and dishonor) are not prohibited.

3. Assignment of wages. An assignment of wages is a provision that gives the institution the right to receive the consumer's wages or earnings directly from the consumer's employer. The following are *not* prohibited:

• an assignment that by its terms is revocable at will by the consumer

• a payroll deduction or preauthorized payment plan (whether or not revocable by the consumer) commencing at consummation of the loan for each payment

• an assignment of wages that has been earned at the time of the assignment

• garnishment

Earnings are defined as compensation paid or payable for personal services rendered or to be rendered by the consumer, whether denominated as wages, salary, commission, or bonus, including periodic payments pursuant to a pension, retirement or disability program.

4. Household goods security interests. A nonpossessory security interest in household goods is prohibited unless they are purchased with credit extended by the bank. The following are *not* prohibited:

• security interests in household goods not purchased with credit extended by the bank if they are placed in the bank's possession;

• security interests in all other real and personal property of the consumer other than household goods as defined by the rule. The term "household goods" is defined as meaning only the clothing, furniture, appliances, linens, china, crockery, kitchenware, and personal effects of the consumer and the consumer's dependents. The following are *not* household goods:

- works of art
- electronic equipment (other than one television and one radio)
- items acquired as antiques (over 100 years of age), including those that have been repaired or renovated without changing their original form or character
- jewelry (other than wedding rings)
- fixtures, automobiles, boats, snowmobiles, cameras and camera equipment (including darkroom equipment), pianos, home workshops, and the like.

*Prohibited Practices*

1. Late charge accounting. The institution may not consider a timely and complete payment delinquent because it collected a late charge on an earlier delinquent payment. For example: if a consumer makes a January payment 15 days late and the February payment in full and on time, the bank may not treat the February payment as delinquent and assess another late charge because of the consumer's failure to pay the late charge for January's delinquent payment. In other words, it cannot "pyramid" late charges on subsequent timely payments merely because an earlier payment was not made or was not timely. However, if a consumer fails to make the January payment and then makes the February payment on time, the bank may assess a late charge every month until the January payment is made; the rule is not intended to permit a consumer to skip a payment and unilaterally extend the term of the loan. The bank may continue to assess a late charge for every period that the delinquent January payment remains unpaid.

2. Cosigner deception. The institution may not misrepresent the nature and extent of a cosigner's liability to any person.

3. Cosigner disclosure. The bank must provide, either in a separate document or in the credit obligation, a clear and conspicuous notice that is substantially similar to the following statement:

NOTICE TO COSIGNER

You are being asked to guarantee this debt. Think carefully before you do. If the borrower doesn't pay the debt, you will have to. Be sure you can afford to pay the debt if you have to, and that you want to accept this responsibility. You may have to pay up to the full amount of the debt if the borrower does not pay. You may also have to pay late fees or collection costs, which increase this amount. The bank can collect this debt from you without first trying to collect from the borrower. The bank can use the same collection methods against you that can be used against the borrower, such as suing you, garnisheeing your wages, etc. If this debt is ever in default, that fact may become a part of *your* credit record. This notice is not the contract that makes you liable for the debt. This notice must be given to the cosigner prior to the time he or she becomes obligated. In the case of open-end credit plans, the notice must be given prior to the time the cosigner becomes obligated for fees or transactions on the account.

**CREDIT REPORT** SEE FAIR CREDIT REPORTING ACT.

**CREDIT REPORTING AGENCY** SEE FAIR CREDIT REPORTING ACT.

**CREDIT SCORING SYSTEM** A statistical system used to determine whether or not to grant credit by assigning numerical scores to various characteristics related to creditworthiness. A credit scoring system evaluates an applicant's creditworthiness mechanically, based on key attributes of the applicant and aspects of the transaction, and that determines, alone or in conjunction with an evaluation of additional information about the applicant, whether an applicant is deemed creditworthy. To qualify as an "empirically derived, demonstrably and statistically sound, credit scoring system" the system must be: (i) Based on data that are derived from an empirical comparison of sample groups or the population of creditworthy and noncreditworthy applicants who applied for credit within a reasonable preceding period of time; (ii) Developed for the purpose of evaluating the creditworthiness of applicants with respect to the legitimate business interests of the creditor utilizing the system (including, but not limited to, minimizing bad debt losses and operating expenses in accordance with the creditor's business judgment); (iii) Developed and validated using accepted statistical principles and methodology; and (iv) Periodically revalidated by the use of appropriate statistical principles and methodology and adjusted as necessary to maintain predictive ability. A creditor may use an empirically derived, demonstrably and statistically sound, credit scoring system obtained from another person or may obtain credit experience from which to develop such a system.

**CREDIT UNION**   A cooperative association organized to accept savings deposits from consumer-members, then offer loans and other financial services at low interest rates or fees. Membership is usually limited to a prescribed affinity group. Most credit unions are organized under the Federal Credit Union Act.

**CREDITOR**   A person who, in the ordinary course of business, regularly participates in the decision of whether or not to extend credit. The term includes a creditor's assignee, transferee or subrogee who so participates. The term also includes a person who, in the ordinary course of business, regularly refers applicants or prospective applicants to creditors, or selects or offers to select creditors to whom requests for credit may be made. The term does not include a person whose only participation in a credit transaction involves honoring a credit card.

**CREDITWORTHINESS**   A creditor's measure of a consumer's past and future ability and willingness to repay debts.

**CRUZEIRO**   Monetary unit of Brazil.

**CURRENCY**   Coin or paper money which circulates as legal medium of exchange and is issued by a government or central bank.

**CURRENT ACCOUNT BALANCE**   The difference between the nation's total exports of goods, services, and transfers and its total imports of them. It excludes transactions in financial assets and liabilities.

**CURRENT ASSETS**   What the business (or individual) owns that is expected to be turned into cash within one year, such as accounts receivable and inventory.

**CURRENT DEBT**   The total of all liabilities due 12 months of less from the date of the current financial statement, excluding any reserves for depreciation. Also referred to as current liabilities.

**CURRENT DEBT TO INVENTORY RATIO**   The dollar amount of current debt divided by the dollar value of inventory indicates the extent to which a business relies upon the funds realized from the disposal of inventories to pay its debts.

**CURRENT LIABILITIES**   Obligations which are due to be repaid within one year.
SEE ALSO CURRENT DEBT.

**CURRENT RATIO**   Total current assets divided by total current liabilities.

**CUSTODIAN**   A bank that performs a variety of services such as the safekeeping of securities, collection of dividends and interest, purchase, sale and delivery of securities, and other duties of a transfer agent.

**CUSTOMER INFORMATION FILE (CIF)**   Computerized control directory of customers and their deposit or loan relationships which allows a bank to look at its customers by total relationship, rather than by individual account only.

# D

**DAILY INTEREST**   Interest which is paid daily from the day of deposit to the day of withdrawal.

**DALASI**   Monetary unit of Gambia.

**DATE OF ACCEPTANCE**   The date upon which a time draft is honored.

**DATE OF MATURITY**   The date upon which a time certificate of deposit is due and available for withdrawal without penalty or the date upon which a loan obligation is payable in full.

**DAYLIGHT OVERDRAFT**   A negative balance created in an account when payments made during business hours exceed incoming funds actually received. The term also refers to an overdraft in a bank's reserve account at the Federal Reserve during business hours.

**DEALER FINANCING**   An arrangement between a bank and a seller of personal property, usually automobiles, motorhomes, trailers, heavy appliances or furniture, whereby the dealer-seller executes with the buyer-borrower a bank contract for the financed purchase of the commodity. The contract is subsequently assigned to the bank with or without recourse in the event of default by the borrower, in exchange for payment by the bank to the dealer of the amount of the contract. Monthly payments are then made by the borrower directly to the bank. The dealer financing arrangement may provide for a dealer rebate, a portion of interest received by the bank on each contract and then paid to the dealer as an incentive, or dealer reserve, an account set up by the bank containing the interest rate differential that accrues to the dealer when the installment sales contract earns interest for the bank. Conditional sales contracts purchased from dealers under such arrangements are commonly referred to as "dealer paper."

**DEBIT**   A dollar entry which increases an asset account and decreases a liability or equity account. Asset and expense accounts generally have debit balances while liability, capital and income accounts have credit balances.

**DEBIT CARD**   A card that resembles a credit card but which debits a transaction account (checking account) with the transfers occurring contemporaneously with the customer's purchases. A debit card may be machine readable, allowing for the activation of an automated teller machine or other automated payments equipment.

**DEBT**   A sum of money, or an amount of materials or services owed to another person according to the terms of a previous agreement or other obligation.

**DEBT COLLECTOR**   A person who regularly collects debts for third parties. SEE FAIR DEBT COLLECTION PRACTICES ACT.

**DEBT CONSOLIDATION**   Combining two or more loans into one with the goal of reducing payments.

**DEBT INSTRUMENT**   A written obligation to repay a debt; usually in the form of a promissory note, but including bills and bonds.

**DEBT RATIO**   An indication of the percentage of a business that is being financed by creditors derived by dividing total debt by total assets. The term may also signify the total-debt-to-net-worth ratio (debt-to-worth) which is used for the same purpose.

**DEBT SERVICE**   The periodic payment of principal and interest.

**DECLINING BALANCE DEPRECIATION**   A weighted depreciation method that charges higher depreciation expenses in earlier years and lesser amounts in later years over the depreciable term. SEE DEPRECIATE.

**DEED**   A common term for an instrument transferring the ownership of real property. Real property is transferred when its title is passed from one person to another, either by an act of the parties or by operation of law. A written transfer of the title to real property is called a "grant" or a "conveyance." A deed is a written instrument which conveys or transfers the title to real property. It is an executed conveyance and acts as a present transfer of the property.

An effective deed must have a grantor and a grantee, must be in writing and signed by the grantor, and must be delivered to the grantee and accepted by him or her. These are the minimum requirements for a valid deed and if they are all present, it is effective to transfer title to the grantee. Frequently used applications are:

• quitclaim deed: forever transfers all right, title and interest in real property to another;

• trust deed: commonly used to secure lenders against loss, the trust deed generally conveys legal title to real property to a trustee, stating explicit authority and conditions binding upon the trustee in his or her dealings with the property;

• warranty deed: a general warranty deed carries with it the express covenant of clear title, guaranteeing that the grantor will defend the title to the property against any and all claims. A special warranty deed is slightly more limited in scope; the grantor warrants that he or she will defend title against grantees, heirs and other claimants.

**DEED OF TRUST**   A formal written document that conveys the title to real property to a trustee as security for a debt. If the debt is not repaid according to the terms of the loan agreement the real property may be sold and the proceeds of sale applied to the balance owing on the loan.

**DEFALCATION** Embezzlement; a misappropriation of funds by a person in a trust or fiduciary position.

**DEFAULT** Failure to meet the terms of a credit agreement.

**DEFERRED AVAILABILITY CASH ITEM** Any item received for collection for which credit has not yet been given.

**DEFINITE TIME** An instrument is payable at a definite time if by its terms it is payable:
- on or before a stated date or at a fixed period after a stated date; or
- at a fixed period after sight; or
- at a definite time subject to any acceleration; or
- at a definite time subject to extension at the option of the holder, or to extension to a further definite time at the option of the maker or acceptor or automatically upon or after a specified act or event.

An instrument which by its terms is otherwise payable only upon an act or event uncertain as to time of occurrence is not payable at a definite time even though the act or event has occurred.

**DELINQUENCY PERCENTAGE** That percentage of the loan portfolio, measured by dollar amount or by number of loans or notes, that is past due.

**DEMAND DEPOSIT** A deposit payable on demand, or a time deposit with a maturity period or required notice period of less than 14 days, on which the depository institution does not reserve the right to require at least 14 days written notice of intended withdrawal. A demand deposit commonly takes the form of a checking account.

**DEMAND DRAFT** A draft payable on sight or immediately upon presentation to the drawee.

**DEMAND LOAN** Also "demand mortgage" or "demand note." The demand feature makes the obligation due and payable upon the demand or "call" of the holder.

**DEPARTMENT OF JUSTICE** The Justice Department's antitrust division is one of the authorities responsible for enforcing federal antitrust laws. Many bankers and federal bank regulators once believed that commercial banks were exempt from antitrust laws. In 1963, however, the Supreme Court clearly ruled in *United States v. Philadelphia National Bank* that there is no exemption. This decision, along with the Bank Merger Acts of 1960 and 1966 and the Bank Holding Company Act of 1956, gives the antitrust division authority to regulate the structure of banking.

The Justice Department can review all bank mergers and holding company bank acquisitions for potential anti-competitive effects. Under the Bank Merger Acts, the primary federal supervisory agency reviewing a proposed bank merger is required to seek an advisory opinion from the Justice Department concerning any probable competitive effects and to notify the Justice Department if approval is granted. Under the Bank Holding Company Act, the Federal Reserve is required to notify the Justice Department immediately when it grants a bank holding company approval to acquire a bank or merge with another holding company. If the Justice Department wants to challenge a proposed acquisition or merger, it must take action under federal antitrust laws within 30 days after approval and before acquisition is consummated.

**DEPOSIT CEILING RATES OF INTEREST**   Maximum interest rates that can be paid on savings and time deposits at federally insured commercial banks, mutual savings banks, savings and loan associations, and credit unions. Ceilings on credit union deposits are established by the National Credit Union Administration. Ceilings on deposits held by the other depository institutions are established by the Depository Institutions Deregulation Committee (DIDC). Under the oversight of the DIDC, deposit interest rate ceilings were phased out over a 6-year period ending in 1986.

**DEPOSIT INSURANCE**   Insurance for the benefit of the depositor against the risk of loss due to failure of the depository institution. SEE FEDERAL DEPOSIT INSURANCE CORPORATION (FDIC).

**DEPOSITARY**   A bank, trust company, other institution or individual entrusted with personal property for safekeeping.

**DEPOSITOR**   Any person or legal entity in whose name funds are deposited to an account established with a depository institution.

**DEPOSITORY INSTITUTION**   A commercial bank, savings bank, savings and loan association, building and loan association, homestead association (including a cooperative bank) or credit union.

**DEPOSITORY INSTITUTION MANAGEMENT INTERLOCKS ACT**   Regulations governing management interlocks relate to the positions individuals hold in depository organizations. Where ownership regulations address the matter of resource concentration through limitations on ownership, interlock regulations address the same matters by prohibiting interlocks between institutions with no significant ownership relationship. The intent is to prohibit possibly anticompetitive behavior where ownership is not a factor.

Originally, management interlocks were prohibited only when one of the banks was a member of the Federal Reserve. Under section 8 of the Clayton Act, member bank management officials — defined as officers, directors, or employees — could not serve in a similar capacity with unaffiliated banks in the same community or a town nearby. The Depository Institution Management Interlocks Act, included in the Financial Institutions Regulatory and Interest Rate Control Act of 1978, broadened and strengthened regulatory control of management interlocks in several ways.

First, the act expands the interlock prohibitions to a broader group of individuals than did the Clayton Act. It extends the definition of management official, for example, to include de facto management officials, such as advisory directors. Additionally, it prohibits individuals who might be considered representatives or nominees of another person from serving as management officials.

Second, the act expands the scope of prohibited interlocks to all depository institutions and organizations and differentiates institutions in metropolitan areas from those in rural areas. Management interlocks are generally prohibited between unaffiliated depository organizations (those with 50 percent or less common ownership) located in the same "relevant metropolitan statistical area," provided one of the organizations has total assets in excess of $20 million. In rural areas, interlocks are prohibited between unaffiliated organizations if both are in the same city, town, or village, or in communities that are contiguous or within ten miles of one another.

Finally, the Depository Institution Management Interlocks Act prohibits interlocks between large depository institutions or holding companies, regardless of location. A management official of a depository institution or holding company with assets of more than $1 billion cannot hold a management position at any other unaffiliated depository organization with assets of more than $500 million.

**DEPOSITORY INSTITUTIONS DEREGULATION AND MONETARY CONTROL ACT OF 1980**  On March 31, 1980, the President signed into law the Depository Institutions Deregulation and Monetary Control Act of 1980. This legislation marks the culmination of many years of effort by members of the Congress, the regulatory agencies, and the financial industry to change some of the rules under which U.S. financial institutions have operated for nearly half a century. In many cases, these rules had been made obsolete by changes in the economy, the functioning of credit markets, technology, consumer demands, and the competitive environment.

The principal goals of the act include: (1) improving monetary control and equalizing its cost among depository institutions, (2) removing the impediments to competition for funds by depository institutions and allowing small savers a market rate of return, and (3) expanding the availability of financial services to the public and reducing competitive inequalities between financial institutions offering them. The major elements expected to contribute to these goals are:

• Imposition of uniform federal reserve requirements on similar classes of reservable liabilities at all depository institutions, including commercial banks, savings and loan associations, mutual savings banks, and credit unions;

• Authorization for collection of data needed to monitor and control the money and credit aggregates;

• Provision for the orderly phase-out of deposit interest rate ceilings;

• Preemption of state usury ceilings on certain types of loans;

• Nationwide authorization of NOW accounts and certain other interest-bearing balances at both banks and thrift institutions that can be used for transactions purposes; and

• Broadening of the asset powers and permissible activities of thrift institutions. Referred to as the Monetary Control Act of 1980, *Title I* of the new legislation was designed to enhance the Federal Reserve's ability to implement monetary policy. The legislation also ensured that all depository institutions share equally whatever burden is necessary for an effective national monetary policy.

There are three major parts to Title I—reporting requirements, reserve requirements, and pricing of Federal Reserve services. With respect to the first two, which are directly related to monetary control, Title I:

• Requires all depository institutions to report their assets and liabilities at such intervals as the Board of Governors of the Federal Reserve System may prescribe:

• Extends reserve requirements imposed by the Board to all depository institutions, including all commercial, savings, and mutual savings banks, savings and loan associations, and credit unions that are federally insured or eligible to apply for federal insurance;

• Requires each depository institution to maintain reserves of 3 percent on its transaction accounts of $25 million or less, plus 12 percent, or such ratio that the Board may set between 8 and 14 percent, on the amount over $25 million. This $25 million "tranche" was indexed to change each calendar year beginning in 1982 by 80 percent of the percentage change in total transaction accounts of all depository institutions during the previous year ending June 30;

• Requires each depository institution to maintain reserves of 3 percent, or such ratio that the Board may set between 0 and 9 percent, on its nonpersonal time deposits. The Board may vary the reserve requirements on nonpersonal time deposits according to maturity.

• Provides for an eight-year phase-in to the new reserve requirements on transaction accounts and nonpersonal time deposits for nonmember banks and thrift institutions and a four-year phase-down (in some cases, a phase-up) to the new requirements for members. However, requirements on new types of accounts or deposits authorized under federal law after April 1, 1980, such as NOW accounts outside New England, New York, and New Jersey, would not be phased in;

• Entitles any depository institution in which transaction accounts or nonpersonal time deposits are held to borrow from the Federal Reserve discount window on the same terms as member banks;

• Permits the Board to impose reserve requirements on certain borrowings from foreign sources, sales of assets by depository institutions in the United States to their foreign offices, and loans to U.S. residents made by foreign offices of depository institutions in the United States. Such Eurocurrency reserve requirements would apply to foreign branches, subsidiaries, and international banking facilities of member and nonmember institutions uniformly;

• Permits the Board, upon a finding by at least five members that extraordinary circumstances require such action and after consultation with the appropriate congressional committees, to impose any level of reserve requirements on any liability of depository institutions for up to 180 days;

• Specifies that reserve requirements may be satisfied by holdings of vault cash, reserve balances held directly at a Federal Reserve Bank, or, in the case of nonmember institutions, reserve balances passed to the Federal Reserve through a correspondent or other designated institution ("pass-through" balances);

• Permits the Board, upon an affirmative vote of five members and after consultation with certain federal financial regulatory authorities, to impose supplemental reserve requirements on every depository institution of up to 4 percent of its transaction accounts, but only if specified conditions are met, including that "the sole purpose of such requirement is to increase the amount of reserves maintained to a level essential for the conduct of monetary policy." The supplemental requirement is to be maintained either in an Earnings Participation Account at a Federal Reserve Bank, on which earnings will be paid quarterly at a rate not exceeding the rate earned on the Federal Reserve's securities portfolio during the previous calendar quarter, or in vault cash.

On August 15, 1980, the Board announced revisions in its Regulation D to implement the reporting and reserve requirement provisions of the act.

*Title II* of the act, titled the Depository Institutions Deregulation Act of 1980, provides for interest rate ceilings on time and savings deposits at depository institutions to be phased out over a period of 6 years. *Title V* of the act overrides existing state usury laws limiting the interest rate that may be paid on a number of specified types of loans. In removing long-standing impediments to the paying and charging of market interest rates, the act introduced a new era in the long evolution of public policy toward competition in financial markets.

*Titles III* and *IV*, Nationwide NOW accounts and new thrift institution powers: New powers for banks and other depository institutions to extend and diversify their balance sheets are provided in Title III, designated the "Consumer Checking Account Equity Act of 1980," and Title IV. Title III provides the first permanent nationwide authorization for depository institutions to offer interest-bearing transaction accounts effective December 31, 1980, and expands other deposit offering and servicing capabilities of these institutions. Specifically, Title III:

• Authorizes most types of depository institutions to offer negotiable order of withdrawal (NOW) accounts;

• Authorizes banks to continue offering automatic transfer services (ATS) for shifting funds from savings to checking accounts;

• Authorizes all federally chartered credit unions to issue share drafts;

• Authorizes savings and loan associations to establish remote service units (RSUs) to facilitate debits and credits to savings accounts, loan payments, and related transactions;

• Increases deposit insurance from $40,000 to $100,000 at federally insured banks, savings and loan associations, and credit unions.

*Title IV* of the act focuses primarily on the asset holdings of nonbank thrift institutions. It aims at overcoming the existing maturity imbalance between the predominantly long-term asset portfolios, mainly fixed-rate mortgage loans, and short-term deposit and non-deposit liability structures of these institutions. Among the powers conferred upon federally chartered savings and loan associations by Title IV are:

• Investment of up to 20 percent of their assets in consumer loans, commercial paper, and corporate debt securities;

• Investment in shares or certificates of open-end investment companies that are registered with the SEC and that restrict their portfolios to the same investment instruments that savings and loan associations are allowed to hold directly;

• Investment of up to 5 percent of their assets in loans for education and community development and unsecured construction loans;

• Issuance of credit cards and extension of credit in connection with them;

• Provision of trust and fiduciary powers under restrictions and protections similar to those applicable to national banks;

• Inclusion of shares of open-end management investment companies among the assets eligible to satisfy liquidity requirements;

• Issuance of mutual capital certificates to be included as part of general reserves and net worth.

For mutual savings banks with federal charters, new powers included:

• Investment of up to 5 percent of total assets in commercial, corporate, and business loans within the home state of the bank or within 75 miles of the bank's home office;

• Acceptance of demand deposits in connection with commercial, corporate, and business loan relationships.

*Title VI* was designated the Truth in Lending Simplification and Reform Act, revising the 1969 Truth in Lending Act to make it easier for creditors to comply with its disclosure provisions. The title requires the Federal Reserve to publish model disclosure forms, exempts agricultural credit from coverage by Truth in Lending, and permits lenders greater tolerance (one-eighth of 1 per centum) in disclosing the annual percentage rate. *Title VII* contains a number of revisions to the national banking laws. It authorizes the Comptroller of the Currency or the Board of Governors of the Federal Reserve System to extend the five-year period that national banks or bank holding companies are currently allowed to dispose of lawfully acquired real estate, removes the limitation of dividends on preferred stock of national banks to 6 percent, provides for revocation of trust powers of national banks, and specifies new minimum ownership requirements for directors of national banks.

*Title VIII*, designated the Financial Regulation Simplification Act of 1980, complements the specific deregulatory provisions of other titles of the act.

*Title IX* imposed a moratorium on takeovers of domestic financial institutions by foreign persons in order to allow Congress time to consider new legislation in response to what had been considered in some quarters as an alarming increase in foreign takeovers of U.S. financial institutions.

**DEPOSITORY INSTITUTIONS DEREGULATION COMMITTEE (DIDC)** The committee responsible for the orderly phase-out over a six-year period of interest rate ceilings on time and savings accounts at depository institutions. Voting members of the DIDC are the Secretary of the Treasury and the Chairmen of the Federal Reserve Board, Federal Deposit Insurance Corporation, Federal Home Loan Bank Board, and National Credit Union Administration. The Comptroller of the Currency serves as a non-voting member.

**DEPRECIATION** The process of reducing the value of assets at periodic intervals over the length of time prescribed by the Internal Revenue Code and charging the reduction amount against earnings.

**DESCRIPTIVE BILLING** Frequently used in the periodic billing of revolving charge accounts, descriptive billing statements do not include original charge receipts but describe each charge transaction in detail on the statement itself.

**DEUTSCHE MARK** Monetary unit of Germany.

**DIDC** SEE DEPOSITORY INSTITUTIONS DEREGULATION COMMITTEE.

**DINAR** Monetary unit of Algeria, Bahrain, Iraq, Jordan, Kuwait, Libya, Tunisia, Yemen.

**DIRECT DEPOSIT** An electronic credit of funds to a deposit account; popular items for direct deposit include Social Security checks, county warrants and corporate payroll checks. SEE AUTOMATIC DEPOSIT PLAN.

**DISCOUNT** The amount of money deducted from the face value of an instrument or the purchase price of a commodity. Also refers to a credit term offered by suppliers such as: "2/10,N/30" or "two-ten, net-thirty" which signifies that a 2% discount is available if the invoice is paid within ten days, otherwise the full amount of the purchase price is due in 30 days. A credit rating of "discount" indicates that a company takes advantage of the 2% reduction and generally signifies a strong cash position. SEE ALSO PREMIUMS.

**DISCOUNT RATE** The interest rate at which eligible depository institutions may borrow funds, usually for short periods, directly from the Federal Reserve Banks.

The law requires the board of directors of each Reserve Bank to establish the discount rate every 14 days subject to the approval of the Board of Governors. The Federal Reserve Act originally envisioned that the discount rate of each Reserve Bank would be set to reflect the banking and credit conditions in its District. Over the years, however, the progressive integration of regional credit markets into a fluid national market has gradually produced a national perspective for discount rate determination.

As a result, the twelve Reserve Banks now post a uniform structure of discount rates except during the short periods when some Reserve Banks already have changed their rate, but the boards of other Reserve Banks have not yet met to take such action.

The basic discount rate applies to all loans made under the programs of adjustment and seasonal credit. This rate also applies to other extended credit for an initial period. However, the rate on extended borrowing is raised above the basic rate according to a schedule if the credit is outstanding over a longer period; an alternative flexible rate that takes into account rates on market sources of funds may be established at a certain point in the rate schedule. When extended credit provided to a particular institution is expected to be outstanding for an unusually long time in relatively large amounts, the period for which each rate in the extended credit rate structure applies may be shortened. The discount rate that would be applicable to loans made to individuals, partnerships. and corporations in unusual and exigent circumstances would be established at the time of the loan.

**DISCOUNT WINDOW** Figurative expression for the Federal Reserve facility for extending credit directly to eligible depository institutions (those with transaction accounts or nonpersonal time deposits).

**DISCRETIONARY TRUST** A trust under which the trustee has discretionary powers to control disbursements of income or principal to the beneficiary.

**DISCRIMINATION** SEE EQUAL CREDIT OPPORTUNITY ACT.

**DISHONOR** An instrument is dishonored when a necessary or optional presentment is duly made and due acceptance or payment is refused or cannot be obtained within the prescribed time or in case of bank collections the instrument is seasonably returned by the midnight deadline, or presentment is excused and the instrument is not duly accepted or paid.

Subject to any necessary notice of dishonor and protest, the holder has upon dishonor an immediate right of recourse against the drawers and indorsers.

Return of an instrument for lack of proper indorsement is not a dishonor.

A term in a draft or an indorsement thereof allowing a stated time for re-presentment in the event of any dishonor of the draft by nonacceptance if a time draft or by nonpayment if a sight draft gives the holder as against any secondary party bound by the term an option to waive the dishonor without affecting the liability of the secondary party and he may present again up to the end of the stated time.

**DISSOLUTION**   Termination of (1) a corporation upon expiration of the corporate charter, by merger, consolidation or action of the shareholders, or by the Secretary of State; or (2) of a partnership by agreement of the partners, or by operation of law due, for example, to death, incapacity or insolvency.

**DOLLAR**   The monetary unit of the United States, including Guam, the Marshall Islands, Puerto Rico, Solomon Islands and the U.S. Virgin Islands. The dollar is also the monetary unit of the following countries: Antigua, Australia, Bahamas, Barbados, British Honduras, British Samoa, Brunei, Canada, Dominica, Ethiopia, Grenada, Guiana Guyana, Hong Kong, Jamaica, Kiribati, Liberia, Montserrat, Nauru Nevis, New Guinea, New Zealand, Singapore, St. Kitts, St. Lucia, St. Vincent, Taiwan, Trinidad and Tobago, Turks and Caicos Islands, Tuvalu, and Zimbabwe.

**DONG**   Monetary unit of Vietnam.

**DOUGLAS AMENDMENT**   The Douglas Amendment in the Bank Holding Company Act prohibits interstate acquisitions of banks by bank holding companies unless specifically authorized by the laws of the state in which the bank is located.
    Since no states had such laws in 1956, the act initially halted interstate banking expansion.

**DOW JONES AVERAGE**   At the end of the trading day, the closing prices of representative stocks traded on the New York Stock Exchange, (30 industrials, 15 public utilities, and 20 transportation) are averaged and used as an accepted indicator of the market's performance.

**DOWN PAYMENT**   An "out of pocket" amount paid by the buyer-borrower, usually calculated as a percentage of the total purchase price of the commodity and commonly referred to in terms such as "20% down" or "10% down." The unpaid balance, plus any appropriate additional charges, is the amount to be financed on a conditional sale contract or direct loan.

**DRACHMA**   Monetary unit of Greece.

**DUAL CONTROL**   A requirement that a function or procedure must be executed in the presence of another authorized person. For example, entry to a safe deposit box should be in the dual control of the customer and an authorized employee of the bank.

**DUAL CUSTODY**   A requirement of joint custody to prevent risk of loss or to protect the safety of employees. For example, the vault combination is kept in dual custody.

**DUE FROM BANK**   SEE ACCOUNT SERVICING BANK.

**DWELLING**   Any building, structure (including a mobile home), or portion thereof which is occupied as, or designed or intended for occupancy as, a residence by one or more natural persons, and any vacant land which is offered for sale or lease for the construction or location thereon of any such building, structure, or portion thereof.

# E

**EARNING ASSET** A bank's earning assets are primarily comprised of its loans and investments.

**EARNINGS CREDIT** The relative value of the funds kept on deposit as used to offset account service charges for a specified period. SEE ACCOUNT ANALYSIS.

**EARNINGS PER SHARE** A corporation's net income calculated as it relates to each outstanding share of common stock.

**ECOA** SEE EQUAL CREDIT OPPORTUNITY ACT.

**EDGE ACT CORPORATION** An organization chartered by the Federal Reserve to engage in international banking operations. The Board of Governors acts upon applications by U.S. and foreign banking organizations to establish Edge corporations. It also examines Edge corporations and their subsidiaries. The Edge corporation gets its name from Senator Walter Edge of New Jersey, the sponsor of the original legislation to permit formation of such organizations.

**EDUCATION LOAN** Also referred to as "student loan," a loan made for the purpose of financing undergraduate, postgraduate, vocational or other educational training.

**EE BOND** EE bonds are savings bonds issued to the general public by the U.S. Government at a discount. Series EE bonds were first issued in 1980, replacing the Series E bond, and are available in denominations from $50 to $10,000. They are sold at 1/2 of their face value and pay varying interest rates.

**EFFECTIVE GROSS INCOME** Total income less deductions for contingencies, vacancies, or bad debts but before deductions for operating expenses.

**EFFECTS TEST** All credit practices are subject to the "effects test." Effects test practices, while not discriminatory in intent, have a disproportionate adverse impact on protected class members (those persons covered by the prohibited bases of the Equal Credit Opportunity Act). Under the effects test, a court might determine that a bank is in violation of the ECOA if a particular practice has a disproportionate adverse impact and is not reasonably related to creditworthiness. For example: a requirement that applicants have unreasonably extensive credit histories in order to receive credit may be illegal discrimination because of its unequal effect upon married women. When a practice is found that may have the effect of discrimination, the banks management and board of directors are encouraged to review the practice with their legal counsel. They should also determine if an alternative business practice exists which serves the same business need, yet is less discriminatory in effect, and consider implementing it. SEE ALSO EQUAL CREDIT OPPORTUNITY ACT.

**EFT** SEE ELECTRONIC FUND TRANSFER.

**EFTA** SEE ELECTRONIC FUND TRANSFER ACT.

**EFTS** SEE ELECTRONIC FUND TRANSFER SYSTEM.

**ELASTICITY** The ability of a bank to adjust its lending practices to meet the demands of economic trends; to meet increased credit and currency demands during economic expansion and to reduce the availability of credit and currency during periods of economic contraction.

**ELECTRONIC FUND TRANSFER (EFT)** Any transfer of funds, other than a transaction originated by check, draft, or similar paper instrument, that is initiated through an electronic terminal, telephone, or computer or magnetic tape for the purpose of ordering, instructing, or authorizing a financial institution to debit or credit an account. The term includes, but is not limited to, point-of-sale transfers, automated teller machine transfers, direct deposits or withdrawals of funds and transfers initiated by telephone. It includes all transfers resulting from debit card transactions, including those that do not involve an electronic terminal at the time of the transaction. The term does not include payments made by check, draft or similar paper instrument at an electronic terminal.

**ELECTRONIC FUND TRANSFER ACT (EFTA) REGULATION E** The Electronic Fund Transfer Act (EFTA) was enacted November 10, 1978, and became effective May 10, 1980. It was implemented by Regulation E. The act establishes the rights, liabilities and responsibilities of participants in electronic fund transfer systems. Electronic fund transfer systems include:
- Automated teller machine transfers
- Telephone bill payment services
- All transfers resulting from debit card transactions, including transactions that do not involve an electronic terminal at the point of sale
- Preauthorized transfers from or to a consumer's account, such as direct deposit of Social Security payments.

The term electronic fund transfer refers to a transaction initiated through an electronic terminal, telephone, computer or magnetic tape that instructs a financial institution to either credit or debit a consumer's asset account. This definition included debit card transactions which are not initiated through an electronic terminal but are processed electronically. An account includes a consumer checking, savings, or share account held by an institution and established by the consumer primarily for family, personal or household purposes. Electronic terminal includes point-of-sale terminals, automated teller machines, and cash dispensing machines. The consumer is usually issued a card or a code (access devices) or both, that may be used to initiate such transfers.

The types of electronic fund transfers *not* covered by the act are:
- check guarantee or authorization services that do not directly result in a debit or credit to the consumer's account;
- any incidental transfer of funds for a consumer within a system that is used primarily to transfer funds between financial institutions or businesses. An example is a wire transfer of funds for a consumer through the Federal Reserve Communications System or other similar network;
- any transaction which has as its primary purpose the purchase or sale of securities or commodities registered by the Securities and Exchange Commission or the Commodity Futures Trading Commission;
- intra-institutional automatic transfers between the institution and a consumer's account;

- trust accounts;
- certain incidental telephone-initiated transfers not under a prearranged plan contemplating periodic or recurring transfers;
- all preauthorized transfers at financial institutions with $25 million, or less, in assets.

The regulation governs the issuance of access devices, including those connected with preexisting overdraft accounts, and the addition of EFT capabilities to existing accepted credit cards. It does not govern the issuance of combined access device-credit cards (other than those that have only an existing overdraft privilege). Those combined devices are covered by Regulation Z, Truth-in-Lending. In general, an institution may issue an access device to a consumer only if:

- it is requested (in writing or orally) or applied for; or
- it is a renewal of, or in substitution for, an accepted access device.

**ELECTRONIC FUND TRANSFER SYSTEM (EFTS)**   A variety of systems and technologies for transferring funds electronically rather than by check. Includes Fedwire, Bankwire, automated clearinghouses (ACHs) and other automated systems.

**ELECTRONIC TERMINAL**   An electronic device, other than a telephone, operated by a consumer through which a consumer may initiate an electronic fund transfer. The term includes, but is not limited to, point-of-sale terminals, automated teller machines, and cash dispensing machines.

**ELIGIBLE PAPER**   The term used to denote acceptances, promissory notes, drafts, bills of exchange and other instruments that the Federal Reserve is permitted by law to accept for discount at its lowest rate of interest.

**EMBEZZLEMENT**   The fraudulent conversion of personal property by a person to whom it was entrusted by or for the owner. SEE ALSO DEFALCATION.

**EMBOSS**   To raise alpha or numeric characters on a bank card for the purpose of visual identification or reading by an embossed character reader (ECR).

**EMINENT DOMAIN**   The soverign power of the state to appropriate real property for the public good, with just and reasonable compensation to the owner. SEE EXPROPRIATION.

**EMPIRICALLY DERIVED CREDIT SCORING SYSTEM**   A credit scoring system is a system that evaluates an applicant's creditworthiness mechanically, based on key attributes of the applicant and aspects of the transaction, and that determines, alone or in conjunction with an evaluation of additional information about the applicant, whether an applicant is deemed creditworthy. To qualify as an empirically derived, demonstrably and statistically sound, credit scoring system, the system must be:

- based on data that are derived from an empirical comparison of sample groups or the population of creditworthy and noncreditworthy applicants who applied for credit within a reasonable preceding period of time;
- developed for the purpose of evaluating the creditworthiness of applicants with respect to the legitimate business interests of the creditor utilizing the system (including, but not limited to, minimizing bad debt losses and operating expenses in accordance with the creditor's business judgment);

    • developed and validated using accepted statistical principles and methodology; and

    • periodically revalidated by the use of appropriate statistical principles and methodology and adjusted as necessary to maintain predictive ability. SEE ALSO JUDGMENTAL SYSTEM FOR EVALUATING APPLICANTS.

**ENCODING**   The imprinting of magnetic ink character recognition (MICR) characters on checks, deposits or other bank documents. The term also refers to the magnetized recording of data in the magnetic stripe on a bank card.

**ENCUMBRANCE**   Any claim, interest or right such as a lien, mortgage or easement on real property.

**ENDORSEMENT**   The placing of one's name, either by signature or by rubber stamp, on an instrument so as to pass title to another party who becomes "holder in due course." "Endorsement" also refers to the stamp on the back of bank card sales drafts and credit slips, and on checks to identify the endorsing bank and date processed. The term may also imply to the act of a third party in the guaranty of payment in the event of default of the maker of a note.

**ENDORSEMENT – QUALIFIED**   An attempt to limit the endorser's liability should the debtor fail to honor the instrument; e.g., an endorsement "without recourse."

**ENDORSEMENT – RESTRICTIVE**   An endorsement that restricts the negotiability of an instrument, e.g., "for deposit only."

**ENDORSEMENT – SPECIAL**   An endorsement that names the party to whom the instrument is to be transferred.

**EQUAL CREDIT OPPORTUNITY ACT (ECOA)**   The Equal Credit Opportunity Act became effective on October 28, 1975, and is implemented by Regulation B. Regulation B prohibits discrimination in any aspect of a credit transaction on the basis of race, color, religion, national origin, sex, marital status, age (providing the applicant has the capacity to enter into a binding contract), receipt of income from public assistance programs, or good faith exercise of any right under the Consumer Credit Protection Act.

    These factors are referred to throughout the regulation as "prohibited bases." In addition, discrimination is unlawful if an application is declined because of the race, color, religion, national origin, sex, marital status, or age of an applicant's business associates or of the persons who will be related to the extension of credit, e.g., those residing in the neighborhood where collateral is located. Illegal discrimination means treating an applicant or a group of applicants less favorably than another group because of a protected basis. Regulation B sets forth certain acts and practices which are specifically prohibited or permitted. To limit discrimination, it imposes a balance between the bank's need to know about a prospective borrower, and the borrower's right not to disclose information inapplicable to the transaction. The regulation deals with taking, evaluating and acting on the application, and the furnishing and maintenance of credit information. It does not prevent a creditor from determining any information necessary to evaluate the creditworthiness of an applicant.

**EQUITY**   The difference between a company's total assets and its total liabilities, the value of the stockholder's ownership in a corporation. Equity includes common stock, preferred stock, retained earnings and other surplus reserves. Equity also refers to the current market value of property less all voluntary and involuntary liens thereon.

**EQUITY CAPITAL**   Equity capital is the capital invested in an organization by shareholders or owners, as opposed to "debt capital."

**EQUITY FINANCING**   The process of raising funds for an organization by selling equity, or ownership, in it usually through the sale of stock.

**ERROR**   As defined by the Electronic Fund Transfer Act, "error" means: an unauthorized EFT, an incorrect EFT to or from the consumer's account, the omission from a periodic statement of an EFT to or from the consumer's account that should have been included, a computational or bookkeeping error made by the institution relating to an EFT, the consumer's receipt of an incorrect amount of money from an electronic terminal, an EFT not identified in accordance with the requirements, or a consumer's request for any documentation required or for additional information or clarification concerning an EFT.

The term "error" does *not* include a routine inquiry about the balance in the consumer's account or a request for duplicate copies of documentation or other information that is made only for tax or other recordkeeping purposes.

**ESCALATION CLAUSE**   A provision in a loan contract permitting the bank to increase or decrease the rate of interest charged if economic conditions change significantly.

**ESCAPE CLAUSE**   A provision in a loan contract permitting one or more of the parties to be relieved of any contractual obligation previously incurred or agreed to under stipulated conditions.

**ESCROW**   A transfer of property by written agreement through a third party who is entrusted with the safekeeping of the property. The third party, generally referred to as an "escrow agent" or "escrow officer," is responsible for the delivery of the property only upon the satisfaction of a condition or conditions precedent.

**ESCUDO**   Monetary unit of Cape Verde and Portugal.

**ESTATE**   All of the real or personal property, including intangibles, owned by an individual at the time of his or her death. May also generally refer to the right, title and interest held by a person in real or personal property.

**ESTATE TAX**   A graduated state or federal excise tax on the transfer of property upon a person's death to be paid before property is transferred to heirs.

**EURODOLLARS**   Deposits denominated in U.S. dollars at banks and other financial institutions outside the United States. Although this name originated because of the large amounts of such deposits held at banks in Western Europe, similar deposits in other parts of the world are also called Eurodollars.

**EXCESS RESERVES**   Each financial institution is required to set aside a certain percentage of customer deposits as determined by the Board of Governors of the Federal Reserve. Those funds held in reserve in excess of the required minimum requirement, whether or not held on deposit with the Federal Reserve, are designated as excess reserves.

**EXCHANGE RATE**  Also called "rate of exchange" the term refers to the price at which one currency can be bought with another currency or with gold. Exchange rates often fluctuate because of economic or political factors.

**EXECUTOR**  The individual or corporation, such as a bank, which is identified in a will and charged with the responsibility of administering the estate upon the death of the maker (testator) of the will and, thus, to dispose of the estate in accordance with the wishes of the deceased. An *executor de bonis non* is that person, named in the will by the testator, whose responsibility is to complete the administration of the estate should the originally named executor fail to do so.

**EXEMPTED SECURITY**  A security that is exempted from most provisions of the securities laws, including the margin rules. Such securities include U.S. government and agency securities, municipal securities designated by the SEC.

**EXIMBANK**  SEE EXPORT-IMPORT BANK OF THE UNITED STATES.

**EXPEDITED FUNDS AVAILABILITY ACT (EFA)**  The Expedited Funds Availability Act (Title VI of Public Law 100-86) was enacted on August 10, 1987, and became effective on September 1, 1988. Regulation CC (12 CFR 229) issued by the Board of Governors of the Federal Reserve System, implements the EFA. The act and regulation set forth the requirements that depository institutions make funds deposited into transaction accounts available according to specified time schedules and disclose funds availability policies to their customers. The regulation also establishes rules designed to speed the collection and return of unpaid checks.

Regulation CC contains three subparts. Subpart A defines terms and provides for administrative enforcement. Subpart B specifies availability schedules or timeframes within which banks must make funds available for withdrawal. It also includes rules regarding exceptions to the schedules, disclosure of funds availability policies, and payment of interest. Subpart C sets forth the rules to ensure the expeditious return of checks, the responsibilities of paying and returning banks, authorization of direct returns, notification of nonpayment of large-dollar returns by the paying bank, check endorsement standards, and other related charges to the check collection system.

Depository banks are permitted to provide availability to customers in a shorter time than that prescribed in the regulation. The regulation does not affect a depository bank's right to accept or reject a check for deposit, to charge back the customer's account based on a returned check of notice of nonpayment, or to claim a refund for any credit provided to the customer.

Nothing in the regulation requires a depository bank to have its facilities open for customers to make withdrawals at specified times or on specific days.

**EXPENDITURE**  The payment, or promise of future payment and the obligation incurred thereunder, for goods or services delivered. If, for example, the goods delivered are determined to be a capital asset, the expenditure may be classified as a capital expenditure.

**EXPENSE**  The term "expense" broadly refers to the cost charged against revenue for goods or services received and is deducted from gross income.

**EXPORT**   To ship an item to a foreign country. The term may refer to the item itself or to the act of moving it out of the country.

**EXPORT CREDIT**   The financing, generally through the use of a letter of credit, of the shipment of goods to a foreign country.

**EXPORT-IMPORT BANK OF THE UNITED STATES**   Also referred to as the Eximbank, or the Ex-Im Bank, this independent agency of the federal government was established in 1934 for the purpose of financing foreign trade. The Export-Import Bank offers direct credit facilities to foreign countries under the provision that loan proceeds must be spent on the purchase of U.S. goods and the loans repaid in U.S. dollars. The agency also offers export guarantees and export credit insurance to domestic exporters.

**EXPORT TRADING COMPANIES**   Under the terms of the Export Trading Company (ETC) Act of 1982, the Federal Reserve Bank may permit U.S. banks to own and operate export trading companies which are permitted to engage in financing, marketing, transacting orders, warehousing, shipping, insuring and all other aspects of international trade. The primary purpose is to help small and medium size businesses develop overseas markets by providing these financing, marketing, shipping and collection services where such functions may otherwise be cost prohibitive.

**EXPROPRIATION**   A modification of the right to private property, or the taking of private property through condemnation proceedings, for public purpose by a governmental agency through its right of eminent domain.

**EXTEND**   To grant credit or time. For example, the phrases "to extend credit" or "to grant a credit extension" generally means to make a loan. The phrase "to extend payments" generally means to offer installment terms of repayment over a set period of time. The phrase "to grant a payment extension" may mean to forgive a currently due monthly payment obligation, or to defer a payment currently due.

**EXTENSION OF CREDIT**   (1) The total amount of any loan, line of credit, or other legally binding lending commitment. (2) The total amount, based on the amount of consideration paid, of any loan, line of credit, or other legally binding lending commitment acquired by a lender by purchase, assignment, or otherwise.

**EXTORTION**   The obtaining of property from another, with his or her consent, or the obtaining of an official act of a public officer, induced by a wrongful use of force or fear, or under color of official right. The type of fear such as would constitute extortion, may be induced by any of the following threats: to do an unlawful injury to the person or property of the individual threatened or of a third person; or to accuse the individual threatened, or any relative or member of his or her family of any crime; or to expose, or to impute to him or them any deformity, disgrace or crime; or to expose any secret affecting him or her.

**EXTRAORDINARY INCOME**   Income which is not derived from the ordinary course of business. For example, whereas income from the sale of inventories might be ordinary to the nature and purpose of the business, income from the sale of a fixed asset, or from a judgment award, would be extraordinary and would generally be accounted for separately from the bulsiness's normal income.

**EXTRAORDINARY LOSS**   Loss which is not derived from the ordinary course of business. Examples of extraordinary loss would include the destruction of raw materials by a tornado or the loss of inventory due to the sinking of a transport vessel.

# F

**FAC**   SEE FEDERAL ADVISORY COUNCIL.

**FACTOR**   The method of raising cash by selling receivables.

**FAIR CREDIT REPORTING ACT(FCPA)**   The Fair Credit Reporting Act became effective on April 25, 1971. The act is designed to regulate the consumer reporting industry, to place disclosure obligations on users of consumer reports, and to ensure fair, timely and accurate reporting of credit information. It also restricts the use of consumer reports and occasionally requires the deletion of obsolete information. Financial institutions may be subject to the act as
  • credit grantors
  • purchasers of dealer paper
  • issuers of credit cards, and/or
  • employers
In general, the act does not apply to commercial transactions, including those that involve agricultural credit.

Although few banks are consumer reporting agencies, most are "users" of information obtained from them. As a user, an institution must identify itself to the consumer reporting agency and certify that the requested information will be used only as specified in the act. A written blanket certification may be given by the financial institution to cover all inquiries to a particular consumer reporting agency. Banks also rely on information from sources other than consumer reporting agencies that report experiences only with their own customers. As a user, a bank must disclose different information depending on its outside source of information.

The obligations imposed on users of credit information allow applicants to correct erroneous reports. The disclosures are triggered by either a denial of credit or an increase in the cost of credit. If credit is approved, but for a lesser amount than the original request, a denial under the act has occurred.

The disclosures required of users of credit information also apply to outside information received on comakers, guarantors, or sureties. Disclosures should be made to the party to whom they relate. In addition, denial of an overdraft or authorization refusal on a credit card purchase based on information from any outside source would trigger the need for disclosures, assuming the information bears upon the consumer's creditworthiness, credit standing, credit capacity, character, general reputation, personal characteristics or mode of living.

The term "consumer reporting agency" applies to anyone who might render a "consumer report." Certain banks function as consumer reporting agencies and, to the extent that they issue consumer reports, are covered by the act. An institution may become a consumer reporting agency if it regularly furnished information about a consumer to other creditors, correspondents, holding companies or affiliates, other than information on its own transactions or experience. However, if the institution furnishes information from outside sources to another party involved in the same transaction, the institution does not become a consumer reporting agency. For instance, such parties could include an insurer or a guarantor, such as the FHA, VA, private insurers or insured student loan programs, and other financial institutions participating in the transaction, or a collection agency engaged in collecting on the transaction. All consumer reporting agencies must:

• make the following required disclosures to consumers upon request and proper identification: (1) nature and substance of all information in its files at the time of the request, (2) sources of information, and (3) recipients of their consumer reports;

• ensure that obsolete information is not reported;

• attempt to resolve accuracy disputes with consumers;

• provide reports only for legitimate purposes;

• keep a dated record of each recipient of information about a consumer, even when inquiry is oral; and

• train personnel sufficiently to explain information furnished to consumers. Financial institutions may be liable for negligent noncompliance as either users of information or as consumer reporting agencies. Civil liability may include actual damages, court costs and attorney's fees. In addition, the court may award any amount for punitive damages in cases of willful noncompliance. Any officer or employee of an institution who obtains a credit report under false pretenses will be subject to a penalty of not more than $5,000 or imprisonment of not more than one year, or both.

**FAIR DEBT COLLECTION PRACTICES ACT (FDCPA)**   The Fair Debt Collection Practices Act (FDCPA), which became effective March 20, 1978, was designed to eliminate abusive, deceptive and unfair debt collection practices. In addition, the federal law protects reputable debt collectors from unfair competition and encourages consistent state action to protect consumers from abuses in debt collection. The FDCPA applies only to the collection of debt incurred by a consumer primarily for personal, family or household purposes. It does not apply to the collection of corporate debt or to debt owed for business or agricultural purposes.

Under the FDCPA, a "debt collector" is defined as any person who regularly collects, or attempts to collect, consumer debts for another person or institution or uses a name other than its own when collecting its consumer debts. That definition would include, for example, an institution that regularly collects debts for an unrelated institution. This includes reciprocal service arrangements where one institution solicits the help of another in collecting a defaulted debt from a customer who has moved.

An institution is not a debt collector under the FDCPA when it collects:

• another's debts only in isolated instances

• its own debts under its own name

• debts it originated and then sold but continues to service (such as mortgage and student loans)

- debts that were not in default when obtained
- debts that were obtained as security for a commercial credit transaction (such as in accounts receivable financing)
- debts incidental to a bona fide fiduciary relationship or escrow arrangement (such as a debt held in the institution's trust department or mortgage loan escrow for taxes and insurance)
- debts regularly for other institutions to which it is related by common ownership or corporate control.

Debt collectors that are not covered include:
- officers or employees of an institution who collect debts owed to that institution in the institution's name
- attorneys-at-law who collect debts for and in the name of the institutions
- legal process servers.

A debt collector may not communicate with a consumer at any unusual time (generally before 8 A.M. or after 9 P.M. in the debtor's time zone) or at any place that is inconvenient to the consumer, unless the consumer or a court of competent jurisdiction has already given permission for such contacts. A debt collector may not contact the consumer at his or her place of employment if the collector has reason to believe the employer prohibits such communications. If the debt collector knows the consumer has retained an attorney to handle the debt, and can easily ascertain the attorney's name and address, all contact must be with that attorney, unless the attorney is unresponsive or agrees to allow direct communication with the consumer. Other than the consumer and the consumer's attorney, the only third parties the debt collector may contact in trying to collect a debt are:
- a consumer reporting agency (if permitted by local law)
- the creditor
- the creditor's attorney
- the debt collector's attorney, unless a court of competent jurisdiction specifically allows direct contact with other persons.

Under the provisions of the FDCPA, a debt collector specifically may not:
- use or threaten to use violence or other criminal means to harm the physical person, reputation, or property of any person
- use obscene, profane, or other language which abuses the hearer or reader
- publish a list of consumers who allegedly refuse to pay their debts (except to a consumer reporting agency or to a legitimate user of consumer reports, where permitted)
- advertise a debt for sale in order to coerce payment
- annoy, abuse or harass persons by repeatedly calling their telephone numbers or allowing their telephones to ring continually
- make telephone calls without properly identifying oneself, except as allowed to obtain location information
- falsely represent or imply that he or she is vouched for, bonded by, or affiliated with the United States or any state, including the use of any badge, uniform, or similar identification
- falsely represent the character, amount or legal status of the debt, or of any services rendered, or compensation he or she may receive for collecting the debt
- falsely represent that he or she is an attorney or that communications are from an attorney

- threaten to take any action which is not legal or intended
- falsely represent or imply that the sale, referral, or other transfer of the debt will cause the consumer to lose a claim or a defense to payment, or become subject to any practice prohibited by the FDCPA
- falsely represent or imply that the consumer committed a crime or disgrace the consumer in any way
- communicate, or threaten to communicate, false credit information or information which should be known to be false, including not identifying disputed debts as such
- use or distribute written communications made to look like or falsely represented to be documents authorized, issued, or approved by any court, official, or agency of the United States or any state if it should give a false impression of its source, authorization, or approval
- use any false representation or deceptive means to collect or attempt to collect a debt or to obtain information about a consumer
- falsely represent or imply that accounts have been sold to innocent purchasers
- fail to disclose clearly, except as allowed in acquiring location information, that he or she is attempting to collect a debt and that information obtained will be used for that purpose
- falsely represent or imply that documents are legal process
- use any name other than the true name of the debt collector's business, company or organization
- falsely represent or imply that documents are not legal process or do not require action by the consumer
- falsely represent or imply that he or she operates or is employed by a consumer reporting agency
- collect any interest, fee, charge or expense incidental to the principal obligation unless it was authorized by the original debt agreement or is otherwise permitted by law
- accept a check or other instrument postdated by more than five days, unless he or she notifies the consumer, in writing, of any intention to deposit the check or instrument. That notice must be made not more than 10 nor less than three business days before the date of deposit
- solicit a postdated check or other postdated instrument or use as a threat or to institute criminal prosecution
- deposit or threaten to deposit a postdated check or other postdated payment instrument before the date on the check or instrument
- cause communication charges, such as those for collecting telephone calls, to be made to any person by concealing the true purpose of the communication
- take or threaten to repossess or disable property when the creditor has no enforceable right to the property or does not intend to do so, or if, under law, the property cannot be taken, repossessed or disabled
- use a postcard to contact a consumer about a debt.

Actions against debt collectors for violations of the FDCPA may be brought in any appropriate U.S. district court or other court of competent jurisdiction. The consumer has one year from the date on which the violation occurred to start such an action.

**FAIR HOUSING ACT**   The Fair Housing Act is Title VIII of the Civil Rights Act of 1968, including the Fair Housing Amendments Act of 1988. Title VIII prohibits discrimination on the basis of race, color, religion, sex, handicap, familial status, or national origin in all aspects of the sale, financing, or rental of housing.

Section 805 of the Act makes it illegal for a lender to deny a loan or to discriminate in fixing terms for loans made to finance the purchase, construction, improvement, or maintenance of housing because of race, color, religion, sex, handicap, familial status, or national origin.

The Fair Housing Act does not require banks to make unsound loans or to provide more favorable terms because of the applicant's status as a member of a group protected by the act. It only requires that the credit decision be based on economic factors applied equally to all applicants.

Examination procedures for bank examiners, as they pertain to fair housing lending, are designed to incorporate the Equal Credit Opportunity Act and the Home Mortgage Disclosure Act as well as the Fair Housing Act. The Office of the Comptroller of the Currency, for example, intends to ensure conscientious bank compliance with the requirements of those statutes. SEE EQUAL CREDIT OPPORTUNITY ACT, FAIR HOUSING HOME LOAN DATA SYSTEM, AND HOME MORTGAGE DISCLOSURE ACT.

**FAIR HOUSING HOME LOAN DATA SYSTEM (FHHLDS)**   To assist in determining compliance with the Fair Housing Act, the Office of the Comptroller of the Currency has developed the Fair Housing Home Loan Data System (FHHLDS). The FHHLDS Regulation became effective on January 1, 1980. It provides for the collection and retention of information necessary to perform a statistical analysis of a bank's home loan decisions to assist examiners in determining if the bank's loan and pricing policies are consistently applied to all applicants.

Mobile home, manufactured home, houseboat, and similar residential dwelling loans not secured by real estate are not covered by the FHHLDS. Monitoring information for such loans must be gathered under the provisions of the Equal Credit Opportunity Act, Regulation B.

The FHHLDS process involves two separate analyses, (1) Phase 1 analyzes a bank's decisions to approve or deny home loan applications, and (2) Phase 2 analyzes the loan terms offered to applicants. A bank receiving fifty or more home loan applications a year must keep a monthly record of its activity for each decision center evaluating home loan applications. The information in the Monthly Home Loan Activity Format includes information for purchase, construction-permanent, and refinance loans using the categories: applications received, loans closed, loans denied, and loans withdrawn.

That information must be completed within 10 days after the end of the month. Banks with fewer than 50 applications must compile the information the month following any quarter when the average volume of home loan applications exceeds four applications a month. After two consecutive quarters, when home loan activity drops to four or fewer applications a month, a bank may discontinue compiling this information the following month. This monthly format enables the OCC to monitor whether a bank's home loan application volume is sufficient for statistical analysis. [fig. Monthly Home Loan Activity Format and Inquiry/Application Log].

**FCPA**   SEE FAIR CREDIT REPORTING ACT.

**FCRS–80**   The Federal Reserve System in mid–1982 began using an improved communications network, Federal Reserve Communications System–80 (FRCS–80) which enables faster, more flexible transfers of funds, securities and other payments and data than possible through the earlier network which opened in August 1970. In addition to transferring funds and securities, the new system handles automated clearing house data, federal recurring payments and administrative messages related to these services. During 1983 the current system replaced a network centered in Culpeper, Va.

FEDWIRE is the name of the Federal Reserve System service which enables the transfer of funds and securities. FRCS–80 is the designation for the series of lines and communications switches through which the funds and securities debits and credits are transmitted. Under the old system, messages among Federal Reserve districts had to go through Culpeper. In the new system, messages are sent by the most direct route, using lines within the network. As a result, messages arrive faster. And, since multiple paths are available, a breakdown in one part of FRCS–80 is less disruptive than a breakdown in the centralized Culpeper system. In essence, FRCS–80 transmission lines resemble triangles, linking several Reserve Banks. Each Reserve Bank in turn is linked to another series of Reserve Banks. The Federal Reserve began pilot testing the FRCS–80 network in autumn 1981 at Reserve Banks in New York, Chicago and Cleveland, as well as the communications center in Culpeper. In addition, the New York Fed and other Reserve Banks in early 1982 began expanding district electronic funds and securities transfer and administrative message networks.

In 1982, in order to broaden network availability, the New York Reserve Bank began a pilot program of placing dial oriented terminals (D.O.T.) at depository institutions. By late 1984, some 160 of these terminals were in operation. With the D.O.T., low-volume users of funds and securities transfer services obtained direct access to the Reserve System's Fedwire service. Low-volume users average fewer than 20 transfers a day.

The D.O.T. is designed to allow low-volume users to send transfer messages through the terminal, rather than relay them by telephone or through correspondents. Medium-volume institutions, those with between 20 and 600 transfers a day, may communicate directly with the New York Fed using direct access remote terminals (D.A.R.T.).

The larger second district depository institutions, those with 600 or more transfers daily, already had computer-to-computer links to the New York Fed.

The three communications links—D.O.T., D.A.R.T., and computer-to-computer—make up the New York Reserve Bank's "Feddirect" funds and securities transfer program. "Feddirect" is a service mark of the New York Fed. Through the "Feddirect" program, district institutions of all sizes have on-line access to the U.S. central bank's Fedwire service.

**FDCPA**   SEE FAIR DEBT COLLECTION PRACTICES ACT.

**FDIC**   SEE FEDERAL DEPOSIT INSURANCE CORPORATION.

**FDPA**   SEE FLOOD DISASTER PROTECTION ACT.

**FED**   SEE FEDERAL RESERVE.

**FEDERAL ADVISORY COUNCIL (FAC)**   This group consists of one member from each federal Reserve District (usually a banker) elected annually by the Board of Directors of each of the 12 Federal Reserve Banks. They meet with the Board of Governors of the Federal Reserve System to discuss business and financial conditions and make advisory recommendations. SEE ADVISORY COMMITTEES.

**FEDERAL DEPOSIT INSURANCE CORPORATION (FDIC)**   Established by the Banking Act of 1933, the Federal Deposit Insurance Corporation directly supervises and examines insured state-chartered banks that are not members of the Federal Reserve System. There were 8451 insured, state-chartered nonmember banks at the end of 1984, accounting for nearly 59 percent of the nation's commercial banks. These banks held $476 billion in deposits, or more than 24 percent of total bank deposits.

Like the Federal Reserve, the FDIC is an independent federal agency. It is managed by three directors, one of whom is the Comptroller of the Currency, and two appointed by the President. The main office is in Washington, and the FDIC has six regional offices.

Although the FDIC supervises a large number of banks, its main function is to insure deposits at commercial banks and mutual savings banks. The insurance is funded through assessments on insured banks. The FDIC has accumulated a deposit insurance reserve fund over the years that amounted to $17.2 billion at the end of 1984. The FDIC can make special examinations of any insured bank when it is necessary to determine the condition of the bank for insurance purposes. Since 1983, for example, the FDIC has participated in the examination of certain problem banks not directly under its supervision.

To guarantee adherence to its supervisory policies concerning the internal affairs of banks, the FDIC has the power to terminate deposit insurance, issue cease and desist orders, remove bank officials, and levy fines.

**FEDERAL FINANCIAL INSTITUTIONS EXAMINATION COUNCIL (FFIEC)**   To promote consistency in the examination and supervision of financial institutions, the Financial Institutions Regulatory and Interest Rate Control Act of 1978 created the Federal Financial Institutions Examination Council, composed of the Comptroller of the Currency, plus one governor of the Federal Reserve System and the chairmen of the FDIC, Federal Home Loan Bank Board, and National Credit Union Administration Board. The council's primary assignment is to "establish uniform principles and standards and report forms for the examination of financial institutions." It also makes recommendations on matters of common concern to supervisors, conducts schools for examiners, and periodically meets with a liaison committee composed of five representatives from state financial regulatory agencies.

Since agencies represented on the council maintain their independence in most states, they are not bound by its recommendations. As a result, while the council has achieved more consistency in dealing with supervisory issues and reporting forms, its recommendations have not always been adopted uniformly.

**FEDERAL FUNDS**   Reserve balances that depository institutions lend each other, usually on an overnight basis. In addition, Federal funds include certain other kinds of borrowings by depository institutions from each other and from federal agencies.

Federal funds are one of the most important money market instruments in the United States and one of the most liquid financial assets. Basically, the federal funds market involves transactions representing the lending and borrowing of reserves by depository institutions over Fedwire. Most transactions are for same-day settlement and are automatically reversed the next business day. Term transactions for more than one day and transactions for forward settlement also can be arranged.

The federal funds market is a primary mechanism by which the banking system's reserves are distributed to institutions with the greatest demand for the available reserves. The transfer of reserves takes place at a competitively determined interest rate, known as the federal funds rate, which the borrower pays for the use of the funds.

Federal funds also are used by non-depository institutions to make large, same-day payments—that is, in "immediately available" funds. For example, a corporation might instruct its bank to make a payment in immediately available funds. Such a payment would be made over Fedwire. The bank would use its reserve account to make the payment and its customer would reimburse it. The market is used by some large depository institutions as a continuous source of funds, and by smaller institutions as a means of earning interest on reserves which otherwise would be unproductive.

The federal funds market is important because of its relation to Federal Reserve monetary policy. Open market operations add reserves to or drain reserves from the banking system and the federal funds rate is sensitive to these central bank actions since it quickly reflects the change in supply or demand for reserves. These actions may influence the banking system's lending decisions.

Since October 1979, Federal Reserve open market strategy usually has focused more on the supply of reserves and less on the cost of funds. The federal funds rate also influences the cost of credit from sources other than banks since interest rates on many short-term financial instruments—such as commercial paper—usually move parallel to the federal funds rate.

The name federal funds originated in the 1920s when, in order to meet reserve requirements, a few New York City banks, which were members of the Federal Reserve, exchanged drafts drawn on their Federal Reserve accounts. The reserve accounts maintained at the district Reserve Banks play a major role in facilitating a bank's daily clearing operations that are part of the normal in and out flow of funds over Fedwire.

Transactions in the federal funds market usually are overnight loans made in immediately usable funds, against which the borrowing commercial bank or other depository institution is not required to maintain reserves. Institutions eligible to lend reserves in this way are limited primarily to commercial banks, certain federal agencies, savings and loan associations, mutual savings banks, credit unions, domestic agencies and branches of foreign banks and, at times, government securities dealers.

Money center and large regional banks are the most active participants in the market, usually borrowing from small institutions. Many small banks intentionally accumulate reserve balances above their requirements in order to sell daily the excess not needed for clearing checks or other purposes.

Banks use the funds market for several purposes, including daily adjustment of reserve positions and to achieve broader asset and liability objectives—as well as daily clearing operations. In addition, bank operations in federal funds have been influenced by changes in banking regulations, as well as by changes in bank portfolio management practices. Federal funds transactions generally are "unsecured." Thus, the institutions providing the funds have no guarantee of repayment other than the promise of the borrower. These transactions, therefore, are conducted among institutions having a high degree of mutual confidence and within established credit limits.

There is no central, physical location where federal funds are traded. The market consists of an informal telephone network connecting the participants. A small number of broker firms that neither borrow nor lend also participate in the market, arranging transactions in exchange for a small commission. Transactions in the brokered market normally range between $5 million and $100 million each.

Additionally, many medium- and large-sized institutions frequently borrow and lend federal funds on the same day, thus performing an intermediary role in the market. These institutions channel funds from those with a lesser need to those with a greater need, frequently borrowing from smaller institutions and lending to larger ones.

**FEDERAL HOME LOAN BANK BOARD (FHLBB)** The agency of the federal government that supervises all federal savings and loan associations and federally insured state-chartered savings and loan associations. The FHLBB also operates the Federal Savings and Loan Insurance Corporation which insures accounts at federal savings and loan associations and those state-chartered associations that apply and are accepted. In addition, the FHLBB directs the Federal Home Loan Bank System, which provides a flexible credit facility for member savings institutions to promote the availability of home financing. The Federal Home Loan Banks also own the Federal Home Loan Mortgage Corporation, established in 1970 to promote secondary markets for mortgages.

**FEDERAL HOUSING ASSOCIATION (FHA) LOAN** A single family mortgage program with a rate ceiling below prevailing market rates to assist home buyers that are unable to obtain conventional mortgage loans from banks, thrifts, and other financial institutions.

**FEDERAL MARGIN CALL** A broker's demand upon a customer for cash, or securities needed to satisfy the required Regulation T downpayment for a purchase or short sale of securities.

**FEDERAL OPEN MARKET COMMITTEE (FOMC)** A 12-member committee consisting of the seven members of the Federal Reserve Board and five of the twelve Federal Reserve Bank presidents. The president of the Federal Reserve Bank of New York is a permanent member while the other Federal Reserve presidents serve on a rotating basis. The Committee sets objectives for the growth of money and credit that are implemented through purchases and sales of U.S. government securities in the open market. The FOMC also establishes policy relating to System operations in the foreign exchange markets.

**FEDERAL RESERVE (FED)** The Federal Reserve System was created by the Federal Reserve Act, passed by Congress in 1913 in order to provide for a safer and more flexible banking and monetary system. For about a hundred years before the creation of the Federal Reserve, periodic financial panics had led to failures of a large number of banks, with associated business bankruptcies and general economic contractions. Following the studies of the National Monetary Commission, established by Congress a year after the particularly severe panic of 1907, several proposals were put forward for the creation of an institution designed to counter such financial disruptions. After considerable debate, the Federal Reserve System was established. Its original purposes were to give the country an elastic currency, provide facilities for discounting commercial credits, and improve the supervision of the banking system.

From the inception of the Federal Reserve System, it was clear that these original purposes were aspects of broader national economic and financial objectives. Over the years, stability and growth of the economy, a high level of employment, stability in the purchasing power of the dollar, and reasonable balance in transactions with foreign countries have come to be recognized as primary objectives of governmental economic policy. Such objectives have been articulated by Congress in the Employment Act of 1946, and more recently in the Full Employment and Balanced Growth Act of 1978. The Federal Reserve Act has also been amended over the years to enable the System to function more effectively in helping to attain the nation's economic goals, with key amendments set forth in the Banking Act of 1935, the 1970 amendments to the Bank Holding Company Act, the International Banking Act of 1978, the Full Employment and Balanced Growth Act of 1978, and Depository Institutions Deregulation and Monetary Control Act of 1980.

The Federal Reserve contributes to the attainment of the nation's economic and financial goals through its ability to influence money and credit in the economy. As the nation's central bank, it attempts to ensure that growth in money and credit over the long run is sufficient to encourage growth in the economy in line with its potential and with reasonable price stability. In the short run the Federal Reserve seeks to adapt its policies to combat deflationary or inflationary pressures as they may arise. And as a lender of last resort, it has the responsibility for utilizing the policy instruments available to it in an attempt to forestall national liquidity crises and financial panics.

Because a sound financial structure is an essential ingredient of an effective monetary policy and a growing and prosperous economy, the Federal Reserve has also been entrusted with many supervisory and regulatory functions. Among other things, it is responsible for the amount of credit that may be used for purchasing or carrying equity securities; it regulates the foreign activities of all U.S. banks and the U.S. activities of foreign banks; it administers the laws that regulate bank holding companies; it supervises state-chartered member banks; and it establishes rules to ensure that consumers are adequately informed and treated fairly in certain credit transactions.

Most countries today have a central bank whose functions are broadly similar to those of the Federal Reserve. The Bank of England, for example, has been in existence since the end of the seventeenth century; the Bank of France was established in 1800 by Napoleon I; the Bank of Canada began operations in 1935. Each of these banks conducts its nation's monetary policy, although, depending on the historical, economic, and political circumstances surrounding its establishment and subsequent development, its specific responsibilities differ from the others', as do its role and its degree of independence within the government. (Board of Governors of the Federal Reserve System).

**FEDERAL RESERVE BANKS**   Many functions of the Federal Reserve System — including operation of the payments mechanism, distribution of coin and currency, examination of banks, and fiscal-agency functions for the Treasury — are implemented through a network of twelve Federal Reserve Banks located in Boston, New York, Philadelphia, Cleveland, Richmond, Atlanta, Chicago, St. Louis, Minneapolis, Kansas City, Dallas, and San Francisco. Branches of Reserve Banks have been established in twenty-five other cities. The Boards' offices in Washington are a headquarters-type facility.

Each Reserve Bank has its own board, consisting of nine outside directors. As provided by law, three Class A directors, who represent member banks, and three Class B directors, who represent the public, are elected by the member banks in each Federal Reserve District. The Board of Governors appoints three Class C directors, who also represent the public, and it designates one of these three as chairman and another as deputy chairman of the Bank's board. No Class B or Class C director may be an officer, director, or employee of a bank, nor may any Class C directors be stockholders of a bank. Each Branch of a Reserve Bank has its own board of directors, comprising five or seven members. The majority (three or four, as the case may be) are appointed by the head-office directors, and the others by the Board of Governors.

The directors of each Reserve Bank oversee the operations of their Bank subject to the overall supervision of the Board of Governors; and, subject to approval of the Board, they establish the discount rates that their Bank charges on collateralized loans to depository institutions. The directors appoint, and recommend the salaries of, the Bank's president and first vice president, subject to final approval by the Board of Governors.

The Federal Reserve Banks derive their earnings primarily from interest on their proportionate share of the System's holdings of securities acquired through open market operations and, to a much lesser extent, from interest on System holdings of foreign currencies and on their loans to depository institutions; pricing of Federal Reserve services was mandated by the Depository Institutions Deregulation and Monetary Control Act of 1980.

Earnings of Federal Reserve Banks are allocated first to the payment of expenses (including assessments by the Board of Governors to defray its expenses), the statutory 6 percent dividend on Federal Reserve stock that member institutions are legally required to purchase, and any additions to surplus necessary to maintain each Reserve Bank's surplus equal to its paid-in capital stock. Remaining earnings are then paid into the U.S. Treasury. About 95 percent of the Reserve Banks' net earnings have been paid into the Treasury since the Federal Reserve System was established. Should a Reserve Bank be liquidated, its surplus — after all obligations had been met — would become the property of the U. S. Government.

**FEDERAL RESERVE FLOAT**   Checkbook money that for a period of time appears on the books of both the payor and payee due to the lag in the collection process. Federal Reserve float often arises during the Federal Reserve's check collection process. In order to promote an efficient payments mechanism with certainty as to the date funds become available, the Federal Reserve has employed the policy of crediting the reserve accounts of depository institutions depositing checks according to an availability schedule before the Federal Reserve is able to obtain payment from others. SEE FLOAT, AND EXPEDITED FUNDS AVAILABILITY ACT, REGULATION CC.

**FEDERAL RESERVE NOTES**   Nearly all of the nation's circulating paper currency consists of Federal Reserve notes printed by the Bureau of Engraving and Printing and issued to the Federal Reserve Banks which put them into circulation through commercial banks and other depository institutions. Federal Reserve notes are obligations of the U.S. government.

**FEDERAL RESERVE SYSTEM**   The central bank of the United States created by Congress, consisting of a seven member Board of Governors in Washington, D.C., 12 regional Reserve Banks, and depository institutions that are subject to reserve requirements. All national banks are members; state chartered banks may elect to become members, and state members are supervised by the Board of Governors and the Reserve Banks. Reserve requirements established by the Federal Reserve Board apply to nonmember depository institutions as well as member banks. Both classes of institutions have access to Federal Reserve discount borrowing privileges and Federal Reserve services on an equal basis.

**FEDERAL TRADE COMMISSION**   The Federal Trade Commission, which investigates business practices that deceive or mislead consumers, shares with other federal regulatory agencies responsibility for the enforcement of the Truth in Lending Act and other consumer protection legislation. The FTC's enforcement responsibilities under these acts are confined primarily to nondepository lending institutions. The commission's rule-making powers are limited to its own enforcement procedures for these acts.

**FEDWIRE**   Fedwire, the Federal Reserve's funds and securities transfer service, is the primary electronic transfer system in the United States. It connects Federal Reserve Banks and branches, U.S. government agencies such as the Treasury, and some 8,000 depository institutions. All Fedwire transfers are completed on the day they are initiated, generally in a matter of minutes. They are guaranteed final by the central bank when the receiving institution is notified of the credit to its account.

The Federal Reserve has been moving funds since the early years of its existence more than 70 years ago. In 1918, in conjunction with the change from a weekly to a daily settlement among Reserve banks, the Federal Reserve installed a private telegraph system connecting the Reserve banks and began to process transfers of funds among member banks. Treasury securities became transferable by telegraph wire in the 1920s. Fedwire, which became largely an electronically based system in the 1970s (although the Fedwire name was not officially used) was upgraded in 1982 to a more reliable system that enabled faster, more secure transfers.

Originally, Fedwire services were offered free to Federal Reserve member commercial banks. However, the Depository Institutions Deregulation and Monetary Control Act of 1980 required pricing of funds and securities transfers as well as other Fed services and gave nonmember depository institutions direct access to Fedwire. Fedwire may be used by depository institutions to move funds resulting from the purchase or sale of federal funds, to move balances to correspondent banks and to send funds to other institutions on behalf of their customers. Transfers on behalf of bank customers include funds associated with the purchase or sale of securities, the replenishment of business demand deposits and other time-sensitive or large payments. The U.S. Treasury and other federal agencies use Fedwire extensively to disburse and collect funds.

Assume an individual or private or governmental organization requests a bank to transfer funds. If the banks of the sender and receiver are in different Federal Reserve districts, the sending bank debits the sender's account, and requests its local Reserve bank to sent a transfer message to the Reserve bank serving the receiver's bank. The sending bank's Reserve bank debits the sending bank's reserve account for the account of the transfer and the receiver's regional Reserve bank credits the receiving bank's reserve balance for the same amount. The two Reserve banks settle with each other through what is called the Interdistrict Settlement Fund, a bookkeeping system which records Federal Reserve interdistrict transactions. Finally, the receiving bank notifies the recipient of the transfer and credits its account. The receiver is free to use the funds immediately. Once the transfer is received it cannot be reversed.

If the sending and receiving banks are in the same Federal Reserve district, the transaction is similar but all of the processing and accounting is done by one Reserve bank.

Fedwire has about 10,000 users nationwide and in 1987 processed 55 million funds transfers with an aggregate value of $153 trillion, or over $695 billion every business day. Nationally, Fedwire is available to 7,000 on-line users—depository institutions with computers or terminals that communicate directly with the Fedwire network. These users represent over 99.5 percent of total users. Fedwire also plays a significant role in the conduct of monetary policy and the government securities market. It is used by the Federal Reserve, the Treasury and depository institutions to transfer U.S. government and agency securities in book-entry form. The wire transfer system improves the efficiency of Federal Reserve open market operations by enabling a liquid market for government securities.

Fedwire and a private sector funds transfer network, the Clearing House Interbank Payment System (CHIPS) handle most large-dollar wire transfers in the U.S. today. Most CHIPS transfers result from international transactions. Because of potential risk on the large-dollar funds transfer networks, the Board of Governors of the Federal Reserve introduced a risk-reduction policy in March 1986. The policy is aimed at controlling and reducing daylight overdrafts which occur when an institution has sent funds over Fedwire in excess of the balance in its reserve or clearing account, or has sent more funds over CHIPS than it has received.

**FHHLDS**   SEE FEDERAL HOUSING HOME LOAN DATA SYSTEM.

**FHLBB**   SEE FEDERAL HOME LOAN BANK BOARD.

**FINANCE CHARGE**   The finance charge is the cost of consumer credit as a dollar amount. It includes any charge payable directly or indirectly by the consumer and imposed directly or indirectly by the creditor as an incident to or a condition of the extension of credit. It does not include any charge of a type payable in a comparable cash transaction. The finance charge includes the following types of charges:

(1) Interest, time price differential, and any amount payable under an add-on or discount system of additional charges.

(2) Service, transaction, activity, and carrying charges, including any charge imposed on a checking or other transaction account to the extent that the charge exceeds the charge for a similar account without a credit feature.

(3) Points, loan fees, assumption fees, finder's fees, and similar charges.

(4) Appraisal, investigation, and credit report fees.

(5) Premiums or other charges for any guarantee or insurance protecting the creditor against the consumer's default or other credit loss.

(6) Charges imposed on a creditor by another person for purchasing or accepting a consumer's obligation, if the consumer is required to pay the charges in cash, as an addition to the obligation, or as a deduction from the proceeds of the obligation.

(7) Premiums or other charges for credit life, accident, health, or loss-of-income insurance, written in connection with a credit transaction.

(8) Premiums or other charges for insurance against loss of or damage to property, or against liability arising out of the ownership or use of property, written in connection with a credit transaction.

(9) Discounts for the purpose of inducing payment by a means other than the use of credit.

The following charges are not finance charges:

(1) Application fees charged to all applicants for credit, whether or not credit is actually extended.

(2) Charges for actual unanticipated late payment, for exceeding a credit limit, or for delinquency, default, or a similar occurrence.

(3) Charges imposed by a financial institution for paying items that overdraw an account, unless the payment of such items and the imposition of the charge were previously agreed upon in writing.

(4) Fees charged for participation in a credit plan, whether assessed on an annual or other periodic basis.

(5) Seller's points.

(6) Interest forfeited as a result of an interest reduction required by law on a time deposit used as security for an extension of credit.

(7) The following fees in a transaction secured by real property or in a residential mortgage transaction, if the fees are bona fide and reasonable in amount:

(i) Fees for title examination, abstract of title, title insurance, property survey, and similar purposes.

(ii) Fees for preparing deeds, mortgages, and reconveyance, settlement, and similar documents.

(iii) Notary, appraisal, and credit report fees.

(iv) Amounts required to be paid into escrow or trustee accounts if the amounts would not otherwise be included in the finance charge.

(8) Discounts offered to induce payment for a purchase by cash, check, or other means.

Premiums for credit life, accident, health, or loss-of-income insurance may be excluded from the finance charge if the following conditions are met:

(1) The insurance coverage is not required by the creditor, and this fact is disclosed.

(2) The premium for the initial term of insurance coverage is disclosed. If the term of insurance is less than the term of the transaction, the term of insurance also

shall be disclosed. The premium may be disclosed on a unit-cost basis only in open-end credit transaction, closed-end credit transactions by mail or telephone and certain closed-end credit transactions involving an insurance plan that limits the total amount of indebtedness subject to coverage.

(3) The consumer signs or initials an affirmative written request for the insurance after receiving the disclosures. Any consumer in the transaction may sign or initial the request.

Premiums for insurance against loss of or damage to property, or against liability arising out of the ownership or use of property, may be excluded from the finance charge if the following conditions are met:

(1) The insurance coverage may be obtained from a person of the consumer's choice, and this fact is disclosed.

(2) If the coverage is obtained from or through the creditor, the premium for the initial term of insurance coverage shall be disclosed. If the term of insurance is less than the term of the transaction, the term of insurance shall also be disclosed. The premium may be disclosed on a unit-cost basis only in open-end credit transactions, closed-end credit transactions by mail or telephone, and certain closed-end credit transactions involving an insurance plan that limits the total amount of indebtedness subject to coverage.

If itemized and disclosed, the following charges may be excluded from the finance charge:

(1) Taxes and fees prescribed by law that actually are or will be paid to public officials for determining the existence of or for perfecting, releasing, or satisfying a security interest.

(2) The premium for insurance in lieu of perfecting a security interest to the extent that the premium does not exceed the fees described in (1), above, that otherwise would be payable.

Prohibited offsets: Interest, dividends, or other income received or to be received by the consumer on deposits or investments shall not be deducted in computing the finance charge.

*Special Rules with Regard to Open-End Credit:* On the initial disclosure statement, the creditor shall disclose to the consumer, in terminology consistent with that to be used on the periodic statement, the circumstances under which a finance charge will be imposed and an explanation of how it will be determined, as follows:

(1) A statement of when finance charges begin to accrue, including an explanation of whether or not any time period exists within which any credit extended may be repaid without incurring a finance charge. If such a time period is provided, a creditor may, at its option and without disclosure, impose no finance charge when payment is received after the time periods' expiration.

(2) A disclosure of each periodic rate that may be used to compute the finance charge, the range of balances to which it is applicable, and the corresponding annual percentage rate. When different periodic rates apply to different types of transactions, the types of transactions to which the rates apply shall be disclosed.

(3) An explanation of the method used to determine the balance on which the finance charge may be computed.

(4) An explanation of how the amount of any finance charge will be determined, including a description of how any finance charge other than the periodic rate will be determined.

The creditor shall furnish the consumer with a periodic statement that discloses to the extent applicable the amount of any finance charge debited or added to the account during the billing cycle, using the tern "finance charge." The components of the finance charge shall be individually itemized and identified to show the amount(s) due to the application of any periodic rates and the amount(s) of any other type of finance charge. (If there is more than one periodic rate, the amount of the finance charge attributable to each rate need not be separately itemized and identified.) (12 CFR Sec. 226.5, 226.6, 226.7)

**FINANCIAL GAP**   The difference between the funds needed to buy new assets and the funds available. The amount that will have to be borrowed in order to support increased sales.

**FINANCIAL INSTITUTION**   An institution that uses its funds chiefly to purchase financial assets (deposits, loans, securities) as opposed to tangible property. Financial institutions can be classified according to the nature of the principal claims they issue: nondeposit intermediaries include, among others, life and property/casualty insurance companies and pension funds, whose claims are the policies they sell, or the promise to provide income after retirement; depository intermediaries obtain funds mainly by accepting deposits from the public. The major depository institutions are listed below. Although historically they have specialized in certain types of credit, the powers of nonbank depository institutions have been broadened in recent years. For example, NOW accounts, credit union share drafts, and other services similar to checking accounts may be offered by thrift institutions.

Commercial banks are allowed to engage in more varied lending activities and to offer more financial services than are the other depository institutions. Commercial banks are owned by stockholders and operated for profit.

Savings and loan associations (sometimes called building and loan associations, cooperative banks, or homestead associations) accept deposits primarily from individuals, and channel their funds primarily into residential mortgage loans. Most savings and loan associations are technically owned by the depositors who receive shares in the association for their deposits.

Mutual savings banks also accept deposits primarily from individuals, and place a large portion of their funds into mortgage loans. These institutions are prominent in many of the northeastern states. Savings banks generally have broader asset and liability powers than savings and loan associations but narrower powers than commercial banks. Savings banks are authorized to offer checking-type accounts.

Credit unions are financial cooperative organizations of individuals with a common affiliation (such as employment, labor union membership, or place of residence). Credit unions accept deposits of members, pay interest (dividends) on them out of earnings, and primarily provided consumer installment credit to members.

Thrift institution is a general term often used for mutual savings banks, savings and loan associations, and credit unions.

**FINANCIAL INSTITUTIONS REFORM, RECOVERY AND ENFORCEMENT ACT (FIRREA)**   Signed into law by President George Bush on August 9, 1989, the major provisions of the Act are as follows:

• REGULATORY APPARATUS. The Federal Savings and Loan Insurance Corporation (FSLIC) and the Federal Home Loan Bank Board (FHLBB) were abolished. Deposit insurance for institutions previously covered by FSLIC was transferred to the Federal Deposit Insurance Corporation's (FDIC) new Savings Association Insurance Fund. Regulation and chartering of thrifts was placed in a new bureau of the Treasury, the Office of Thrift Supervision (OTS). The 12 district banks resumed their original role of allocating housing credit, and became supervised by a new Federal Housing Finance Board. Examiners formerly housed in the district banks were transferred to the OTS.

• FUNDING. $20 billion of funding for thrift resolutions was placed on-budget in fiscal 1989, and $30 billion was to be raised through an off-budget agency, the Resolution Finding Corporation in 1990 and 1991.

• PREMIUMS. Thrift premiums are to rise to 23 basis points in 1991, fall to 18 basis points in 1994, and are placed on a par with banks at 15 basis points in 1998.

• CAPITAL. Thrifts must meet minimum 1.5% tangible capital and 3% core capital within 120 days after the law was enacted, phasing up to 3% tangible core capital by 1995. Risk based supplementary capital levels are to be determined by federal banking regulators in the future.

• GOODWILL. Supervisory goodwill is a "qualifying intangible" component of core capital, but must be phased out by 1995.

• FREDDIE MAC. The Federal Home Loan Mortgage Corporation's ties to the thrift regulator were severed. Freddie Mac became an independent agency with an 18-member board of directors.

• CONSUMER ISSUES. Data-gathering requirements under the Home Mortgage Disclosure Act were expanded to combat redlining, and the rules now apply to mortgage bankers. Public disclosure of a revamped system of Community Reinvestment Act ratings is required. Low income housing groups will have a "first look" at RTC properties.

• HOUSING PROGRAMS. District banks must earmark a portion of advances for mortgages to low income borrowers. The set-aside must be at least $100 million by year end 1995. The banks must also make advances at cost for community development programs.

• SUPERVISION OF STATE CHARTERED THRIFTS. Primary federal supervision of state chartered thrifts remains in the hands of the Bank Board's successor agency, the OTS.

• DIRECT INVESTMENTS. Direct investments are forbidden for all thrifts and those already on the books must be divested by 1995.

• JUNK BONDS. Junk bond investments are forbidden for all thrifts. They must be divested or placed in a separately capitalized affiliate by 1995.

• CHECKING ACCOUNTS. Federal thrifts may offer checking accounts to all customers.

• DISTRICT BANK ACCESS. Banks and credit unions with 10% of their assets in residential mortgages may join the Federal Home Loan Bank System and obtain advances. They must purchase stock as if they had 30% of assets in home mortgages.

• QTL TEST. Beginning July 1, 1991, thrifts must meet a 70% qualified thrift lender test, with qualifying assets more rigidly defined than before. Penalties for failure are also tougher.

• DISTRICT BANK LEVY. District banks will pay a flat $300 million a year toward interest on Refcorp bonds. The levy will not rise with inflation as the House sought. The Federal Housing Finance Board may suspend contributions in some cases.

• THE RESOLUTION TRUST CORPORATION is established to liquidate troubled thrifts. It is managed by the FDIC, and governed by a five member oversight board consisting of the Treasury Secretary, HUD Secretary, Federal Reserve Chairman, and two private citizens. It may issue notes and guarantees up to 85% of its assets.

• BANK HOLDING COMPANY ACQUISITION OF THRIFTS. Bank holding companies may buy healthy thrifts immediately upon enactment of the Act. These institutions may be converted to bank charters, but must continue paying SAIF premiums for five years.

• LOAN TO VALUE RATIOS. Statutory loan-to-value requirements approved by the Senate were dropped from the final bill, but the federal regulators must ensure that general limits are adopted for banks and thrifts alike. Regulators must use the Senate-passed standards as a guideline: 95% LTV for mortgages, 80% for completed projects, 70% for finished land, and 65% for undeveloped.

• LOGO. The President unveiled a new deposit insurance logo that states that accounts are federally insured to $100,000. The eagle-motif design contains a pledge of the government's full faith and credit, but mentions no government agency. Thrifts must display this logo; banks may adopt it or retain their existing FDIC stickers.

• ENFORCEMENT. The Justice Department has new budget authority of $65 million a year for investigating and prosecuting thrift claims, and $10 million is authorized to federal courts. Additionally, fines and sentences for crimes against financial institutions are increased. The grounds for civil money penalties are expanded, and these fines may run as high as $1 million a day. The bill also increases the statute of limitations to ten years from five years, giving the Justice Department additional time to investigate and prosecute wrongdoers.

**FINANCIAL PRIVACY**   SEE RIGHT TO FINANCIAL PRIVACY ACT.

**FINANCING PATTERNS**   The relationship between the need for funds to support sales and the availability of those funds. The relationship between the use of profits, the use of debt, and the repayment of debt in acquiring assets to support sales. Also, the requirements for funds to support both seasonal and permanent growth, and the sources of those funds.

**FINANCING STATEMENT**   SEE UCC-1 STATEMENT.

**FIRREA**   SEE FINANCIAL INSTITUTIONS REFORM, RECOVERY AND ENFORCEMENT ACT.

**FISCAL AGENCY SERVICES**   Services performed by the Federal Reserve Banks for the U.S. government. These include maintaining deposit accounts for the Treasury Department, paying U.S. government checks drawn on the Treasury, and issuing and redeeming savings bonds and other government securities.

**FISCAL POLICY**   Government policy regarding taxation and spending. Fiscal policy is made by Congress and the Administration.

**FIXED ASSETS**   Those assets which tend to be of a more permenent, long-term nature such as equipment, vehicles, buildings, etc.

**FIXED COSTS**   Expenses that do not vary with sales; those costs that are incurred whether or not any sales take place.

**FIXED RATE**   A traditional approach to determining the finance charge payable on an extension of credit. A predetermined and certain rate of interest is applied to the principal.

**FLOAT**   Float is checkbook money which, for a period of time, appears on the books of both the check writer and the check receiver due to a lag in the check collection process. The lag is caused by a number of factors and results in various types of float. Federal Reserve float is the addition to depository institution's reserve accounts which arises unintentionally during the Federal Reserve's check collection process. The Federal Reserve credits the reserve accounts of depository institutions depositing checks within two business days of the deposit, even through more time may be needed to process the checks and collect funds from the depository institution on which the checks are drawn. This crediting procedure sometimes results in an addition to the reserves of some depository institutions before reserves are taken from other depository institutions. Thus, float is generated.

The check collection cycle begins with the deposit of a check at a depository institution. If a check is drawn on that institution, the collection is completed internally. If the check is drawn on another depository institution, other steps are required before funds can be transferred from the depository institution upon which the check is drawn. Checks may be sent by the depository institution receiving them as deposits directly to the depository institution on which they are drawn. In such cases, the two institutions settle directly with each other. Alternatively, checks may be sent to correspondent banks which provide clearing and collection services. Checks also may be cleared through a clearing association of which both depository institutions are members. Checks which are not handled through any of these arrangements are likely to be processed through the Federal Reserve's check collection system.

The majority of checks cleared through a Reserve Bank are processed on high-speed computer equipment. The depositing depository institution will receive credit, according to the Federal Reserve's published time schedules, ranging from the date the checks are received to a maximum, in certain circumstances, of three business days later. On the day credit is due, the depository institution's reserve account balance at the Reserve Bank is increased and, on the day payment is made, the paying institution's reserve balance is reduced. Assuming the collection process goes smoothly, the day the credit is available for use by depositing institutions corresponds to the day payment is received.

However, a variety of reasons may prevent the Reserve Bank from obtaining payment from the depository institution on which checks are drawn on the day credit automatically is given.

Checks received in poor condition must be processed at Reserve offices on semi-automatic equipment, slowing the collection process. Or, delays may occur due to unexpected volume or equipment malfunctions. Another factor may be transportation. A Federal Reserve Bank's time schedule for granting credit for checks is based on shipping times between Federal Reserve offices and depository institutions. When checks do not reach their destination as scheduled, credit is given anyway. At that moment, float is created.

The Federal Reserve System has implemented a series of operational changes to substantially reduce Federal Reserve float. Depository institutions are charged for any float remaining after these changes, as required by the Monetary Control Act of 1980.

In 1987 the Federal Reserve System adopted a uniform standard holiday schedule which eliminated float created when some depository institutions and one regional Reserve Bank might be open while others are closed. The uniform schedule ended the potential for an increase in non-standard holiday float which had been estimated at $15 million a day in check services. It should be noted that Federal Reserve float affects the monetary aggregates since it creates reserves in the overall banking system. Therefore, depending upon monetary objectives, Federal Reserve open market operations may have to be used to offset movements in float.

Another kind of float is commercial bank float, which appears on the balance sheets of banks as "cash items in the process of collection." Cash items include checks, postal money orders, food coupons and other items payable on demand. Banks generally credit customer accounts when deposits are made, but do not allow customers to use those funds for a specified time to allow banks to collect the funds. Thus, since uncollected funds appear in two accounts simultaneously (the check writer's and the check depositor's) float occurs.

Another situation which sometimes occurs is "mail float" which is a misnomer, since it is not float in the traditional sense and does not involve the Federal Reserve, depository institutions or bank reserves. "Mail float" occurs when anyone writes and mails a check, but continues to use the funds allocated in the mailed check. In many cases, the check writer considers the payment made once the check has been mailed. However, "mail float" exists until the check is delivered to the recipient and the traditional clearing process begins, which may be several days after the check is written. During the interval, the writer of the check continues to have use of the funds, and, in this sense, "mail float" continues.

**FLOOD DISASTER PROTECTION ACT (FDPA)**    The Flood Disaster Protection Act of 1973 became effective on December 31, 1973. The Act requires regulators of federal financial institutions to promulgate regulations prohibiting:
*   federally regulated lending institutions from making, increasing, extending or renewing any loan (applicability of the FDPA is not limited to consumer loans) secured by improved real estate or a residential mobile home located or to be located in a flood hazard area of a community participating in the national flood insurance program (NFIP), unless the property securing the loan is covered by flood insurance;
*   the use of federal financial assistance for acquisition or construction of a structure in a flood hazard area, unless the community participates in the national flood insurance program and flood insurance has been purchased. The term "federal financial assistance" includes loans, grants, guarantees, and similar forms of direct and indirect assistance from federal agencies such as FHA or VA mortgage insurance. For communities participating in the NFIP, that term also includes conventional loans from federally insured, supervised or approved lending institutions.

The principal objectives of the Flood Disaster Protection Act are:
* to provide adequate amounts of federally subsidized flood insurance to owners of improved real property located in flood hazard areas of communities that participate in the NFIP, and
* to reduce or avoid future flood losses and provide a preventative alternative to massive doses of federal disaster relief funds normally made available to flood stricken areas.

**FLUCTUATING CURRENT ASSETS**  Current assets—cash, accounts receivable, inventory, etc.,—whose levels rise and fall in direct relation to annual seasonal sales increases and decreases.

**FOREIGN EXCHANGE DESK**  The foreign exchange trading desk at the New York Federal Reserve Bank. The desk undertakes operations in the exchange markets for the account of the Federal Open Market Committee, and as agent for the U.S. Treasury and for foreign central banks.

**FOREIGN EXCHANGE TRANSACTIONS**  Purchase or sale of the currency of one nation with that of another. Foreign exchange rates refer to the number of units of one currency needed to purchase one unit of another, or the value of one currency in terms of another.

**FRANC**  Monetary unit of Benin, Cameroon, Central African Republic, Chad, Congo, Equatorial Guinea, France, Gabon, Guinea, Ivory Coast, Luxembourg, Madagascar, Niger, Rwanda, Senegal, Switzerland, and Togo.

**FUNDAMENTAL BUSINESS PURPOSE**  The charter of the business.

**FUTURES**  Contracts that require delivery of a commodity of specified quality and quantity, at a specified price, on a specified future date. Commodity futures are traded on a commodity exchange and are used for both speculation and hedging.

# G

**GAAP**  SEE GENERALLY ACCEPTED ACCOUNTING PRINCIPLES.

**GAIN**  The opposite of loss; profit, pecuniary benefit or advantage.

**GAP ANALYSIS**  The matching of maturities of loan and deposit portfolios at a positive spread to guarantee profit. Gap analysis, which emphasizes short term position and liquidity risk, may be compared to "duration analysis"

$$\frac{\text{sum of (discounted cash flow} \times \text{period)}}{\text{sum of discounted cash flow}}$$

which focuses on the long term effects of rate changes.

**GARN-ST. GERMAIN DEPOSITORY INSTITUTIONS ACT OF 1982**  The Garn-St. Germain Depository Institutions Act of 1982 was signed into law on October 15 of that year by President Ronald Reagan. A multi-purpose legislation, the act sought to accelerate the deregulation process started by the Depository Institutions and Monetary Control Act of 1980, enhance the competitiveness of all types of financial institutions and to provide flexibility to regulatory agencies allowing them to better deal with distressed financial institutions. Garn-St.Germain contained the following eight titles:

## TITLE I
### THE DEPOSIT INSURANCE FLEXIBILITY ACT
The Federal Deposit Insurance Corporation (FDIC), Federal Savings and Loan Insurance Corporation (FSLIC) and National Credit Union Administration (NCUA) were given additional powers to allow them to more effectively assist financially troubled institutions, primarily through the ability to arrange interstate and cross-industrial acquisitions and mergers.

## TITLE II
### THE NET WORTH CERTIFICATE ACT
Title II provided a vehicle for insured institutions to exchange capital notes with the Federal Deposit Insurance Corporation or the Federal Savings and Loan Insurance Corporation for the purpose of strengthening the institution's net worth.

## TITLE III
### THE THRIFT INSTITUTIONS RESTRUCTURING ACT
The lending and investment powers of federally insured thrift institutions were broadened, interest rate differentials on deposits were scheduled for elimination effective January 1, 1984, prohibitions against enforcing due-on-sale clauses in mortgage contracts were preempted and a new deposit instrument, the Money Market Deposit Account (MMDA) was created to be "directly equivalent and competitive with money market mutual funds." The MMDA had the following characteristics:
- minimum initial and average balance of $1,000
- no interest rate limitation, providing the average balance remains at least $1,000
- if the average balance falls below $1,000, the interest rate paid on the account may not be greater than the interest paid on NOW accounts
- account is available to all depositors
- account is limited to 6 preauthorized transfers per month. No more than 3 of these may be made by draft. Telephone transfers are categorized as preauthorized transfers and thus fall under the 6 transfer limit. Transfers made by mail, messenger, ATM or in person are not limited.

## TITLE IV
### PROVISIONS RELATING TO NATIONAL AND MEMBER BANKS
The major thrust of Title IV was the amendments to the National Banking Act which revised obsolete lending and borrowing limits and modified real estate lending authority of national banks.

## TITLE V
### FEDERAL CREDIT UNION ACT AMENDMENTS
The Federal Credit Union Act was amended to simplify the organization process, and broaden residential mortgage lending authority of credit unions.

## TITLE VI
### PROPERTY, CASUALTY, AND LIFE INSURANCE ACTIVITIES OF BANK HOLDING COMPANIES

With specific exceptions, Title VI restricted the property and casualty insurance activities of bank holding companies and their subsidiaries. Some of the exceptions as set forth in the act include:

- grandfathered activities authorized as of May 1, 1982
- permitted credit life, disability and involuntary unemployment insurance
- permitted bank holding companies to engage in general insurance agency activities in cities of fewer than 5,000 population or where inadequate insurance agency activity exists, and
- permitted nearly 3,000 bank holding companies with assets under $50 million to participate in insurance agency activities.

## TITLE VII
### MISCELLANEOUS PROVISIONS

Numerous varied provisions were included in Title VII, such as making industrial banks eligible for FDIC insurance, exempting certain student loan transactions from Truth-in-Lending, amending the International Banking Act of 1978, amending the Bank Service Corporation Act, and establishing phase-in of reserve requirements for banks that withdrew from the Federal Reserve System between July 1, 1979, and March 31, 1980.

## TITLE VIII
### ALTERNATIVE MORTGAGE TRANSACTION PARITY ACT

Title VIII permits nonfederally chartered housing creditors to engage in alternative mortgage transactions, creating a parity with federally chartered housing creditors.

**GARNISHMENT**   The order of a court of competent jurisdiction to an employer directing the employer to withhold and set aside all or a portion of an employee's (garnishee's) wages or other compensation and to pay that amount to the court in favor of a third party plaintiff or directly to the plaintiff.

**GENERAL ENDORSEMENT**   A non-restrictive endorsement; the signature or other acceptable endorsement of a person or firm making the item payable to the bearer and therefore negotiable.

**GENERAL FUND**   Money not already earmarked for another purpose or assigned to another specific accounting fund.

**GENERAL LEDGER**   Containing various departmental subsidiary records, the general ledger is the overall record of every transaction that takes place in the bank during a business day affecting asset accounts, liability accounts, capital accounts, suspense accounts, expense accounts or income accounts.

**GENERAL LIEN**   A lien against an individual, not against a particular or specific item of property owned by the individual.

**GENERAL PARTNER**   A partner who, among other things, is liable for the debts of the partnership.

**GENERAL POWER OF APPOINTMENT**   Under the provisions of a trust agreement, a general power of appointment grants in the donee (the one who has the power) the ability to pass an interest in real or personal property to anyone, including himself, as the ultimate recipient of the asset(s) of the trust.

**GENERAL WARRANTY DEED**   A deed which carries with it the guarantee that the grantor will defend the title against any claim, that title passes free of debt or cloud.

**GENERALLY ACCEPTED ACCOUNTING PRINCIPLES (GAAP)**   Created by the Financial Accounting Standards Board (FASB), an independent, self-regulatory organization formed in 1973 to standardize accounting applications of firms and private practitioners.

**GIFT CAUSA MORTIS**   A gift made in anticipation of death usually for the purpose of avoiding inheritance taxes.

**GIFT INTER VIVOS**   A gift made during the donor's life, usually not made in anticipation of death. SEE GIFT CAUSA MORTIS.

**GIFT TAX**   A graduated federal, and in some jurisdictions local, tax paid by the donor.

**GINNIE MAE**   SEE GOVERNMENT NATIONAL MORTGAGE ASSOCIATION.

**GLASS-STEGALL ACT OF 1933**   The Banking Act of 1933, carrying the names of its sponsors, which was signed into law by President Franklin D. Roosevelt on June 16 of that year. The act created the Federal Open Market Committee (FOMC) and authorized deposit insurance. Largely in response to the collapse of banks during the depression, the act prohibited commercial banks from engaging in investment banking activities. In recent years Glass-Stegall has been challenged by the banking industry through, for example, the introduction of money market accounts, municipal revenue bonds, discount brokerage services, personal financial planning services, and commercial paper.

**GNMA**   SEE GOVERNMENT NATIONAL MORTGAGE ASSOCIATION.

**GNMA MORTGAGE-BACKED SECURITIES**   An investment vehicle collateralized by FHA or VA mortgages, guaranteed by the Government National Mortgage Association, and issued by mortgage bankers.

**GNP**   SEE GROSS NATIONAL PRODUCT.

**GO-BACKS**   Checks returned by the drawee bank to the payor bank for any of several reasons, including insufficient funds, closed account, lack of endorsement, uncollected funds, irregularity, or stop payment.

**GO PUBLIC**   The term used to indicate a public offering of equity in a business previously closely held.

**GOLD COVER**   A now defunct requirement that U.S. Federal Reserve Notes be backed by a gold reserve of 25% of the value of the currency outstanding. The Gold-Cover Repeal Act of 1968 thus freed more than $10 billion in gold reserves previously required to back the Federal Reserve Notes.

**GOURDE**   Monetary unit of Haiti.

**GOVERNMENT NATIONAL MORTGAGE ASSOCIATION (GINNIE MAE or GNA)**   An agency of the U.S. Department of Housing and Urban Development (HUD). The agency was created in 1968, spawned from the Federal National Mortgage Association ("Fannie Mae" or "FNMA") to help finance additional housing by offering permanent financing for low rent housing. This is accomplished through a mortgage-backed securities program which attracts new sources of capital to FHA and VA mortgages; the Government National Mortgage Association guarantees timely repayment of privately issued securities backed by pools of FHA and VA mortgages.

**GRACE PERIOD**   That period allowed after a payment due date but before a late charge is applied. A common grace period is 10 days; thus a contract provision may call for a late charge to be due and payable on the 11th day after the day a payment is due.

**GRADUATED PAYMENT**   Repayment terms calling for gradual increases in the payments on a closed-end obligation. A graduated payment loan usually involves negative amortization. Thus, the Federal Housing Administration (FHA) which has insured Graduated Payment Mortgages since 1976, generally requires that down payments be larger that those required under a fixed-payment mortgage. Graduated Payment Mortgages are also eligible for pooling into GNMA securities (SEE GOVERNMENT NATIONAL MORTGAGE ASSOCIATION) and represent a substantial portion of FHA-insured mortgages.

**GRANDFATHERED ACTIVITIES**   Nonbank activities, some of which would normally not be permissible for bank holding companies and foreign banks in the United States, but which were acquired or engaged in before a particular date. Such activities may be continued under the "grandfather" clauses of the Bank Holding Company Act and the International Banking Act.

**GROSS DEPOSITS**   All deposits, demand and time, including government deposits and those due banks.

**GROSS ESTATE**   All property, real or personal, tangible or intangible, owned by a person before any deductions for taxes, debts, encumbrances or other liabilities.

**GROSS INCOME**   Income before expenses have been deducted.

**GROSS LEASE**   A agreement under which the lessor or real property agrees to be liable for all expenses which normally would be paid by the owner of such property.

**GROSS MARGIN**   The amount available to cover operating and financial expenses derived by subtracting the cost of goods sold from net sales.

**GROSS NATIONAL PRODUCT (GNP)**   The total value of goods and services produced in the economy of a country for a defined period of time, usually one year.

**GROSS PROFIT**   Total operating income less the cost of goods sold.

**GROSS RECEIPTS**   The total of all receipts prior to deducting expenses.

**GROSS REVENUE**   Total revenues, generally reflected as gross sales, before any deductions have been made for returns, allowances, or discounts.

**GUARANI**   Monetary unit of Paraguay.

**GUARANTEE**   A written statement assuring quality, quantity, performance, value, benefit or performance. "Payment guaranteed" or equivalent words added to a signature mean that the signer engages that if the instrument is not paid when due he will pay it according to its tenor without resort by the holder to any other party.

   "Collection guaranteed" or equivalent words added to a signature mean that the signer engages that if the instrument is not paid when due he will pay it according to its tenor, but only after the holder has reduced his claim against the maker or acceptor to judgment and execution has been returned unsatisfied, or after the maker or acceptor has become insolvent or it is otherwise apparent that it is useless to proceed against him.

**GUARANTEE OF SIGNATURE**   SEE SIGNATURE GUARANTEE.

**GUARANTEED INTEREST CERTIFICATE**   A form of negotiable instrument which is registered and represents the guaranteed portion of a Small Business Administration loan. Guaranteed Interest Certificates may be sold by lenders in the secondary market.

**GUARANTEED STUDENT LOANS**   Loans made by banks, savings and loans or credit unions to students to pay for costs of education; the interest is paid by the U.S. government while the student is actively enrolled.

**GUARANTOR**   That party to a guaranty agreement who contracts to ensure the performance of one of the other parties. Generally, the guarantor is that person who contracts himself or herself to assume liability for the debt of the borrower in the case of the borrower's default.

**GUARANTY**   A three party agreement. Generally, a guaranty agreement involves a lender or creditor, a borrower or debtor, and a guarantor. SEE GUARANTOR.

**GUARDIAN**   A person or trust department or institution appointed by a court of competent jurisdiction to care for the person and/or property of a minor or incompetent person. If the appointment is for the purpose of representing the minor or incompetent person in court proceedings, the appointee is referred to as "guardian ad litem".

**GUARDIANSHIP**   A personal trust arrangement where a court appointed-party protects, manages and maintains the property of, and for the benefit of, a minor or incompetent person.

**GUARDIANSHIP ACCOUNT**   A bank account held in the name of a guardian who manages the funds therein for the benefit of a minor or an incompetent person.

**GULDEN**   Monetary unit of the Netherlands.

# H

**H BOND**   A United States Government Savings Bond discontinued in 1980.

**HANDLING CHARGE**   A charge levied by either a merchant bank or a card-issuing bank for the processing of interchange transactions. SEE INTERCHANGE.

**HAZARD INSURANCE**   A policy written to protect real estate against loss from certain hazards, among which may be included fire, windstorm, other natural causes, or vandalism.

**HEAD TELLER**   Generally the senior teller. A bank teller who, among other varied responsibilities, supervises other tellers and maintains appropriate levels of cash and currency in order to meet the daily demands of the bank's customers while at the same time minimizing risks of loss.

**HEDGE**   To minimize risk of loss, such as controlling the risk of one transaction by entering into an offsetting transaction. For example, a bank can hedge the holding of large amounts of foreign currency by arranging for the sale of the same amount of currency for future delivery at a fixed price.

**HEIR**   A person who inherits property. A direct heir, sometimes referred to as an "heir of the body," is one who is in direct line of the decedent, for example a son or mother. A collateral heir is a person not in direct line, such as a nephew or aunt. An heir-at-law inherits property from a decedent who dies intestate.

**HEREDITAMENT**   Real or personal property that can be inherited. A corporeal hereditament is visible and tangible property. An incorporeal hereditament is neither visible nor tangible and may, for example, be an inherited right.

**HH BOND**   A United States Government Savings Bond issued at face value. These bonds pay interest semiannually and mature in 10 years.

**HIDDEN ASSETS**   Property of a corporation not easily identifiable on the corporation's financial statement.

**HIGH CREDIT**   The highest outstanding balance or amount of credit a borrower has historically reached.

**HIGH-RATIO LOAN**   Generally a mortgage loan, the amount of which exceeds 80 percent of the value of the property securing it.

**HIGHEST AND BEST USE**   That activity which produces the highest legal net income possible to land, thus giving the land its highest value.

**HMDA**   SEE HOME MORTGAGE DISCLOSURE ACT OF 1975.

**HOLD**   A restriction placed on all or part of the funds in an account. For example, a hold may be placed on an item received for deposit. Funds are "held" to allow time for collection.

**HOLDER**   A person who is in possession of a document of title or an instrument or a certificated investment security drawn, issued, or endorsed to him or his order or to bearer or in blank.

**HOLDER IN DUE COURSE**  A holder who takes an instrument for value, in good faith, and without notice that it is overdue or has been dishonored or of any defense against or claim to it. A payee may be a holder in due course.

A holder does not become a holder in due course of an instrument by purchase of it at judicial sale or by taking it under legal process, by acquiring it in taking over an estate, or by purchasing it as part of a bulk transaction not in the regular course of business of the transferer. A purchaser of a limited interest can be a holder in due course only to the extent of the interest purchased.

In the examples that follow, the payee, "P," is a holder in due course:

[a] A remitter, purchasing goods from P, obtains a bank draft payable to P and forwards it to P, who takes it for value, in good faith, and without notice.

[b] The remitter buys the bank draft payable to P, but it is forwarded by the bank directly to P, who takes it in good faith and without notice, in payment of the remitter's obligation to him.

[c] A and B sign a note as co-makers. A induces B to sign by fraud, and without authority from B delivers the note to P, who takes it for value, in good faith and without notice.

[d] A defrauds the maker into signing an instrument payable to P. P pays A for it in good faith and without notice, and the maker delivers the instrument directly to P.

[e] D draws a check payable to P and gives it to his agent to be delivered to P in payment of D's debt. The agent delivers it to P, who takes it in good faith and without notice in payment of the agent's debt to P.

[f] D draws a check payable to P but blank as to the amount, and gives it to his agent to be delivered to P. The agent fills in the check with an excessive amount, and P takes it for value, in good faith and without notice.

[g] D draws a check blank as to the name of the payee, and gives it to his agent to be filled in with the name of A and delivered to A. The agent fills in the name of P, and P takes the check in good faith, for value and without notice.

To the extent that a holder is a holder in due course, he takes the instrument free from all claims to it on the part of any person, and all defenses of any party to the instrument with whom the holder has not dealt except:

(1) infancy, to the extent that it is a defense to a simple contract; and

(2) such other incapacity, or duress, or illegality of the transaction, as renders the obligation of the party a nullity; and

(3) such misrepresentation as has induced the party to sign the instrument with neither knowledge nor reasonable opportunity to obtain knowledge of its character or its essential terms; and

(4) discharge in insolvency proceedings; and

(5) any other discharge of which the holder has notice when he takes the instrument.

Unless he has the rights of a holder in due course, any person takes an instrument subject to:

(1) all valid claims to it on the part of any person; and

(2) all defenses of any party which would be available in an action on a simple contract; and

(3) the defenses of want or failure of consideration, nonperformance of any condition precedent, non-delivery, or delivery for a special purpose; and

(4) the defense that he or a person through whom he holds the instrument acquired it by theft, or that payment or satisfaction to such holder would be inconsistent with the terms of a restrictive indorsement. The claim of any third person to the instrument is not otherwise available as a defense to any party liable thereon unless the third person himself defends the action for such party.

**HOLDER IN DUE COURSE DOCTRINE**   A provision of the Uniform Commercial Code which has been weakened to some extent by subsequent legislation. The doctrine holds that if a note, such as a conditional sales contract, is held by a holder in due course, the borrower may not withhold payment because of dissatisfaction with the merchandise.

**HOLDER OF RECORD**   An owner of stock who, according to the records of the corporation, owned the stock on a specified date referred to as the "holder of record date," generally for the purposes of payment of dividends.

**HOLDING COMPANY**   A company that owns the securities of another, generally with voting control. A "bank holding company" means any company, including a bank, that has direct or indirect control of a bank. The term includes a foreign banking organization only if it owns or controls a bank in the United States. "Company" includes any bank, corporation, general or limited partnership, association or similar organization, business trust, or any other trust unless by its terms it must terminate either within 25 years and 10 months after the death of individuals living on the effective date of the trust. The term does not include any organization, the majority of the voting securities of which are owned by the United States or any state. "Voting securities" means shares of common or preferred stock, general or limited partnership shares or interests.

**HOLOGRAPHIC WILL**   A will that is entirely written, dated and signed by the hand of the testator himself or herself. It is subject to no other form and need not be witnessed. No address, date or other matter written, printed or stamped upon the document, which is not incorporated in the provisions which are in the handwriting of the decedent, shall be considered as any part of the will.

**HOME BANKING**   A general term which describes the ability of a customer to gather information or pay recurring bills or transfer funds between accounts through the use of a touch tone telephone or personal computer. Because the term does not include the ability to deposit or withdraw funds, it is not considered branch banking. Home banking services are not offered by all institutions and the features differ among those institutions that do offer such services.

**HOME EQUITY LOAN**   A personal loan which is secured by a lien on the borrower's real property. A home equity loan is generally a "second trust deed" secured loan or "second mortgage." It may be structured as a fixed term loan or a line of credit. Although generally secured by a junior lien on the borrower's primary residence, some institutions will take a lien on the borrower's other property, such as a vacation home.

**HOME IMPROVEMENT LOAN**   A consumer loan made for the purpose of repairing or remodeling a single family dwelling. A home improvement loan is generally a fixed term home equity loan. SEE HOME EQUITY LOAN.

**HOME LOAN**   A home loan is a real estate loan for the purchase, construction and permanent financing or the refinancing of residential real property which will be used as the applicant's principal residence. Residential real property includes one-to-four family residences and individual units of condominiums and cooperatives. Real estate loans include loans made in reliance upon the security of a mobile home and the parcel of land to which it is permanently affixed.

**HOME MORTGAGE DISCLOSURE ACT OF 1975 (HMDA)**   Implemented by Federal Reserve Regulation C, effective June 28, 1976. In 1988, HMDA was amended and extended permanently under provisions of the Housing and Community Development Act of 1987. The regulation's coverage was expanded to include mortgage banking subsidiaries of bank and savings and loan holding companies, and savings and loan service corporations that originate or purchase mortgage loans in its definition of "financial institutions." The act emerged from public concern over credit shortages in certain urban neighborhoods. Congress found that some financial institutions had contributed to the decline of certain geographic areas by their failure, pursuant to their chartering responsibilities, to provide adequate home financing to qualified applicants on reasonable terms and conditions.

The act and the implementing regulation provide the public with information that helps to show whether financial institutions are serving the housing credit needs of the neighborhoods and communities in which they are located. They also assist public officials in distributing public sector investments in a way that will attract private investments in neighborhoods where they are needed. As a disclosure law, HMDA relies upon public scrutiny for its effectiveness. It neither prohibits any specific activity of lenders nor establishes a quota system of mortgage loans to be made in any MSA or county. It allows the public to review a lender's mortgage loan record in a particular area and help form a judgment about a lender's responsiveness in providing adequate home financing. Home mortgage disclosure data may also be used in conjunction with several Community Reinvestment Act assessment factors.

Financial institutions must make complete loan disclosure statements available to the public by March 31 following the calendar year for which the loan data was compiled, and continue to make that data available for five years.

The date must be made available in the home office and if the institution has branch offices in other Metropolitan Statistical Areas (MSA) in at least one branch office in each of those MSAs. Loan disclosure statements at a branch office location need contain data only relating to property in the MSA where the branch is located. The Federal Financial Institutions Examinations Council (FFIEC) aggregates the loan disclosure data for all financial institutions in each MSA, showing lending patterns by location, age of housing stock, income level and racial characteristics. These data are available to the public at central depositories located in each MSA. Banks must compile and report data on number and dollar amounts of home purchase and home improvement loans that they originate and purchase for each calendar year.

**HOMEOWNER'S INSURANCE**   A combination of hazard insurance and personal liability protection.

**HOT CARD**   A bank credit card or access device which is generally being used without authorization or is lost or stolen.

**HOT MONEY**   Temporary deposits, usually of substantial amounts.

**HUD**   Department of Housing and Urban Development. This federal agency was formed in 1975 to assume responsibility for establishing and monitoring national programs dealing with housing needs and urban development and renewal.

**HULL INSURANCE**   A policy written on the structure of a marine vessel as opposed to its cargo or freight.

**HURDLE RATE**   The minimum acceptable rate of return to justify an undertaking or investment.

**HYPOTHECATE**   To pledge real or personal property as collateral for a debt. For example, a savings account, certificate of deposit, securities, or other assets may be hypothecated generally without transfer of title or physical possession, subject to the terms of a hypothecation agreement, to collateralize a loan to a third party.

# I

**IBF**   SEE INTERNATIONAL BANKING FACILITY.

**IMF**   SEE INTERNATIONAL MONETARY FUND.

**IMMEDIATE CREDIT**   Instant access to funds. The opposite of "deferred availability," immediate credit is given, for example, on checks drawn "on-us" or, perhaps, for checks drawn on other local banks by prior agreement.

**IMPORT**   To receive merchandise or services from another country.

**IMPORT LETTER OF CREDIT**   A commercial letter of credit issued by a bank for the purpose of financing the importation of goods and services from abroad. SEE LETTER OF CREDIT.

**IMPORT QUOTA**   Aggregate quantitative limit imposed by one country on the import of certain specific goods generally established to protect domestic manufacturers or producers of the same or like commodity.

**IMPOUND**   To take physical control of an item and hold it in legal custody.

**IMPROVED PROPERTY LOAN**   An extension of credit secured by one of the following types of real property: farmland, ranchland or timberland committed to ongoing management and agricultural production; 1- to 4-family residential property that is not owner-occupied; residential property containing five or more individual dwelling units; completed commercial property; or other income-producing property that has been completed and is available for occupancy and use, except income-producing owner-occupied 1- to 4-family residential property.

**IN-STORE BANKING**   Also referred to as "supermarket banking," the operation of branch banks inside supermarkets. Predicated on the principle that the average consumer visits a supermarket in excess of 2 times each week, some banks have established small, full service or nearly-full service banking units within these stores for the convenience of the consumer and in an effort to gain additional share of the local market.

**INACTIVE ACCOUNT**   A deposit account in which no activity has occurred for a specified period of time. Also referred to as a "dormant" account. "Inactive account" may also be a cardholder account in which no charges have been made.

**INCOME**   Accrued or earned money, or an equivalent thereof, arising from the sale of goods or performance of services.

**INCOME ACCOUNT**   A general ledger account which is credited with various sources of revenue. At the end of the accounting period, this account is closed out and the balance is transferred to either retained earnings or dividends.

**INCOME AND EXPENSE STATEMENT**   Synonymous with "profit and loss statement" or "P & L," an accounting summary of revenue and costs of operation during the specified accounting period.

**INCOME PROPERTY**   Real property, generally not a principal residence, which generates revenue such as commercial, industrial or residential rental property.

**INCOME STATEMENT**   The summary of the revenues, costs and expenses of a company during an accounting period.

**INCOME TAX**   Tax levied by a local, state or federal authority on the earnings of a legal entity such as a person, partnership, or corporation.

**INDEFEASIBLE**   A right or document that is perfected or otherwise incapable of being rendered void.

**INDEMNIFY**   The act of returning to the position as it was prior to loss. Indemnification generally requires compensation for actual loss sustained.

**INDEMNITY**   An agreement of protection against loss. For example, an indemnity bond protects the insured from loss due to the nonperformance of another or the failure of another to adequately fulfill his or her obligation.

**INDENTURE**   A contract underlying a bond issue which sets forth the maturity date, interest rate and other terms including the rights and responsibilities of the parties.

**INDEX**   A statistical average, generally weighted, that measures change over a defined period.

**INDIRECT LIABILITY**   The liability of an endorser or guarantor, as compared to the direct liability of the maker.

**INDIRECT LOAN**   Generally a conditional sales contract between buyer and seller which is assigned by seller with or without recourse to a bank. The seller is paid in full upon assignment, or paid the face amount of the contract less a predetermined reserve. The buyer is notified of the assignment and his or her obligation to make installment payments as defined by the contract directly to the bank, rather than the seller.

**INDIVIDUAL RETIREMENT ACCOUNT (IRA)**   A savings account with preferential tax treatment. Effective January 1, 1982, all wage earners were permitted to make tax deductible contributions to Individual Retirement Accounts. An individual taxpayer could contribute up to $2000 annually ($2,250 with a nonworking spouse) and allow the earnings to accumulate tax free until the taxpayer reached age 59 1/2. Lump sum or periodic distributions could then be withdrawn, assumably at the time the taxpayer would be in a lower tax bracket.

**INDUSTRIAL DEVELOPMENT BOND**  A community-issued, tax-exempt municipal bond. Industrial development bonds are used to raise capital to finance private business development and attract industry.

**INFLATION**  A rise, over time, in the average level of prices, which creates a decrease in purchasing power along with general increases in wages and production costs.

**INHERITANCE TAXES**  State tax levied on property inherited.

**INSOLVENCY**  The inability to pay debts as they mature. The inability to convert assets to cash to meet matured current obligations.

**INSTALLMENT CREDIT**  Generally a loan that, according to the terms of its repayment agreement, is to be repaid in a defined number of periodic payments ("installments"), due on a certain day of each succeeding month.

**INSTALLMENT NOTE**  A promissory note in which the principal is paid in specified installments, together with interest on the unpaid balance until the loan is paid in full.

**INSTITUTIONAL LENDER**  A financial institution that directly invests in real estate mortgages or indirectly through purchases of mortgages or mortgage-backed securities in the secondary market.

**INSURANCE BINDER**  Written evidence of temporary insurance coverage. Hazard or title insurance coverage for a generally short time, upon the expiration of which coverage must be extended by a permanent policy of insurance.

**INSURANCE POLICY**  A written document, including endorsements, which is the contract of insurance.

**INSURED BANK**  A member institution of the Federal Deposit Insurance Corporation.

**INSURED DEPOSIT**  Bank deposits which are guaranteed by the FDIC against loss due to bank failure.

**INSURED LOAN**  A loan insured by the Federal Housing Administration or a private mortgage insurance company.

**INTANGIBLE ASSET**  Nonmaterial resource such as goodwill, patent or franchise rights.

**INTER VIVOS**  "Between living people" (Latin). SEE INTER VIVOS TRUST.

**INTER VIVOS TRUST**  A "living trust" which is operative during the lifetime of the trustor, as distinguished from a trust under will or testamentary trust.

**INTERCHANGE** The movement of debit and credit transaction data between merchant banks and cardholder banks, subject to agreement. The term also refers to the use of electronic funds transfer (EFT) services such as the transfer and settlement of data originated by the use of a foreign credit card for purchase from a local merchant.

**INTERCHANGE FEE** A handling charge levied by the merchant bank or the card-issuing bank for the processing of interchange transactions.

**INTEREST** The cost of using money; the fee which is charged for the use of the principal.

**INTEREST (DEPOSITS)** Any payment made to a depositor as compensation for the use of deposit funds. Payment of interest does not include normal banking expenses absorbed by the bank. Services, such as free checking accounts, loans at reduced interest rates and free money orders, are examples of absorbed fees that are not considered payment of interest.

Before 1980, the payment and advertising of interest on deposits, including interest rate ceilings, the establishment of deposit account characteristics and required early withdrawal penalties on time deposits, were governed primarily by the Federal Reserve Board's Regulation Q. The Depository Institutions Deregulation and Monetary Control Act of 1980 provided for an orderly phase-out of interest rate ceilings under the direction of the Depository Institutions Deregulation Committee (DIDC). On March 31, 1986, the DIDC ended and all interest rate ceiling authority expired, as did the authority to require early withdrawal penalties.

Banks may establish any deposit account desired without regard to interest rate ceilings and without requiring early withdrawal penalties. Deposit contracts remain subject to local laws. The advertising of interest on deposits and disclosure of any bank-required early withdrawal penalties are governed by Regulation Q.

The Federal Reserve Board's Regulation D (12 CFR 204) has preserved certain deposit account characteristics and early withdrawal penalties for reserve requirement purposes.

Numerous factors affect the actual amount that a customer will receive in interest. The terms and conditions and methods of computation are as important as the interest rate. They include opening balance requirements, minimum balance requirements, access privileges, grace periods, service charges, balances upon which the interest is calculated, frequency of compounding and crediting earned interest, compounding formula used, etc. The various methods of earnings computation, combined with the infinite possibilities of compounding, indicate the wide options available to a bank for determining interest. To maximize interest earnings, consumers must gear their personal savings habits to the bank's policies and consider factors other than a simple annual interest rate.

The more frequently the bank compounds interest, the higher the effective annual yield. Some commonly used (from least to most favorable to the consumer) compounding methods are: none, semiannual, quarterly, monthly, weekly, daily, and continuous. The amount of interest a consumer may earn also will vary depending on how the bank computes the balance on which interest is paid. There are four basic methods for determining the balance on which interest is paid. A simple example will illustrate how those different methods work:

Assume you have a passbook account that pays interest at the rate of 5 percent a year. Assume further that you begin a calendar quarter (July 1) with a $5000 balance, withdraw $4000 on August 1, deposit $10,000 on September 1 and withdraw $1000 on September 30. Finally, assume that all months have 30 days and a year 360.

*Low Balance:* Under the low balance method shown in the table, you only receive interest on your lowest balance during the quarter. In the example given, this is $1000. Thus, interest for the quarter would be $1000 times 5%, divided by 4 ($12.50).

*FIFO:* The term "FIFO" stands for "First In — First Out." Under that method, each withdrawal is deducted from the balance at the beginning of the quarter and from later deposits (in the order made) if the beginning balance is insufficient. The method is also referred to as the "Day of Deposit to End of Interest Period Method." In the example given, the two withdrawals totaling $5000 are deducted from the beginning balance of $5000. As a result, the balance from July 1 until September 1 is effectively zero and no interest is earned during that period. Only one month's interest, amounting to $41.66 is earned on the $10,000 deposited on September 1.

*LIFO:* The term "LIFO" stands for "Last In — First Out." Under that method, each withdrawal is deducted from the immediately preceding deposit. In the example given, the first withdrawal of $4000 is deducted from the beginning balance of $5000, leaving on July 1 an effective balance of $1000. Interest is earned on the $1000 for three months. The second withdrawal of $1000 on September 30 is deducted from the most recent deposit of $10,000 leaving a balance of $9000, as of September 1, on which interest is earned for one month. The combined interest on those balances comes to $50.

*Day of Deposit to Day of Withdrawal*: This is the most favorable method for the saver. It is also referred to as "daily interest." Under this method, interest is earned on the exact amount in the account each day. In the example given, interest is earned on the $5000 balance for July, on the $1000 balance for August, on the $11,000 balance for the first 29 days in September, and on the $10,000 balance for the last day in September. The combined interest on those balances amounts to $70.70.

Those computations have been simplified by assuming that each month has exactly 30 days. In reality, the arithmetic may be more complicated. Nevertheless, the example does provide an insight into how the different computation methods work and shows that one bank can pay almost 6 times as much interest as another bank, even though both banks advertise interest at 5%. Although other examples might show different results, in all cases, the most favorable method to the saver for calculating the balance on which interest is paid is Day of Deposit to Day of Withdrawal.

**INTEREST (LOANS)**   The price borrowers pay to lenders for credit over specified periods of time. The amount of interest paid depends on a number of factors such as the dollar amount lent or borrowed, the length of time involved in the transaction, the stated (or nominal) annual rate of interest, the repayment schedule, and the method used to calculate interest.

**INTEREST ACCRUED**   Interest earned but not yet due or payable.

**INTEREST BEARING** Subject to interest, used to describe a mortgage, note or bond upon the balance of which interest is computed. For example, the borrower of a debt evidenced by an interest bearing note agrees to pay the face amount of the note plus interest on the outstanding balance.

**INTEREST ONLY LOAN** A loan which calls for the periodic payment of accrued interest without a reduction in principal. In theory, the entire principal amount borrowed would be due at maturity while the interest charged on the loan would have been paid prior to maturity, generally in periodic installments.

**INTEREST PENALTY** A fee or additional charge imposed when the terms of a financial agreement are altered.

**INTEREST RATE** The cost of money, expressed as a percentage and usually calculated on an annual basis.

**INTERMEDIATION** The movement of funds from an ultimate lender (a bank depositor) through the bank and to a borrowing customer.

**INTERNAL RATE OF RETURN (IRR)** The rate of return on an investment.

**INTERNAL REVENUE SERVICE** A federal agency which administers the rules and regulations of the Department of the Treasury, including, but not limited to the collection of federal income taxes.

**INTERNATIONAL BANK FOR RECONSTRUCTION AND DEVELOPMENT** SEE WORLD BANK.

**INTERNATIONAL BANKING FACILITY (IBF)** In general, these facilities can accept time deposits from foreign customers free of reserve requirements and interest rate limitations, and can lend to foreigners if the funds are for the conduct of foreign business outside of the United States. International Banking Facilities allow banks to participate in the Eurodollar market without the expense of maintaining an overseas branch, generally by locating a functional unit within a bank in the United States. This allows U.S. chartered depository institutions, U.S. offices of Edge Act corporations, and U.S. agencies and branches of foreign banks to conduct banking business with foreign residents in a regulatory environment without having to use an offshore facility.

**INTERNATIONAL MONETARY FUND (IMF)** An international organization with 146 members, including the United States. The main functions of the International Monetary Fund are to lend funds to member nations to finance temporary balance of payments problems, to facilitate the expansion and balanced growth of international trade, and to promote international monetary cooperation among nations. The IMF also creates special drawing rights (SDRs) which provide member nations with a source of additional reserves. Member nations are required to subscribe to a Fund quota, paid mainly in their own currency. The IMF grew out of the Bretton Woods Conference of 1944.

**INTESTATE** Without a will. When a person dies leaving property but without leaving a will, that person is intestate. A court of competent jurisdiction will appoint an administrator to distribute the property according to the local state law.

**INTESTATE SUCCESSION** The distribution of property, generally to the next of kin, of a person who dies intestate.

**INVENTORY**   A business asset consisting of raw materials, intermediate product and parts, work in progress and finished goods. Inventories may be considered as intended for either internal consumption or for sale. The term also refers to a detailed listing of all items owned by a business and their corresponding value. Inventory can also mean an accounting by an administrator or executor of the real and personal property of a deceased person.

**INVENTORY FINANCING**   The use of a dealer's inventory as security for a loan. "Flooring" is a form of inventory financing where, for example, the bank advances funds to a piano dealer who holds certain pianos in trust for the bank and issues a trust receipt until the goods are sold, at which time the funds are repaid to the bank. Another form of inventory financing is "warehouse financing," where goods are held in trust as collateral for the loan. As the goods are sold, they are released by the trustee to the purchaser; the trustee forwards the sale proceeds to the bank to repay the loan.

**INVENTORY TURNOVER**   A measurement of the rate of usage of a company's goods as indicated by the number of times, on the average, that inventory is replaced during a period. The ratio is calculated by dividing Cost of Goods Sold by Average Inventory.

**INVESTMENT BANKING**   The financing, usually through the underwriting of new security issues, of the capital requirements of an enterprise. Common functions include the determination by the investment banker of the type and terms of the new security issue, the formation of a syndicate to market the security either privately or to the public and the maintenance of an orderly and fair trading market in the early days of a new issue. Investment bankers generally help with the long term financing requirements of a business where commercial banks generally focus on the short term credit requirements.

**INVESTMENT COMPANY**   A company or trust that engages primarily in investing its capital in the securities of other companies. "Closed-end" investment companies offer shares which are readily transferable on the open market and are bought and sold like other securities. "Open-end" investment companies, most generally mutual funds, sell their own new shares to investors and stand ready to buy back their old shares.

**INVESTMENT CREDIT**   Credit given to a business for the purchase of identified fixed assets.

**INVESTMENT INCOME**   Any and all income derived from the investment in securities or other property.

**INVESTMENT TAX CREDIT**   An incentive granted by the Internal Revenue Service for making long term investments. The incentive is a reduction in the business' federal tax obligation by a specified percentage of the new investment costs.

**INVOICE**   A bill for goods sold or services rendered.

**INVOLUNTARY LIEN**   A lien placed on real property without the consent of the owner. For example, the deed of trust securing a home equity loan would represent a lien placed against real property with the agreement and consent of the owner/

borrower. On the other hand, a lien placed against the property for the unpaid balance of federal or property taxes would likely be an involuntary lien.

**IRA**   SEE INDIVIDUAL RETIREMENT ACCOUNT.

**IRR**   SEE INTERNAL RATE OF RETURN.

**IRREVOCABLE LETTER OF CREDIT**   An irrevocable document which, when issued to a firm or a person by a bank, substitutes the bank's credit for that of the person or firm. Where a revocable letter of credit may be cancelled at any time by the issuing bank, an irrevocable letter of credit must be honored without exception. SEE LETTER OF CREDIT.

**IRREVOCABLE TRUST**   A trust which, by its terms, cannot be revoked or set aside by the settler acting alone or without the express consent of the beneficiaries.

**ISSUE**   Securities which are issued by a company and sold to the public, or the act of distributing such securities.

**ISSUED AND OUTSTANDING**   Stocks or bonds which have been authorized for sale, have been sold, and are held by investors. Excluded from this term are repurchased securities held as treasury stock, or securities which have been retired.

**ISSUER IDENTIFICATION NUMBER**   The identification number of the issuer as set forth in American National Standard specifications for Credit Cards, ANSI x4.13−1983, and embossed Credit Cards Specifications, Numbering System and Registration Procedure, ISO 2894−1974.

**ISSUER IDENTIFIER**   The portion of a primary account number that, when combined with the majority industry identifier, identifies the card issuer and/or primary processing endpoint.

**ITEM**   A very broad term encompassing all instruments payable in money such as "cash items," "non-cash items," "city items," "local items," "collected items," and so forth.

**ITEMIZED STATEMENT**   A detailed item-by-item recap of account activity during a predesignated period of time.

# *J*

**JAJO**   January, April, July, October. The first month of each quarter; used most commonly in reference to interest or dividend payments.

**JOINT ACCOUNT**   An investment account, charge account, bank account, or any other account which is owned by and held in the names of two or more individuals, each sharing equally in the rights and liabilities of the account. Generally, any bank account which is held in the names of two or more people is referred to as a joint account regardless of whether more than one person may sign checks or make withdrawals.

**JOINT AND SEVERAL ACCOUNT WITH RIGHT OF SURVIVORSHIP** A joint account which may be accessed by either joint owner. Upon the death of either owner, the survivor retains the right to the account's funds.

**JOINT AND SEVERAL GUARANTY** An endorsement or guaranty that enables the entire liability to be enforced against any or all of the obligors.

**JOINT LIABILITY** A liability shared by two or more people who must be acted upon as a group in the event of legal proceedings.

**JOINT OWNERSHIP** The common ownership of real or personal property by two or more people. SEE, FOR EXAMPLE, JOINT TENANCY.

**JOINT POLICY STATEMENT ON BASIC FINANCIAL SERVICES** A 1985 combined regulatory agency position on the offering of basic financial services:
"The Board of Governors of the Federal Reserve System, Federal Deposit Insurance Corporation, Federal Home Loan Bank Board, National Credit Union Administration, Office of the Comptroller of the Currency, Conference of State Bank Supervisors, and National Association of State Savings and Loan Supervisors are issuing this joint policy statement to encourage the efforts of trade associations and individual depository institutions regarding the offering of 'basic financial services.'
"The economic environment in which financial institutions operate has changed over the past few years, due in part to increased competition from outside the traditional depository institution structure, increased cost of funds following deregulation of interest rates, and interest rate volatility. As a consequence, many institutions have had to adopt new strategies to market their services, generate income, manage risk, and reduce costs. Some institutions have begun to price their products explicitly, consolidate or eliminate services they believe to be unprofitable, and close branch offices. In many instances, institutions have increased service charges, imposed new fees, and raised minimum balance requirements.
"Although such adaptation may be a necessary response to competitive markets, considerable concern has developed about the potential impact of these changes in effectively denying or reducing convenient access of many individuals to the payments system and to safe depositories for small savings. Because credit availability often depends on an account relationship with a financial institution, access to credit for low-income or young consumers also may be adversely affected.
"Although a significant number of consumers have never had a deposit account, some research studies reflect declines in account ownership that may be cause for concern. For example, between 1977 and 1983 the proportion of families headed by a younger person having checking accounts decreased, as did the number of families from the lowest income group, regardless of age. The proportion of young families having either a savings or checking account also declined. Although the cause of these declines is not always clear, the surveys do suggest that a significant number of individuals or families do not have a deposit relationship of any kind.
"Legislation dealing with basic financial services has been introduced at both the federal and state level as a result of these concerns. The industry also has responded. Many financial institutions independently have undertaken to develop and implement new measures to meet minimum consumer needs. They are offering

basic services, such as low-cost transaction and savings accounts with low or no minimum balances, accounts for consumers who use a limited number of checks or drafts, and other accounts on which minimal charges are made for account maintenance. Institutions that have for years offered such services to particular groups of customers are now advertising their availability more widely. Other institutions are exploring and finding ways to maintain a physical presence in low- and moderate-income neighborhoods even while reducing the expense normally associated with full branch facilities. Trade groups too have joined in these efforts to encourage the offering of such services at affordable prices. The American Bankers Association and Consumer Bankers Association, for example, have called upon their members to address the continuing interest in basic banking services.

"The member agencies of the Federal Financial Institutions Examination Council and the associations of state supervisors wish to encourage such efforts by trade associations and individual depository institutions that promote the offering of basic financial services, consistent with safe and sound business practices. Although the specific type of services will, of course, vary because of differences in local needs and in the characteristics of individual institutions, we encourage efforts to meet certain minimum needs of all consumers, in particular:

- The need for a safe and accessible place to keep money,
- The need for a way to obtain cash (including, for example, the cashing of government checks),
- The need for a way to make third-party payments.

We believe that industry trade associations have a key role to play in this effort, and are in a position to encourage a constructive response without the rigidities of legislation or regulation. We realize that some associations have such programs already underway. These programs could usefully:

- Encourage members to offer and publicize appropriately low-cost basic financial services, such as those listed above;
- Survey the current availability of such services among member institutions;
- Make available to members not providing such services material reflecting the successful experiences of other organizations."

**JOINT TENANCY**  Equal ownership and equal right of usage of real or personal property by two or more people. "Joint tenancy with right of survivorship" means that in the case of the death of one joint tenant, the surviving joint tenants immediately become owners of the property.

**JOINT VENTURE**  Two or more people joined together to undertake a commercial purpose. Whereas a partnership of two or more people will continue until dissolved, a joint venture may continue only as long as the single commercial purpose for which it was formed.

**JOINT WILL**  One document representing the last will and testament of each of two or more individuals. At one time joint wills were invalid. Today, it is generally accepted that such a will is valid unless it appears that the will was to operate only on the death of the survivor of the co-testators. A valid joint will, then, operates and is probated upon the death of each co-testator as if there were two separate documents.

**JOURNAL**  A book of original entry.

**JUDGMENT** The decision of a court of law. The term is frequently used in reference to the sum of money due as a result of such a decision and resulting court order.

**JUDGMENT CREDITOR** The person to whom the court has awarded a judgment of money against a debtor.

**JUDGMENT DEBTOR** The person whom the court has ordered to pay a specified amount to the judgment creditor.

**JUDGMENTAL SYSTEM OF EVALUATING APPLICANTS** Any system for evaluating the creditworthiness of an applicant other than an "empirically derived, demonstrably and statistically sound, credit scoring system." SEE EMPIRICALLY DERIVED, DEMONSTRABLY AND STATISTICALLY SOUND, CREDIT SCORING SYSTEM. SEE ALSO EMPIRICALLY DERIVED CREDIT SCORING SYSTEM.

**JUMBO CD** A time certificate of deposit with a value of $100,000 or more. SEE ALSO CERTIFICATE OF DEPOSIT.

**JUNIOR LIEN** A lien that is subordinate to the rights and claims of the holder of a superior lien. For example, a second mortgage is generally junior to a first mortgage.

**JUNK BONDS** Speculative-grade bonds with Standard and Poor's ratings below BBB- or Moody's ratings below Baa3; those ratings are generally given to new firms that do not have a performance record. High yield, low rated debt securities sold at a low price usually to help finance corporate acquisitions.

**JURISDICTION** The authority of a court to hear and adjudicate a case. The authority of nations or states to create or prescribe penal or regulatory norms and enforce them through administrative and judicial action. Federal maritime and territorial jurisdiction extends to the high seas and other waters within the admiralty and maritime jurisdiction of the United States and not within the jurisdiction of any state. It also extends to vessels and aircraft of American ownership or registry on or above such waters. For the most part, federal legislative competence turns on delegated substantive powers under the Constitution and not on locale. American states control their land territory and immediate coastal waters as established through federal law. Municipalities derive their legislative powers from state constitutions and legislation, but there is no federal constitution objection to the exercise of municipal powers over residents and activities in adjacent areas that affect a legislating and enforcing municipality.

# K

**K** The abbreviation for one thousand, kilobyte, or one thousand kilobytes.

**KEOGH PLAN (HR-10)** A retirement plan for self-employed individual proprietors and partnerships, to which yearly tax deductible contributions can be made. Effective January 1, 1982, a self-employed person or an individual who has outside self-employment income can put as much as $15,000 every year in a Keogh plan. A sole proprietor is treated as his or her own employer, while a partnership is considered to be the employer of each partner. A sole proprietor is capable of making contributions to a plan in a dual capacity—as an employer and as an employee. A partner may also make contributions as an employee, but employer contributions are made by the partnership, with each partner deducting his or her distributive share.

**KEY CURRENCY**   An arrangement in international trade whereby many countries agree to settle foreign transactions with the currency of a particular country. The country issuing the key currency is referred to as the key currency nation.

**KEY MAN INSURANCE**   A policy of insurance on the life of an individual, the death of whom would be deemed to have significant financial impact on a business. Sometimes banks will require key man insurance to be placed on a key executive of a borrowing business if the bank feels that the death of this individual would hurt the business' ability to meet its debt obligations. Key man insurance is a means of protecting the business . . . and the bank . . . from the adverse results of the loss of an individual possessing special skills, knowledge or experience.

**KINA**   Monetary unit of Papua New Guinea.

**KIP**   Monetary unit of Laos.

**KITING**   The unauthorized, interest free use of bank credit through an attempt to draw against insufficient funds, generally for fraudulent purposes. A depositor can "acquire" fictitious transaction account balances by taking advantage of the time it takes banks to process, clear, present and pay checks.

**KORUNA**   Monetary unit of Czechoslovakia.

**KRONA**   Monetary unit of Iceland.

**KRONE**   Monetary unit of Denmark and Norway.

**KWACHA**   Monetary unit of Mawawi and Zambia.

**KWANZA**   Monetary unit of Angola.

**KYAT**   Monetary unit of Myanmar.

# L

**L**   Federal Reserve Board definition of money supply equalling M3 plus term Eurodollars held by U.S. residents other than banks, bankers' acceptances, commercial paper, U.S. Savings Bonds, Treasury bills and other liquid Treasury securities and other liquid assets not included elsewhere.

**LABOR BANK**   An industrial bank whose stock is owned by labor unions and labor union members.

**LABOR ORGANIZATION**   A group of workers who are organized for the purpose of increasing the welfare of the group and its members through the collective bargaining for wages, health benefits, etc.

**LACHES**   A delay that results in disadvantage, usually referring to the failure to litigate or otherwise protect one's interest within a reasonable or prescribed period of time.

**LADDERED MATURITIES**   The equal staggering of the maturities of securities or certificates of deposit so that over a period of time the shortening of their maturities provides a steady flow of income which is reinvested.

**LAGGED RESERVE**   A bank reserve accounting system followed by the Federal Reserve from the late 1960s through the early 1980s requiring banks to hold reserves in one period against deposits outstanding in an earlier period. A bank's lending is not normally constrained by the amount of excess reserves it has at any given moment. Loans are made, or not made, depending on the bank's expectations about its ability to obtain the funds necessary to pay its customer's checks and maintain required reserves in a timely fashion. In fact, because Federal Reserve regulations in effect from 1968 through 1982 specified that required reserves for a given week should be based on the deposit levels two weeks earlier ("lagged" reserve accounting), deposit creation actually preceded the provision of supporting reserves. In mid-1982, it was decided to move toward "contemporaneous" reserve accounting in order to improve monetary control.

**LAND CONTRACT**   An installment contract for the purchase of land with title transferring to the buyer upon the payment of the final installment.

**LAND DEVELOPMENT LOAN**   An extension of credit for the purpose of improving unimproved real property prior to the erection of structures. The improvement of unimproved real property may include the laying or placement of sewers, water pipes, utility cables, streets, and other infrastructure necessary for future development.

**LAND TRUST**   An association formed for the purpose of holding real property. Title to the property is held in the name of one or more trustees for the benefit of the land trust members. The interest of each land trust member is evidenced by land trust certificates.

**LAPSED LEGACY**   A gift which falls into the residuary estate because the donee has died within the lifetime of the testator.

**LAST IN—FIRST OUT (LIFO)**   An inventory valuation method which assumes that the most recent purchases are the first to be used. In consideration of price fluctuation, this method gives an accurate estimate of inventory values. SEE ALSO INTEREST—DEPOSITS.

**LAST TRADING DAY**   The final day during which future contracts may be traded for delivery in a particular month.

**LAST WILL AND TESTAMENT**   A legally enforceable declaration of a person's wishes regarding the distribution of his or her estate and other matters to be attended to after, but not operative until, his or her death. Although of no particular significance today, historically "will" referred to real property and "testament" referred to personal property. Today, "will" is accepted as referring to the intent of the testator regarding all forms of property, real and personal. Because a will may be changed or amended at any time during the lifetime of the testator, the term "last will" serves to indicate that all prior wills are void, having been revoked by the "last" one.

**LATE CHARGE**   A fee or penalty charged for a delinquent installment loan payment or for failure to make minimum payments on a credit card account.

**LATE PAYMENT**   An installment payment made after the contracted due date.

**LAUNDERED MONEY**   Funds sent through numerous accounts or depositories one after another in an attempt to conceal the source of the money.

**LAW OF DIMINISHING RETURNS**   Incremental additions of one factor of production to a fixed factor of production will ultimately decrease the additional output received from the added factor.

**LBO**   SEE LEVERAGED BUY OUT.

**LDC**   SEE LESS DEVELOPED COUNTRY.

**LEAD BANK**   The managing bank in a loan syndication.

**LEADING EDGE**   On the face of a check the leading edge is the right edge, that closest to the date and signature areas. When the check is turned over, the leading edge then becomes the left edge and it is the three inch area from the leading edge that is reserved for the endorsement of a subsequent collecting bank.

**LEASE**   A contract in which a lessor grants to a lessee the right to use or occupy property owned by the lessor for a specified time. A consumer lease is a contract in the form of a lease or bailment, which meets all of the following criteria:
- it must have a duration of more than four months;
- the total lease obligation must not exceed $25,000;
- the property leased must be used principally for family, personal or household purposes;
- the lease must be to a natural person; and
- the lease must be for the use of personal property. SEE CONSUMER LEASING ACT.

**LEASE—PURCHASE AGREEMENT**   An arrangement where a portion of the lease fee or rent may be applied to the purchase price of the asset leased.

**LEASEBACK**   An arrangement, also referred to as sale/leaseback, whereby the seller of an asset simultaneously contracts to rent or otherwise use the asset for a fee, thus remaining in possession of the asset.

**LEASEHOLD**   Land held under a lease agreement.

**LEASEHOLD IMPROVEMENT**   Improvement to land held under a lease agreement.

**LEDGER**   The final book of entry that records a business' financial transactions and may be a general ledger comprised of the entries of one or more subsidiary ledgers.

**LEDGER BALANCE**   The book balance of an account according to the bank's records. The ledger balance differs from the "available" or "collected" balance by the amount of uncollected funds.

**LEGACY**   A gift (bequest) of personal property made in a will. A legacy may be: specific—a particular piece of property, such as a "1957 Chevrolet Bel Air convertible, Serial No. 1234567890"; demonstrative—one payable in money out of a certain designated fund or account; general—a sum certain gift of money; or residual—all of the remaining personal property after payment of all obligations of the estate and distribution of all other legacies.

**LEGAL ENTITY**   A responsible being which, in the eyes of the law, has the ability to sue or be sued and which can enter into a binding contract. Other than an individual, a legal entity might include a proprietorship, partnership, corporation, association or other organization.

**LEGAL RATE OF INTEREST**   The maximum interest rate allowed by applicable state law which can be charged on a loan or revolving credit obligation.

**LEGAL RESERVES**   The percentage of a bank's cash assets which must be retained as a protection for depositors as established by the Federal Reserve act of 1933 and 1935 and by various state laws.

**LEGAL RESIDENCE**   That one place where a person lives whether or not he or she spends a majority of time there. Federal law recognizes only one legal residence per individual.

**LEGAL TENDER**   Authorized currency, backed by the government of the country in which it is issued, that must be accepted in payment of public and private debts.

**LEGAL TITLE**   Ownership of property to the extent that the ownership is recognized by and enforceable in a court of law.

**LEGATEE**   The recipient of a legacy, a gift of personal property under the provisions of a will.

**LEK**   Monetary unit of Albania.

**LEMPIRA**   Monetary unit of Honduras.

**LEND**   To extend credit; to finance. To advance or make available a certain sum of money for a certain period in reliance on the promise of timely repayment by the borrower.

**LENDER OF LAST RESORT**   As the nation's central bank, the Federal Reserve has the authority and financial resources to act as "lender of last resort" by extending credit to depository institutions or to other entities in unusual circumstances involving a national or regional emergency, where failure to obtain credit would have a severe adverse impact on the economy.

**LENDING INSTITUTION**   A bank, finance company, savings and loan, credit union, or other organization that lends money.

**LEONE**   Monetary unit of Sierra Leone.

**LESS DEVELOPED COUNTRY (LDC)**   A country indicating the following: a poverty level of per capita income, a high rate of population growth, a significant number of working population employed in agriculture, a high adult illiteracy rate, high unemployment, and limited export.

**LETTER OF ADMINISTRATION**   A certificate of authority issued by the court to an administrator authorizing the settlement of the estate of a decedent who failed to name an executor. The administrator may be an individual or trust institution.

**LETTER OF ATTORNEY**   SEE POWER OF ATTORNEY.

**LETTER OF CONSERVATORSHIP**   A certificate of authority corresponding with a Letter of Guardianship issued by a court to an individual or corporate fiduciary to serve as conservator of the property of a person subject to the jurisdiction of the court.

**LETTER OF CREDIT**   An instrument under which a bank agrees to substitute its credit for that of its customer. For example, XYZ imports widgets from exporter ABC in Singapore. ABC may insist that XYZ's bank establish a commercial letter of credit so drafts may be drawn against that credit for immediate payment. In this transaction, XYZ Co. is referred to as the "Account Party"; XYZ's bank is the "Issuer" and ABC is the beneficiary. If the terms of the letter of credit are transmitted to ABC through ABC's bank, that bank is referred to as the "Advising Bank" which has no liability under the letter of credit, only for the proper notification of its customer, ABC. A "Confirming Bank," if one is used, is one which agrees to become liable under the terms of the letter of credit to the same extent as the issuer. A "Standby letter of credit" is generally used as a performance bond or to support a contract bid. If a letter of credit is irrevocable, it must be honored without exception. If a letter of credit is revocable, it may be cancelled at any time by the issuing bank. The term "revolving letter of credit" refers to a letter of credit that covers a whole series of commercial transactions on advisement that previous drafts have been paid. A "traveler's letter of credit," once highly popular, would authorize correspondent banks of the issuer to advance funds to a traveling holder. Today, traveler's letters of credit have been generally replaced by traveler's checks.

**LETTER TESTAMENTARY**   A certificate of authority issued by a court to the executor named in a will authorizing him to settle the estate.

**LEVEL PAYMENT AMORTIZATION PLAN**   A loan repayment schedule calling for equal periodic payments although the amounts credited to principal and interest vary with each payment.

**LEVERAGE**   The increased rate of return that is made on net worth by using debt to acquire assets.

**LEVERAGED BUY OUT (LBO)**   The purchase, with borrowed money, of the controlling interest in a company.

**LEVERAGE FACTOR**   The ratio of debt (including preferred stock) to total assets.

**LEVERAGE RATIO**   A minimum level of capital as prescribed by bank regulators to guard against institutions becoming highly leveraged. For example, the Comptroller of the Currency and the Board of Directors of the Federal Reserve have recommended that the leverage ratio of core capital (which consists of common stockholder's equity, noncumulative perpetual preferred stock and surplus, minority interests in the equity of consolidated subsidiaries and certain intangibles) be 3 percent of total assets.

**LEVY** An assessment. A levy may represent a tax assessment or the judicial process of taking property from a defendant to satisfy the judgment rendered for the plaintiff.

**LIABILITIES** The amount a bank owes, the most significant of which generally consists of the funds on deposit. Debts or obligations stated in terms of money. Current liabilities are the short term debts (generally repayable in less than one year) of a business.

**LIBOR** SEE THE LONDON INTERBANK OFFERING RATE.

**LICENSEE** A bank which has been authorized by a licensing authority such as VISA, U.S.A. Inc., or MasterCard International Inc., to issue bank cards and operate a bank card plan.

**LIEN** A voluntary or involuntary legal attachment filed against real property as security for the payment of an obligation. Upon default, the lien holder may be allowed to take possession of the property.

**LIFE BENEFICIARY** The beneficiary of a trust who, in accordance with the trust agreement, will remain beneficiary for the term of his or her natural life, or for the term of the natural life of a named third person.

**LIFE ESTATE** A possessory interest in real or personal property for the life of the life tenant or some other named third party. If the estate is for the life of a third party, it is called an "estate per auter vie."

**LIFE INSURANCE** Insurance against loss of income and providing for payment of a stipulated amount to a named beneficiary, or beneficiaries, upon the accidental or natural death of the insured.

**LIFE INSURANCE TRUST** An inter vivos trust, the principal of which will be the proceeds of a life insurance policy.

**LIFE TENANT** The person who owns an estate or interest in real property for the term of his or her life or for the term of the life of a named third person. SEE ALSO LIFE ESTATE AND LIFE INTEREST.

**LIMIT CONTROL** The function within a bank card department which monitors cardholder balances, continually comparing them to authorized credit limits and taking appropriate action when credit limits are exceeded.

**LIMITED CHECK** A check which, on its face, limits the amount for which it can be cashed. Such a limiting provision may read: "Void if issued for an amount in excess of $500." Another form of limitation is date, such as "Void unless presented for payment within 90 days of date issued."

**LIMITED PARTNERSHIP** An association formed by two or more persons, having as members one or more general partners and one or more limited partners. The limited partners are not bound by the partnership obligations; that is, they are not, as are the general partners, individually liable for such obligations. The Uniform Limited Partnership Act states the formalities necessary to form such a partnership and requires a signed and sworn certificate stating: the partnership name; character of business; location of its principal place of business; name and residence address of each partner with designations of who are general, and who limited, partners; the term during which the partnership is to exist; the amount of cash and property, the latter to be described and the agreed valuation to be stated, to be contributed by each limited partner; additional contributions, if any, and the times at which or the events upon which such shall be made, by each limited partner; the time, if agreed, when each limited partner is to have returned to him his contribution; the "share of the profits or the other compensation by way of income which each limited partner shall receive by reason of his contribution"; the right of a limited partner, if given, to substitute an assignee-contributor in his place with the terms and conditions of the substitution; the right, if given, of partners to admit additional limited partners; the right, if given, of priority among limited partners as to their contributions or as to compensation by way of income; the right, if given, of continuation of the business after the death, retirement or insanity of a general partner by the remaining general partners; and the right, if given, of a limited partner to demand and receive property other than cash in return for his contribution. The act provides that a limited partner does not become liable as a general partner "unless, in addition to the exercise of his rights and powers as a limited partner, he takes part in the control of the business."

**LINE OF CREDIT**   The maximum amount of credit a bank will extend to a borrower over a defined future time period. A "confirmed" line of credit is communicated to the customer whereas a "guidance" line is for internal bank use only. A "nonrevolving" line of credit is confirmed to the borrower who has the approval to draw upon the line once during the prescribed period. In contrast, a "revolving" line of credit, sometimes referred to as a "revolver," is a specified amount upon which the borrower may draw funds as often as desired during the prescribed time period, and the balance may fluctuate from zero to the maximum available under the provisions of the line.

**LIQUID**   Capable of conversion to cash. Assets are considered liquid if they consist of cash or readily marketable securities.

**LIQUIDATE**   To convert to cash.

**LIQUIDATED CLAIM**   A claim or debt, the amount of which is set and agreed upon by the parties involved, and no bona fide dispute regarding the amount exists between those parties.

**LIQUIDATED DAMAGES**   An agreed sum of money paid as damages for breach of contract.

**LIQUIDATION CONTROL**   Ownership, either individual or collective, of 66 2/3% or more of the shares of a corporation. These "two-thirds majority" owners can liquidate the corporation at will.

**LIQUIDITY (BANK)**   A bank is liquid when it can raise cash to honor loan commitments or unexpected deposit withdrawals without significant loss. Liquidity measures can help management and directors determine how liquid the bank is and how much it relies on volatile short-term liabilities. Some measures to consider are:

*Temporary investments divided by total assets* shows how much of bank assets can be readily converted into cash. Temporary investments are short-term items such as federal funds sold, repurchase arrangements, or debt securities with remaining maturities of one year or less.

*Temporary investments divided by volatile liabilities* shows how much of the bank's volatile liabilities (short-term items like federal funds purchased and certificates of deposit of $100,000 or more) are matched by short-term assets.

*Net loans divided by core deposits* shows how much of the loan portfolio is funded by stable deposits. Core deposits are demand and savings deposits and certificates of deposits of less than $100,000.

*Volatile liability dependence* shows the degree to which volatile liabilities fund long-term assets. This figure is the result of dividing the difference between volatile liabilities and temporary investments by loans and longer term investments.

*Net loans divided by deposits* shows how much of the bank's deposits are lent, and the bank's ability to fund additional loan volume with these deposits.

**LIQUIDITY BALANCE**   A definition of the balance of payments which broadens the concept of payment, relative to the official reserve transactions balance, to include sales of liquid short-term debt instruments by both private transactors and the government.

**LIQUIDITY PREFERENCE HYPOTHESIS**   Hypothesis regarding the terms structure of interest rates holding that there is a liquidity premium on implied future rates, which increases as the maturity is more distant. The assumption that the yield curve reflects the net present value of all expected interest rates that will prevail in the future, as modified by a willingness to pay a liquidity premium for relatively short maturities.

**LIQUIDITY PREMIUM**   A premium placed on very short term assets due to their liquid nature.

**LIQUIDITY RATIO**   The ability of a business to meet its current debt with cash payment is measured by:

(1) Current Assets to Current Liabilities ratio. By dividing the firm's current assets by its current liabilities, the resulting ratio measures the ability of the company to meet its current debts; and

(2) Cash, Securities and Accounts Receivable to Current Liabilities ratio. This "quick ratio" or "acid test" is the critical liquidity test of a company's ability to pay its current debt because inventory and less liquid assets are excluded from current assets. It is determined by dividing cash, securities and accounts receivable by current liabilities.

**LIQUIDITY RISK**   Risk of loss due to inadequate liquidity.

**LIRA**   Monetary unit of Italy, Malta, and Turkey.

**LISTED SECURITIES**   Stocks or bonds which have met the necessary requirements and have been accepted for trading on an organized securities exchange, such as the New York Stock Exchange or the American Stock Exchange. Unlisted securities are generally traded over-the-counter.

**LIVING TRUST**   SEE INTER VIVOS TRUST.

**LOAD**   The sales commission paid by a buyer of shares of an open-end mutual investment fund.

**LOAD FUND**   A mutual fund that charges a separate commission cost instead of deriving all management fees from its portfolio income. The mutual fund sells its shares through an agent or broker who, as a middleman, charges a sales commission. In contrast, no load funds are sold directly to the investor with little or no fees or commissions.

**LOAN**   A contract between a borrower and a lender in which the borrower agrees to pay certain interest for the use of lender's funds for a specified period of time. Loans differ in structure and may, for example, be secured or unsecured, demand or installment, short or long term, business or personal, etc. An extension of credit.

**LOAN APPLICATION**   A sometimes verbal but generally written form that a potential borrower completes to formally request an extension of credit. Loan applications are generally a "fill-in-the-blanks" format which ask the borrower for pertinent information which the bank will use in determining creditworthiness and ability to repay.

**LOAN COMMITMENT**   A binding promise by a lender to advance credit to a borrower, generally at a defined interest rate for a stated term and for a specified purpose. The loan commitment may also require the borrower to comply with certain stated conditions.

**LOAN COMMITMENT FEE**   A fee charged for preparation and extension of a loan commitment and in consideration of the banks "reserving" loan funds for the borrower on an interest-free basis until the committed loan is actually executed.

**LOAN COMMITTEE**   A group of experienced lending officers responsible for approving or declining loan applications. Loan committees generally review and make decisions on large loans, the amount of which exceed lending limits conferred upon individual loan officers.

**LOAN FEE**   Any fee associated with the review, approval, documentation, execution, or perfection of an extension of credit.

**LOAN LOSS PROVISION**   An operating expense for loan losses.

**LOAN LOSS RESERVE**   A reserve account against which loan losses are charged. The account is established based on a bank's historical loan loss experience or anticipated losses to compensate for expected loan losses either domestically or internationally.

**LOAN MATURITY**   The date upon which a loan becomes due and payable.

**LOAN OFFICER**   An employee of the bank who is responsible for the loan interview, evaluation and extension process.

**LOAN ORIGINATION**   (1) All of the steps necessary to solicit, interview, evaluate and extend credit resulting in a viable asset to the bank. (2) The time of inception of the obligation to extend credit (i.e., when the last event or prerequisite, controllable by the lender, occurs causing the lender to become legally bound to fund an extension of credit).

**LOAN PARTICIPATION**   The making of one loan to a single borrower by more than one lender. The participating lenders each obligate themselves to a portion of the loan; thus, each assumes a relative portion of the risk and enjoys a representative portion of the loan income.

**LOAN SYNDICATION**   A group of banks that join together to make a loan that is too large for one member bank to make. SEE LOAN PARTICIPATION.

**LOAN-TO-VALUE RATIO**   A lending formula most commonly used in real estate purchase or improvement lending. The percentage or ratio is derived at the time of loan origination by dividing an extension of credit by the total value of the property(ies) securing or being improved by the extension of credit plus the amount of any readily marketable collateral and other acceptable collateral that secures the extension of credit. The total amount of all senior liens on or interests in such property(ies) should be included in determining the loan-to-value ratio. When mortgage insurance or collateral is used in the calculation of the loan-to-value ratio, and such credit enhancement is later released or replaced, the loan-to-value ratio should be recalculated.

**LOBBY**   The main banking floor or room where business is transacted in the bank. The operations area includes the teller line and that part of the bank behind the teller line, generally where the vault and safe deposit areas are located. The platform is that part of the lobby where new accounts are opened and loans are transacted. The manager and loan officers generally are located on the platform.

**LOCAL CHECK**   A check payable by or at a local paying bank, or a check payable by a nonbank payor and payable through a local paying bank.

**LOCAL PAYING BANK**   A paying bank located in the same check processing region as the physical location of the branch or proprietary ATM of the depository bank in which the check was deposited, or both the branch of the depository bank at which the account is held and the nonproprietary ATM at which the check is deposited.

**LOCK BOX**   A specialized fee generating service where the bank acts as an agent for a business by actually receiving and collecting payments made to that business. Receivables thus collected are then credited to the business' account with the bank and a detailed accounting is provided to the business customer.

**LOCK IN**   The process in which a quoted rate of interest is guaranteed to remain the same for an agreed upon period of time. The term also refers to the situation where an investor cannot sell a security because the profit on such a sale would immediately become subject to capital gains taxation.

**LONDON INTERBANK OFFERING RATE (LIBOR)**   The rate offered by banks in London for Eurodollar deposits.

**LONG TERM DEBT**   Generally debt which is due and payable in more than one year.

**LONG TERM FINANCING**   Debt that is scheduled to be completely repaid at some point past one year in the future.

**LOSS**   The sale of an item at less than its cost or value; an unrecoverable cost; the items of expense as reflected in a statement of profit and loss.

**LOSS CARRYBACK**   The process of offsetting a current year's loss against prior years' income in an effort to reduce taxable income for previous years.

**LOSS CARRY-FORWARD** or "loss carryover," the functional opposite of a loss carryback. Losses sustained in prior years are deducted from profits in the current, and subsequent, years in order to reduce taxable income.

**LOSS CARRY-OVER**   SEE LOSS CARRY-FORWARD.

**LOSS ON SALE OF ASSETS**   An expense account in which is recorded losses that occur when assets are sold or otherwise liquidated for less than the book value.

**LOSS PAYABLE ENDORSEMENT** A clause which provides for insurance payment to the lienholder as well as the insured property owner to the extent of the the parties' interest in the property at the time of loss.

**LOSSES**   The amount charged off to bad debt or fraud loss.

**LOST CARD**   A bank card which has been reported to the issuing bank as lost or misplaced by the cardholder, thus limiting exposure to the cardholder for unauthorized use.

**LOST IN TRANSIT**   Any item lost in the process of clearing. The term also refers to an item lost somewhere between a credit card processing center and either the local office handling the item or the clearing house.

**LUMP SUM DISTRIBUTION**   The distribution of a participant's entire interest in a qualified pension plan. In the case of a participant other than a self-employed person, the distribution must be made because of the participant's death, or separation from the service of the employer, or it must be made after he or she has attained age 59½. In the case of a self-employed person, the distribution must be made because of the individual's death or it must be made after he or she reached age 59½, unless he or she was previously disabled. According to the IRS, a participant who remains on the same job after a merger, liquidation or consolidation of his corporate employer is not "separated" from his or her employment for purposes of the lump-sum distribution rules.

# *M*

**M-1**   The sum of currency held by the public, plus traveler's checks, and demand deposits held at commercial banks.

**M-1A**   Money supply definition which includes M-1 (above) with the exception of demand deposits held by foreign banks.

**M-1B**   Money supply definition which includes M-1A plus NOW accounts and other demand deposits at all depository institutions including Automatic Transfer Service accounts, credit union share drafts and demand deposits at mutual savings banks.

**M-2**  Money supply definition which includes M-1B plus savings and time deposits (under $100 thousand) at all depository institutions, commercial bank overnight repurchase agreements (REPOs), overnight Eurodollars and money-market mutual fund shares.

**M-3**  Money supply definition which includes M-2 plus large ($100 thousand plus) time deposits at all depository institutions and term (longer than overnight) repurchase agreements (REPOs) at commercial banks and savings and loan associations.

**M-4**  An older money supply definition which included M-2 plus negotiable certificates of deposit of $100,000 or more with large weekly reporting banks.

**M-5**  An older money supply definition which included M-3 plus negotiable certificates of deposit of $100,000 or more with large weekly reporting banks.

**McFADDEN ACT**  1927 legislation which exclusively guaranteed the rights of states to control the branching activities of banks, including national banks, within individual state borders and banned interstate banking.

**MACHINE LANGUAGE**  A set of symbols and characters along with accompanying rules that conveys instructions or data to a computer; data expressed in code that is read directly by a computer.

**MACHINE READABLE**  Data written in a code of symbols and characters that may be interpreted directly by a computer without further translation.

**MAGNETIC ENCODING**  The encoding of data through the use of electronic impulse on ferro-magnetic material.

**MAGNETIC INK**  Ink containing magnetic substance particles which allows the ink to be "read" by electronic sensors.

**MAGNETIC INK CHARACTER RECOGNITION (MICR)**  The process by which magnetic ink is used to encode a check with the amount of the check, the account number, the bank's identification number and the serial number of the check. That information is optically scanned and recorded during the check clearing process.

**MAGNETIC STRIPE**  The magnetic tape affixed to the back of a bank card or other credit or debit card or access device which contains, in magnetic code, all pertinent identifying data relevant to the account linked to the card. The tape is usually plastic or mylar and coated with iron oxide on which data are stored.

**MAIL DEPOSIT**  A bank deposit received through the mail as opposed to over the counter.

**MAIL FLOAT**  SEE FLOAT.

**MAINTENANCE CHARGE**  A service charge assessed in order to reimburse the bank for the expenses of keeping records, preparing statements and other functions relative to the account charged.

**MAJOR INDUSTRY IDENTIFIER**  The first digit of the primary account number of a credit card. The digit signifies the industry issuing the card.

**MAJORITY-OWNED SUBSIDIARY**  A company whose outstanding voting capital stock is more than 50 percent owned by another company. The company which owns the majority of the outstanding voting capital stock may be a parent company or another majority-owned subsidiary of the parent company.

**MAKER**   The principal obligor, or drawer. The invididual or other legal entity who executes an instrument such as a note or a check as the responsible party.

**MARGIN**   With regard to securities, this term refers to a fractional amount of full value, or the equity outlay (downpayment) required for an investment in securities purchased on credit.

**MARGIN CALL**   A demand for additional collateral because of a change in price. If a borrower collateralizes his loan with marketable securities, and the declining market for the securities forces their value downward, the bank will request that the borrower maintain the originally agreed upon margin by providing more collateral or by paying down the loan.

**MARGIN LOAN**   A loan from a broker to a customer whereby the customer uses the proceeds of the loan to purchase stock from the broker.

**MARGIN REQUIREMENT**   The minimum amount a customer must provide in order to purchase securities on credit. Requirements for stock margins are set by the Federal Reserve.

**MARGIN STOCK**   Any stock listed on a national securities exchange, any over-the-counter security approved by the SEC for trading in the national market system, or appearing on the Board of Governors of the Federal Reserve System's list of over-the-counter margin stock, and most mutual funds. The Federal Reserve System sets the requirements for the minimum amount a customer must provide to purchase securities on margin (credit).

**MARGINAL TAX RATE**   The amount of tax paid on each additional dollar of income.

**MARITAL DEDUCTION**   The portion of a decedent's estate which may pass to the surviving spouse without being subject to federal estate taxation.

**MARKET PENETRATION**   The portion of a defined market held or controlled by a bank. For example, "5% deposit penetration" suggests that a financial institution holds 5% of the total deposit dollars held by all financial institutions in the defined market.

**MARKET POTENTIAL**   Salability, marketability. The potential sales of a commodity in a particular market for a defined time period.

**MARKET SEGMENTATION**   The act of catagorizing the general population of a defined area into heterogeneous groups in order to design optimal marketing strategies for each group.

**MARKET VALUE**   The best price property will bring on the open market. The current value of a security as determined by either the value of the last recorded sale on the present date, the value at the close of market on the preceding business day, or the closing value at the date of the report in which the market value is shown.

**MARKKA**  Monetary unit of Finland.

**MARKUP**  The difference between sales price or offering price and the acquisition price.

**MASTER FILE**  A file composed of records having similar characteristics. For example, a cardholder master file would contain such information as account numbers, names, addresses, credit limits, expiration dates, number of cards issued, etc.

**MASTER TRUST AGREEMENT**  An arrangement designating the custodianship and accounting for all employee benefits assets of a corporation or a controlled group of corporations to a single trustee. A master trust facilitates the uniform administration of the assets of multiple plans and multiple investment managers.

**MATCHED FUNDING**  The process of funding a loan or other asset by issuing a liability with the same maturity or duration.

**MATCHED SALE-PURCHASE AGREEMENTS**  When the Federal Reserve makes a matched sale-purchase agreement, it sells a security outright for immediate delivery to a dealer or foreign central bank, with an agreement to buy the security back on a specific date (usually within 7 days) at the same price. Matched sale-purchase agreements are the reverse of repurchase agreements and allow the Federal Reserve to withdraw reserves on a temporary basis.

**MATURITY**  The date upon which a note, bill of exchange, time draft, bond, or any other negotiable instrument becomes due and payable. Presentation and request for payment is usually made on the maturity date.

**MDT**  SEE MERCHANT DEPOSIT TRANSMITTAL.

**MECHANICS LIEN**  A claim created by law for the purpose of securing priority of payment of the price or value of work performed and materials furnished in erecting or repairing a building or other structure, and as such attaches to the land as well as buildings and improvements erected thereon.

**MEDIUM OF EXCHANGE**  A commodity which is generally accepted in payment for goods and services and in the settlement of debts.

**MEMBER BANK**  A depository institution that is a member of the Federal Reserve. All national banks are required to be System members, and state-chartered commercial banks and mutual savings banks may elect to become members. Member banks own stock in Federal Reserve Banks and elect some of the Reserve Bank directors.

**MERCHANT**  Any legal entity which is contractually affiliated with a bank card plan for the purpose of accepting bank cards in payment of goods and services.

**MERCHANT ACCOUNTING**  The recording by a bank of the number and dollar amount of all sales drafts and credit slips submitted by each merchant.

**MERCHANT AGREEMENT**  The written contract between a bank and a merchant containing the respective rights, duties and warranties of each with respect to the acceptance and handling of bank card transactions and related matters.

**MERCHANT APPLICATION**  The formal, written request prepared by a merchant at the time the merchant enters into a bank card plan with a bank. The application contains basic information about the merchant such as its type of business, locations and bank references.

**MERCHANT BASE**  The total number of merchants under agreement with or belonging to a bank card plan.

**MERCHANT DEPOSIT TRANSMITTAL (MDT)**  The form used by merchants to deposit sales drafts and credit vouchers.

**MERCHANT DEPOSITORY ACCOUNT**  A demand deposit account established by a merchant with a bank for payment of sales drafts submitted to the bank for collection under the terms of the merchant agreement.

**MERCHANT DISCOUNT**  Generally expressed in terms of percentage, the fee paid by the merchant to the bank for accepting and processing credit or debit card transactions. It is usually a percentage of each retail sale which is withheld, generally in the aggregate on a monthly basis from the total sales deposited by the merchant's bank. The merchant discount rate will vary by merchant based, in part, on the volume of sales, average sale price, competition, other bank relationships and processing costs.

**MERCHANT IDENTIFICATION CARD**  An embossed card supplied to each merchant to be used in imprinting the merchant summary slip which is included in the sales draft envelope. The information embossed on the card will include the merchant account number, name, location and checking account number.

**MERCHANT MEMBERSHIP FEE**  A charge levied against each merchant-member of a bank card plan for the privilege of affiliation.

**MERGER CONTROL**  Ownership of 80% or more of the shares of a corporation. If Corporation A owns 80% or more of the shares of Corporation B, then B's dividends can be passed through to A without being taxed.

**METES AND BOUNDS**  The boundary lines of land, with their terminal points and angles.

**METICAL**  Monetary unit of Mozambique.

**MICR**  SEE MAGNETIC INK CHARACTER RECOGNITION.

**MINIMUM PAYMENT**  The smallest installment payment allowed under the terms and conditions of the payment agreement; for example, the smallest monthly payment a cardholder can make and remain in compliance with the terms and conditions of the cardholder agreement.

**MINORITY INTEREST**  SEE MINORITY SHAREHOLDER.

**MINORITY SHAREHOLDER**  A less than 50 percent individual or collective interest in the outstanding shares of a corporation.

**MINT**  The place where coin is manufactured.

**MMDA**  SEE MONEY MARKET DEPOSIT ACCOUNT.

**MONETARY CONTROL ACT OF 1980**  Title 1 of the Depository Institutions Deregulation and Monetary Control Act of 1980, the act broadened the Federal

Reserve's authority to manage bank reserves and required the Federal Reserve to charge specific fees for Reserve Bank service such as check collection.

## Reporting Requirements

• Requires all depository institutions to make reports of their liabilities and assets as the Federal Reserve Board may determine to be necessary or desirable;

• Requires that the reports be made directly to the Board in the case of member banks and in the case of other depository institutions whose reserve requirements exceed zero;

• Provides that the reports are to be made through the FDIC, the FHLBB, the NCUAB, and state officers and agencies as appropriate for other depository institutions.

## Reserve Requirements

• Requires each depository institution (banks, savings banks, S&Ls, and credit unions) to maintain reserves against its transactions accounts in the ratio of 3 percent for that portion of its total transactions accounts of $25 million or less. (Transactions account is defined to include demand deposits, NOW accounts, telephone transfers, ATS and share drafts.);

• Requires each depository institution to maintain reserves in the ratio of 12 percent — or in such other ratio as the Board may prescribe within a range of 8–14 percent — for that portion of its total transactions accounts in excess of $25 million;

• Requires each depository institution to maintain reserves against its nonpersonal time deposits in the ratio of 3 percent — or in such other ratio as the Board may prescribe within a range of 0–9 percent;

• Directs the Board to index the $25 million breakpoint on transactions balances by issuing a regulation by December 31, of each year, beginning in 1981, which would increase or decrease the breakpoint by 80 percent of the percentage increase or decrease in transactions accounts of all depository institutions which occurred during the 12 month period immediately preceding June 30 of that year.

• Permits the Board upon an affirmative vote of five of its members to impose reserve requirements on any liability of depository institutions and outside the limitations on ratios as otherwise prescribed, for a period of up to 180 days. These reserve requirements can be reviewed for additional 180 day periods.

## Supplemental Reserve

• Permits the Board, upon an affirmative vote of five members, to impose an additional reserve requirement on every depository institution of not more than 4 percent of its transactions accounts. The supplemental reserve requirement may be imposed only if:

- the sole purpose is to increase the amount of reserves to a level essential for the conduct of monetary policy;
- it is not imposed for the purpose of reducing the cost burdens resulting from the basic reserve requirements;
- it is not imposed for the purpose of increasing the amount of balances needed for clearing purposes; and
- the total amount of basic reserves required at the time it is imposed is not less than the amount of reserves that would be required if the initial ratios for the basic reserves (12 percent on transactions balances and 3 percent on nonpersonal time) were in effect.

• provides that the supplemental reserve shall be maintained by the Federal

Reserve Banks in an Earnings Participation Account, and it shall receive earnings during each calendar quarter at a rate not more than what the Federal Reserve's securities portfolio earned during the previous calendar quarter.

• Terminates the supplemental reserve automatically at the close of the first 90 day period during which the average amount of basic reserves is less than the amount that would be required if the initial ratios on basic reserves were in effect.

• Permits reserves to be imposed on Eurodollar borrowings and nonmember foreign branches, subsidiaries and international banking facilities to the same extent as they are imposed on foreign branches, subsidiaries and IBFs of member banks. The Board may impose reserves on borrowings from, loans to U.S. residents by, and purchases of assets from domestic offices by foreign offices of any depository institution.

• Exempts deposits payable only outside the United States, i.e., banks in Puerto Rico, from the reserve requirement imposed under this act. But, Eurodollar reserve requirements may be imposed on such deposits.

• Entitles any depository institution that holds transactions accounts or non-personal time deposits to the same discount and borrowing privileges as member banks.

• Provides an 8 year phase-in of reserve requirements for nonmember depository institutions. For each 12-month period during the 8 years, the amount of reserves maintained would increase by one-eighth of the total reserves required.

• Specifies that the 8-year phase-in would not apply to any category of accounts or deposits authorized by federal law after the date of enactment of the Monetary Control Act, e.g., NOW accounts other than those already authorized in New England, New York and New Jersey.

• Provides for a 4-year phase-down of reserve requirements for member banks.

• Provides for a 4-year phase-in of reserve requirements for a bank which becomes a member bank during the 4 years beginning on the effective date of the act.

• Requires any institution which was a member bank on July 1, 1979, and which withdrew from membership in the Federal Reserve System before the date of enactment of this act, to maintain reserves beginning on the date of enactment of this act in an amount equal to what would be required if it were a member bank.

• Exempts from reserve requirements any financial institution which is organized solely to do business with other financial institutions, does not do business with the general public and is owned primarily by the financial institutions with which it does business.

• Reserve requirements are satisfied by maintaining vault cash or reserve balances at a Federal Reserve Bank. Reserves of nonmember depository institutions may be passed to the reserve bank through a correspondent or a Federal Home Loan Bank or the Central Liquidity Facility.

• Vault cash may be used to satisfy the supplemental reserve requirement but shall be excluded in any computation of earnings.

• Balances maintained to meet reserve requirements may be used to satisfy liqidity requirements imposed under other provisions of federal or state law.

• Exempts notes that are held in the vaults of the Federal Reserve Banks from collateral requirements; expands the kinds of collateral for Federal Reserve notes to include obligations of, or fully guaranteed as to principal and interest by, a foreign government or agency of a foreign government.

• Limits member banks to keeping on deposit with any depository institution that does not have access to the discount window no more than 10 percent of its own paid-up capital and surplus.
• Removes the 10(b) penalty rate on advances on ineligible paper.

Pricing for Services

• Requires the Board to publish for comment a set of pricing principles and a proposed schedule of fees for Federal Reserve Bank services no later than the first day of the sixth month after the date of enactment.
• Requires the Board to begin to put into effect a schedule of fees for services no later than the first day of the 18th month after the date of enactment.
• The services covered by the fee schedule are:
  − currency and coin services;
  − check clearing and collection services;
  − wire transfer services;
  − automated clearing house services;
  − settlement services;
  − securities safekeeping services;
  − Federal Reserve float; and
  − any new service which the Federal Reserve offers.

Effective Dates

• This Act shall take effect on the first day of the sixth month which begins after the date of enactment except that:
  − depository institutions holding transactions accounts will have access to the discount window on the date of enactment, and
  − institutions that withdrew from the Federal Reserve on or after July 1, 1979, will have to keep reserves at the same level as member banks beginning on the date of enactment.

**MONETARY POLICY**   The management of money supply to ensure availability of credit specific with economic objectives. In the United States, the Federal Reserve System makes monetary policy. Decisions with regard to the overall conduct of monetary policy are made by the twelve-member Federal Open Market Committee, or FOMC. This committee, which meets in Washington eight times a year, consists of the seven members of the Board of Governors, the president of the Federal Reserve Bank of New York, and the presidents of four other Reserve Banks who serve in rotation. The presidents of the remaining Federal Reserve Banks participate in the deliberations of the committee but do not vote. The process of setting the discount rate, one of the tools of monetary policy, involves both the Boards of Directors of the Reserve Banks and the Board of Governors of the Federal Reserve System. The founders of the System believed it was necessary to separate the people who frame the government's spending decisions from the people who control the supply of money, and devised the System's institutional structure with this view in mind. For example, the Federal Reserve is structured to be self-sufficient in the sense that it meets its operating expenses primarily from the interest earnings on its portfolio of securities.

The objectives of U.S. monetary policy are high employment, stable prices (no inflation) and growth in output on a sustainable basis. These ultimate goals, as they are often described, are not directly under the control of the Federal Reserve.

Instead, the Federal Reserve takes actions with respect to the tools of monetary policy — for example, open market purchases and sales of securities, and changes in the discount rate — that are expected to contribute indirectly to the achievement of the ultimate goals. The precise magnitude and timing of the effects of Federal Reserve actions on the economy are never perfectly predictable. Since the mid–1970s, the Federal Reserve's strategic approach in implementing monetary policy has been to focus on control of the monetary aggregates. Under this strategy, the Fed has established target ranges for its various measures of the money supply that are estimated to be consistent with achieving its ultimate goals. Movements in the money supply relative to target are then used as an important factor in determining what policy actions are necessary to achieve the ultimate objectives. Thus, the Fed takes actions with respect to the tools of monetary policy, observes their effects on the monetary aggregates, and infers from those effects what impact its actions would ultimately have on the economy. If money begins to deviate from target, the Federal Reserve may have to adjust policies to make them once again consistent with achieving the ultimate objectives.

Because of the economy's changing complexity, the Federal Reserve does not follow this procedure rigidly. No single monetary policy indicator can be considered reliable under all circumstances. Thus, although the monetary aggregates often provide useful information about future economic developments, they also have provided misleading signals at different times. As a consequence, the Federal Reserve interprets monetary growth within the wider context of emerging data on the strength of business activity, developments in foreign exchange markets, progress against inflation, and conditions in domestic and international credit markets. In particular instances, the Federal Reserve may therefore choose to permit the monetary aggregates to deviate from pre-established target ranges, or to revise the target ranges.

**MONEY**   Anything that serves as a generally accepted medium of exchange, a standard of value, and a means to save or store purchasing power. In the United States, paper currency (nearly all of which consists of Federal Reserve Notes), coin and funds in checking and similar accounts at depository institutions are examples of money. In its strict technical sense, "money" means coined metal, usually gold or silver, upon which the government stamp has been impressed to indicate its value. In its more popular sense, "money" indicates any currency, tokens, bank notes, or other circulating medium in general use as the representative of value. SEE ALSO MONEY SUPPLY.

**MONEY MARKET**   The unorganized market in which short term (typically 90 days or less) debt securities are purchased and sold to banks, other financial institutions, the U.S. Treasury and other governments, specialized dealers and the managers of money market funds.

**MONEY MARKET CERTIFICATE**   A certificate of deposit in a minimum denomination of $10,000 with a maturity of 6 months. The interest rate on money market certificates is related to the yield on 6-month Treasury bills, in accordance with regulations issued by the Depository Institutions Deregulation Committee.

**MONEY MARKET DEPOSIT ACCOUNT (MMDA)**   A savings account authorized by the Garn-St. Germain Depository Institutions Act of 1982 to allow banks and thrifts to become competitive with money market mutual funds. Market rates of interest are paid by MMDAs with balances in excess of $1,000 subject to no regulatory limits. If the balance drops below $1,000, MMDAs pay the same rate as Negotiable Order of Withdrawal (NOW) accounts. SEE ALSO NEGOTIABLE ORDER OF WITHDRAWAL ACCOUNT.

**MONEY MARKET FUND**   A mutual fund in which investments are made in such short-term credit instruments as Treasury bills, acceptances, short term notes, or certificates of deposit (usually 60 days or less). Customers earn high interest rates on the accounts and may write checks against the accounts. SEE ALSO MUTUAL FUNDS.

**MONEY ORDER**   A negotiable instrument typically purchased from a commercial bank or the United States Post Office for a fee and used in lieu of a personal check.

**MONEY SUPPLY**   The total amount of money available in the economy, expressed as follows:
  • M1 — The sum of currency held by the public, plus traveler's checks, demand deposits, other checkable deposits (i.e., negotiable order of withdrawal [NOW] accounts, and automatic transfer service [ATS] accounts, and credit union share drafts.
  • M2 — The sum of M1 plus savings accounts and small-denomination time deposits, plus shares in money market mutual funds (other than those restricted to institutional investors), plus overnight Eurodollars and repurchase agreements.
  • M3 — The sum of M2 plus large-denomination time deposits at all depository institutions, large denomination term repurchase agreements, and shares in money market mutual funds restricted to institutional investors.
  • L — A broad measure of liquid assets comprised of M3 plus other liquid assets not elsewhere included, such as Eurodollars hold by U.S. residents, banker's acceptances, Treasury bills and other securities, and U.S. Savings Bonds.
    In formulating monetary policy, the Federal Reserve has used several measures of the money supply that correspond to different concepts of money. Since one of money's traditional roles is as a medium of exchange, one of these measures consists of the things that people generally accept in payment. Hence, one measure of the nation's money supply is the total of the public's holdings of currency and deposits on which checks can be written, including traveler's checks. (Instruments with limitations on the frequency with which checks can be written are excluded.) This measure is called M1, and is often referred to as the "transaction definition" of money.
    Until relatively recently, commercial banks were unique in being able to offer deposits on which checks could be written. As late as 1980, these traditional checking accounts, called demand deposits, accounted for more than 90 percent of all checkable deposits. Since the 1970s, regulatory and institutional changes have both expanded the range of checkable deposits that banks can offer to households, and made it possible for thrift institutions — savings and loan associations, mutual savings banks and credit unions — also to issue some types of checkable deposits.
    Thus, the deposit component of M1 now includes not only demand deposits issued by banks, but also "other checkable deposits," or OCDs, which include

Automatic Transfer and NOW accounts offered by banks and thrifts, and share draft accounts offered by credit unions. These new types of checkable deposits pay explicit interest and can be held only by households, whereas demand deposits can be held by any type of depositor and are not permitted by law to pay explicit interest.

The other monetary aggregates compiled by the Federal Reserve, called M2 and M3, are based on broader definitions of money. These measures recognize the number of different types of deposits and other financial assets that can be readily converted into spendable forms, even though they themselves cannot be used directly to make payments. The Federal Reserve uses these broader measures of money to gauge the amount of readily spendable funds at the public's disposal. Passbook savings and time accounts at banks and thrifts are familiar examples of these "liquid assets" as they typically are called. The relatively new money market deposit account, or MMDA, also falls into this category. Accounts at money market mutual funds are yet another example.

**MONTHLY PAYMENT LOAN**   A loan repaid through scheduled monthly installments.

**MOODY'S RATING**   A rating of bond or securities quality named after John Moody. Bonds are rated AAA (best quality or "gilt edge"), AA (high quality or "high grade"), A (high-medium-grade), BAA (lower-medium-grade; neither highly protected nor poorly secured). Preferred and common stocks are rated high quality, good quality, and medium quality.

**MORTGAGE**   The conventional mortage is a contract which binds all or a portion of a person's property in favor of another without divestiture of possession. The borrower [mortgagor] gives to the lender [mortgagee] a lien on property as security for the payment of an obligation. The lien is removed upon termination of the obligation. Generally, the term applies to the encumbrance of real property. Personal property, however, may also be mortgaged under what is called a chattel mortgage.

A "first mortgage" is the first, in time or right, of a series of two or more mortgages covering the same property. A "second mortage" takes rank immediately after a first mortgage. Note, however, that the term designates the second in a series of mortgages which may not necessarily mean a second lien. For example, a tax lien may intervene between first and second mortgages; this would result in the second mortgage becoming a third lien. A purchase money mortgage is granted to secure the unpaid balance of a purchase price. A conventional mortgage is a mortage loan that is neither insured by the Federal Housing Administration (FHA) or by the Veterans Administration (VA).

**MORTGAGE BANKER**   An individual or company in the business of originating mortgages and then selling them to institutional or individual investors, while retaining the right to collect, for a fee, the payments on each mortgage as they become due during the life of each mortgage loan.

**MORTGAGE INSURANCE**   A policy written by a mortgage insurance company to insure a portion of the mortgage loan in favor of the lender. This allows the lender to accept a lower down payment on a conventional mortgage loan.

**MORTGAGE LOAN**   A loan, secured by real property, to finance the purchase or construction of improvements to real property such as a single family dwelling, condominium, or commercial building.

**MORTGAGE PORTFOLIO**   The total of all mortgage loans included in the assets of a financial institution or those serviced by a mortgage banker.

**MORTGAGEE**   The lender in a mortgage loan agreement.

**MORTGAGOR**   The borrower in a mortgage loan agreement.

**MUNICIPAL BOND**   A bond issued by a government agency or authority, usually political subdivisions such as cities or counties. Municipal bonds are typically referred to as "tax exempts" in that the interest paid on most issues is generally exempt from federal, state and local income taxes.

**MUTILATED CURRENCY**   Paper currency and coin that is withdrawn from circulation due to its poor condition.

**MUTUAL FUNDS**   Investment companies in which shareholders' investments are pooled and diversified by a portfolio manager. Governed by the Investment Company Act of 1940 and monitored by the Securities and Exchange Commission, mutual funds are sold as load, low-load and no-load, depending on the fee structure, and are distinguished by their investment objectives, such as:
- *Aggressive-growth funds*—long-term capital gains and speculative securities
- *Growth funds*—long-term growth, less speculative
- *Growth-income funds*—capital appreciation or dividend income, more balanced
- *Income funds*—current income; preservation of capital
- *Balanced funds*—balanced set percentage of assets invested for capital appreciation and for income
- *Municipal Bond funds*—federal tax exempt; state tax exempt for residents of the state in which the bond is issued
- *Money Market mutual funds*—short-term securities including Treasury bills, acceptances, and certificates of deposit.

**MUTUAL SAVINGS BANK**   A savings institution owned by depositors, managed by a board of trustees and maintained without capital stock. SEE FINANCIAL INSTITUTION.

**MUTUAL WILLS**   The separate wills of different persons, containing similar or reciprocal provisions in favor of each other or the same beneficiary.

# N

**NABW**   SEE NATIONAL ASSOCIATION OF BANK WOMEN.

**NACHA**   SEE NATIONAL AUTOMATED CLEARING HOUSE ASSOCIATION.

**NASD**   SEE NATIONAL ASSOCIATION OF SECURITIES DEALERS.

**NATIONAL ASSOCIATION OF BANK WOMEN (NABW)**  An organization of women financial executives founded in New York in 1921. The organization's objective is the furtherance of its members' careers through management and other educational programs.

**NATIONAL ASSOCIATION OF SECURITIES DEALERS (NASD)**  An organization of member broker-dealers with self regulatory jurisdiction over its members. Those self-regulatory activities include the conduct of examinations for compliance with net capital requirements and other regulations, and market surveillance of the over-the-counter (OTC) securities market. NASDAQ, a subsidiary of the NASD, facilitates the trading of approximately 5,000 of the most active OTC issues through an electronically connected network.

**NATIONAL AUTOMATED CLEARING HOUSE ASSOCIATION (NACHA)**  A private association providing a common basis for the exchange of information and support services among regional or local automated clearing house associations.

**NATIONAL BANK**  A bank that is chartered under the authority of the National Bank Act by the Comptroller of the Currency (OCC) and required to be a member of the Federal Reserve System and the Federal Deposit Insurance Corporation.

**NATIONAL BANK ACT OF 1863**  An act of Congress providing for the incorporation of banks under federal supervision.

**NATIONAL BANK EXAMINATION**  A comprehensive audit of a bank supervised by the Office of the Comptroller of the Currency.

**NATIONAL BANK EXAMINER**  An auditor employed by the Office of the Comptroller of the Currency whose job is to perform periodic examinations of assigned national banks to determine compliance with the provisions of the National Bank Act and all pertinent federal laws and regulations.

**NATIONAL BANKRUPTCY ACT OF 1898**  The first bankruptcy act which established federal laws which, under specific circumstances, granted financial relief for corporate and consumer borrowers. The increased demand for credit and the "play now, pay later" lifestyle of American society after World War II catapulted consumer debt to its highest level in history, resulting in an overburdening of the courts. Bankruptcy law decisions were handed down inconsistently in different jurisdictions, often to the detriment of both the banks and the borrowers.

Congress, attempting to streamline and provide consistent application of the federal bankruptcy rules, passed the Bankruptcy Reform Act of 1978 which became effective on October 1, 1979. The 1978 act clarified and modified the Wage Earner Plan by adding to the Bankruptcy Code Chapter 13, "adjustment of Debts of an Individual With Regular Income." Other changes included the prohibition of a setoff once the plan had been filed until the stay was lifted under motion and court approval, changes in the reaffirmation procedure, and the establishment of a list of federal exemptions.

Congress' plan backfired. Under the provisions of the 1978 act, consumers found it attractive to "load up" unsecured debt in anticipation of filing bankruptcy and the resulting eventual discharge of unsecured debt. Thus, a continuing of the "play now, pay later" mentality coupled with more lenient advertising rules for attorneys who "specialized" in debt relief resulted in an increase in the consumer bankruptcy rate of more than 100 percent. The Bankruptcy Amendments and Federal Judgeship Act of 1984 was signed into law on July 10, 1984. Its purpose was to curb the abuse of the 1978 reform by encouraging repayment plans, appointing more than 200 new bankruptcy judges, and applying substantive restrictions to the Code in order to prevent misuse by debtors. The Bankruptcy Code was again amended on November 28, 1986, in an effort to provide relief to America's farmers which was not available under Chapters 7 or 13 of the Code. The agricultural crisis left crop and livestock lenders with unprecedented levels of uncollected debt. Farm foreclosures had reached an all-time high and the bankruptcy laws needed to be tailored to meet the needs of the overburdened and insolvent farmer. Congress, in its attempt to ease the farm crisis, directly impacted every agricultural lender in the United States by creating, as part of the act, a new chapter to the Bankruptcy Code, the "family farmer" provisions of Chapter 12.

**NATIONAL CREDIT UNION ADMINISTRATION (NCUA)** The regulatory agency that charters, supervises and insures federal credit unions. State-chartered credit unions that apply and qualify for insurance may also be insured by NCUA. The NCUA also operates a credit facility for member credit unions.

**NATIONAL DEBT** Money owed by the United States government to others.

**NATIONAL FLOOD INSURANCE PROGRAM** A two phase program for providing flood insurance protection for communities under the Federal Emergency Management Association (FEMA). In cooperation with FEMA, every state has appointed an agency that serves as a liaison between the federal government and the communities in the state for developing a flood insurance program. Licensed property and casualty insurance agents and brokers provide the link between the NFIP and the insured. There are two phases to the NFIP.

*PHASE I* The Emergency Flood Insurance Program serves as an interim program for communities entering the NFIP. It provides lower limits of coverage ("first layer") on eligible structures at federally subsidized rates. Under this phase, FEMA issues initial flood hazard boundary maps which are used to determine whether properties are located in a flood plain area having special flood or mudslide hazards.

*PHASE II* Once a detailed study of the community is completed and FEMA issues flood insurance rate maps for the area, Phase II, the regular program, provides full insurance coverage (first and second layers), flood insurance rate maps and additional flood plain management requirements for the community. The maps delineate communities by degrees of probability of flood hazard and include more specific area identification on the flood hazard boundary maps. They also provide base flood elevations, where there is at least a 1% chance of flood loss each year. The NFIP covers improved real estate or mobile home located, or to be located in an area that has been identified by FEMA as having special flood hazards, including:

• construction loans for buildings under construction that are walled and roofed;

• mobile homes that are anchored to a permanent site to resist flotation, collapse, or lateral movement by providing over-the-top frame ties to ground anchors, unless it is a mobile home on a foundation continuously insured at the same time by the NFIP at least since September 30, 1982; dealers' inventories of mobile homes on foundations;

- condominiums or townhouses that are contiguous to the ground, capable of separate ownership and having legal descriptions;
  - high-rise condominiums with common ownership; and
  - other types of residential, industrial, and agricultural buildings with any walled and roofed structure that is principally above ground and affixed to a permanent site.

Each building is insured separately, as is each mobile home, including those in dealer inventories, that are eligible for coverage. Policies for high-rise condominiums are issued to the condominiums owners association and policies on individual units are issued to unit owners. Each unit is eligible for contents coverage on personal property contained within a fully enclosed building. Personal property insurance coverage is available for machinery, equipment, fixtures, and furnishings contained in real property or a mobile home.

National flood insurance is not available on the following:
- unimproved land, bridges, dams, and roads;
- mobile homes on or after October 1, 1982, not affixed to a permanent site (anchored) to resist flotation, collapse, or lateral movement by providing over-the-top and frame ties to ground anchors;
- travel trailers and campers;
- buildings entirely on, in, or over water into which boats are floated;
- buildings newly constructed or substantially improved on or after October 1, 1982, in an area designated as an undeveloped coastal barrier within the Coastal Barrier Resource System established by the Coastal Barrier Resources Act (Public Law 97-348).

**NCUA**   SEE NATIONAL CREDIT UNION ADMINISTRATION.

**NEGATIVE AMORTIZATION**   Amortization means that monthly payments are large enough to pay the interest and reduce the principal on a mortgage or other term loan. Negative amortization occurs when the monthly payments do not cover all of the interest cost. The interest cost that isn't covered is added to the unpaid principal balance. This means that after making many payments, the borrower could owe more than he or she did at the beginning of the loan. Negative amortization can occur when an ARM (adjustable rate mortgage) has a payment cap that results in monthly payments not high enough to cover the interest due.

**NEGOTIABILITY**   The ability of an instrument to be transferred from one individual to another by endorsement and delivery; the quality which makes an instrument transferable by endorsement.

**NEGOTIABLE INSTRUMENT**   A bill of exchange, check, draft, promissory note or other written instrument made payable to order or to the bearer and transferred by endorsement and delivery or by delivery alone. In accordance with the terms of the Uniform Negotiable Instruments Act, "An instrument, to be negotiable, must conform to the following requirements: (a) it must be in writing and signed by the maker or drawer; (b) it must contain an unconditional promise or order to pay a certain sum in money; (c) it must be payable on demand, or at a fixed or determinable future time; (d) it must be payable to order or to bearer; and (e) where the instrument is addressed to a drawee, he must be named or otherwise indicated therein with reasonable certainty."

**NEGOTIATED ORDER OF WITHDRAWAL (NOW) ACCOUNT**  A type of deposit account offering the payable on demand features of a checking account and the interest bearing features of a savings account, commonly referred to as a form of interest bearing checking account. The account holder can withdraw funds by writing a negotiable order of withdrawal payable to a third party.

**NEGOTIATION**  The transfer of an instrument in such form that the transferee becomes a holder. If the instrument is payable to order it is negotiated by delivery with any necessary endorsement; if payable to bearer it is negotiated by delivery. An endorsement must be written by or on behalf of the holder and on the instrument or on a paper so firmly affixed thereto as to become a part thereof. An endorsement is effective for negotiation only when it conveys the entire instrument or any unpaid residue. If it purports to be of less it operates only as a partial assignment. Words of assignment, condition, waiver, guaranty, limitation or disclaimer of liability and the like accompanying an endorsement do not affect its character as an endorsement.

Negotiation is merely a special form of transfer, the importance of which lies entirely in the fact that it makes the transferee a holder as defined in UCC Section 1-201 (SEE HOLDER IN DUE COURSE).

Any instrument which has been specially endorsed can be negotiated only with the endorsement of the special endorsee. An instrument endorsed in blank may be negotiated by delivery alone, provided that it bears the endorsement of all prior special endorsees.

**NET CHARGE OFF**  The balance charged to bad debts, less recoveries received and applied, during a specified period.

**NET EARNINGS**  Net income. Gross earnings less gross operating expenses, including all costs, allowances for depreciation, and expenses have been deducted.

**NET LEASE**  A rental agreement whereby the lessor will incur all maintenance costs, taxes, insurance and all other expenses usually paid for by the owner.

**NET PROFIT**  The income which remains after all expenses have been deducted from revenue during a given period of time.

**NET WORTH**  The difference between total assets and total liabilities, also referred to as equity.

**NEVER USED**  The designation of a bank cardholder account which has never been active.

**NEW YORK CLEARING HOUSE ASSOCIATION (NYCHA)**  The clearing house association for New York City banks.

**NEW YORK STOCK EXCHANGE (NYSE)**  The oldest and largest stock exchange in the United States, organized under its existing name in 1863 from the New York Stock and Exchange Board.

**NIGHT DEPOSITORY**  Also referred to as the "night drop," it is a vault accessible through the wall of a bank through which depositors may gain access by use of a pass key or envelope drawer. This facility is popular with merchants who deposit cash, checks and credit card drafts after hours. The contents of the depository are counted under dual custody during the next banking day when funds are credited to the depositor's account.

**NO LOAD FUNDS** Mutual funds which do not contain a sales charge or commission.

**NOMINAL ASSET** An insignificant asset, the value of which is usually represented by some token value, such as "goodwill."

**NOMINEE** One who is authorized to act for another in some limited way; for example, an appointed agent into whose name funds are transferred by agreement to facilitate the purchase or sale of securities in a case where it might be inconvenient to obtain the signature or other authorization of the principal to make such transfer.

**NONACCRUAL OF INTEREST** Banks shall not accrue interest on (1) any asset which is maintained on a cash basis because of deterioration in the financial position of the borrower, (2) any asset for which payment in full of interest or principal is not expected, or (3) any asset upon which principal or interest has been in default for a period of 90 days or more unless it is both well secured and in the process of collection. A nonaccrual asset may be restored to an accrual status when none of its principal and interest is due and unpaid or when it otherwise becomes well secured and in the process of collection.

For purposes of applying the third test for the nonaccrual of interest listed above, the date on which an asset reaches nonaccrual status is determined by its contractual terms. If the principal or interest on an asset becomes due and unpaid for 90 days or more on a date that falls between call report dates, the asset should be placed in nonaccrual status as of the date it becomes 90 days past due and it should remain in nonaccrual status until it meets the criteria for restoration to accrual status described above.

A debt is "well secured" if it is secured by (1) collateral in the form of liens on or pledges of real or personal property, including securities, that have a realized value sufficient to discharge the debt (including accrued interest) in full, or (2) the guaranty of a financially responsible party. A debt is "in the process of collection" if collection of the debt is proceeding in due course either through legal action, including judgment enforcement procedures, or, in appropriate circumstances, through collection efforts not involving legal action which are reasonably expected to result in repayment of the debt or in its restoration to a current status.

The reversal of previously accrued but uncollected interest applicable to any asset placed in nonaccrual status and the treatment of subsequent payments as either principal or interest should be handled in accordance with generally accepted accounting principles. Acceptable accounting treatment includes a reversal of all previously accrued but uncollected interest applicable to assets placed in a nonaccrual status against appropriate income and balance sheet accounts.

**NONBANK BANK** An institution created under an interpretation of law which allows nonbanking companies to open banking offices and commercial banks to open limited service branches across state lines despite the then effective statutory ban on interstate banking.

**NONBORROWED RESERVES** The amount reflected by the bank's total reserves minus that amount borrowed from the Federal Reserve.

**NONCASH ITEM**   An instrument that a bank decides to handle as a collection item, as opposed to offering immediate credit. The customer's account is not credited until settlement of the item occurs.

**NONLOCAL CHECK**   A check deposited in a different check processing region than the paying bank. There are a total of 48 Federal Reserve check processing offices in the United States and the territory served by each office constitutes a region.

**NON-PAR CHECK**   A check that cannot be collected at face value for any reason.

**NONPERFORMING LOAN**   A loan which is not paying according to original agreement, generally upon which interest payments are not being collected.

**NONRECOURSE AGREEMENT**   An arrangement under which a vendor sells a conditional sales contract to a bank without liability in case of default on behalf of the borrower for the primary obligation.

**NONREVOLVING LINE OF CREDIT**   A line of credit upon which the borrower may draw only once, as opposed to a revolving line of credit upon which the borrower may draw upon more than once under the preapproved terms of the credit facility.

**NONSUFFICIENT FUNDS (NSF)**   A phrase indicating that a check has been written against an account, the balance of which is not sufficient to cover the amount of the check.

**NOTARY PUBLIC**   An individual commissioned by a state who, as a public officer, authenticates the identification of parties to writings, or may take affidavits, depositions and protests of negotiable instruments for nonpayment or nonacceptance.

**NOTE**   Written evidence of a debt, signed by the maker (borrower) and promising to pay a certain sum of money at a specified date and location to a lender.

**NOTICE OF DISHONOR**   An instrument is dishonored when, upon presentment, it is refused for payment. A notice of dishonor may be given to any person who may be liable on the instrument by or on behalf of the holder or any party who has himself received notice, or any other party who can be compelled to pay the instrument. In addition, an agent or bank in whose hands the instrument is dishonored may give notice to his principal or customer or to another agent or bank from which the instrument was received. Any necessary notice must be given by a bank before its midnight deadline and by any other person before midnight of the third business day after dishonor or receipt of notice of dishonor. Notice may be given in any reasonable manner. It may be oral or written and in any terms which identify the instrument and state that it has been dishonored. A misdescription which does not mislead the party notified does not vitiate the notice. Written notice is given when sent although it is not received.

**NOVATION**   Substitution; the replacement of one debt for another. Generally, novation refers to the replacement of a new debtor for a former one.

**NOW ACCOUNT**   SEE NEGOTIATED ORDER OF WITHDRAWAL ACCOUNT.

**NSF**   SEE NONSUFFICIENT FUNDS.

**NUNCUPATIVE WILL**   An oral will made by a person on his or her deathbed or in the sense of impending death. It must be declared in the presence of at least two witnesses and subsequently reduced to writing and submitted into probate in accordance with local statute.

**NYCHA**   SEE NEW YORK CLEARING HOUSE ASSOCIATION.

**NYSE**   SEE NEW YORK STOCK EXCHANGE.

# O

**OBLIGATION**   The responsibility of the obligor to pay when due and the legal right of the creditor to enforce payment.

**OCC**   SEE OFFICE OF THE COMPTROLLER OF THE CURRENCY.

**OFFICE OF THE COMPTROLLER OF THE CURRENCY**   The Administrator of National Banks, the OCC is that part of the Treasury Department which has the responsibility for supervision and examination of national banks. SEE ALSO COMPTROLLER OF THE CURRENCY.

**ON DEMAND**   Payable upon presentation.

**ON-US ITEM**   A depositor's check which is drawn on, and payable at, the bank of account, is described as "on-us" when presented for payment to the drawee bank.

**OPEN END CREDIT**   A charge account or revolving line of credit which may be used repeatedly subject to a credit limit. An open end lease usually involves a balloon payment at the end of the lease term based on the value of the property at the end of the lease.

**OPEN MARKET COMMITTEE**   A committee comprised of the presidents of five of the Federal Reserve District Banks plus the Board of Directors of the Federal Reserve System. SEE ALSO FEDERAL RESERVE.

**OPERATING CONTROL**   Ownership, individual or collective, of 51% or more of the shares of a corporation. These "majority" shareholders can generally hire, fire, determine dividend policy and make all operating decisions for the corporation.

**OPERATIONS OFFICER**   That officer level employee who oversees the operations department of a bank. The overall scope of responsibility may extend to bookkeeping, proof, wire transfer, notes and other non-lending functions.

**ORGANIZATION COSTS**   The direct costs incurred to incorporate and charter a bank. Such direct costs include, but are not limited to, legal, accounting and consulting fees and printing costs directly related to the chartering or incorporating process, filing fees paid to chartering authorities, and the costs of economic impact studies. Organization costs incurred by newly chartered banks should be capitalized and amortized using the straight-line method over a period not to exceed five years. Pre-opening expenses such as salaries and employee benefits, rent, depreciation, supplies, directors' fees, training, travel, postage and telephone, are not considered organization costs and should not be capitalized. In addition, allocated internal costs (e.g., management salaries) shall not be capitalized as organization costs.

**OTHER ACCEPTABLE COLLATERAL**   Any collateral in which the lender has perfected a security interest, that has a quantifiable value, and is accepted by the lender in accordance with safe and sound lending practices. Other acceptable collateral should be appropriately discounted by the lender consistent with the lender's usual practices for making loans secured by such collateral. Other acceptable collateral includes, among other items, unconditional irrevocable standby letters of credit for the benefit of the lender.

**OVERDRAFT**   An extension of credit which creates a negative deposit balance. An overdraft can be either planned or unplanned. An unplanned overdraft occurs when a depository institution honors a check or draft drawn against a deposit account when insufficient funds are on deposit and there is no advance contractual agreement to honor the check or draft. When a contractual agreement has been made in advance to allow such credit extensions, overdrafts are referred to as planned or prearranged. Any overdraft, whether planned or unplanned, is an extension of credit and should be treated and reported as a "loan."

**OVERDRAFT CHECKING ACCOUNT**   A prearranged agreement in which a line of credit allows the depositor to write checks for more than the account balance and pay interest on the amount that exceeds the balance. SEE ALSO OVERDRAFT.

**OVERNIGHT REPURCHASE AGREEMENT**   A form of a short-term loan agreement in which one party sells a security to another party, agreeing to repurchase it the following day at the same price.

**OWNER OCCUPIED**   Used in conjunction with the term "1- to 4-family residential property" to mean that the owner of the underlying real property occupies at least one unit of the real property as a principal residence.

# P

**P&L STATEMENT**   SEE PROFIT AND LOSS STATEMENT.

**PAID CHECK**   A check that has been negotiated, cancelled and paid.

**PAR VALUE**   The face value of stock.

**PARTICIPATION**   An ownership interest, such as in a loan, mortgage, or pool of mortgages or securities.

**PARTICIPATION CERTIFICATE**   A written representation of a beneficial interest in a pool of mortgages or loans or syndicated Eurocredit; a formal credit instrument carrying a contractual interest obligation on a specified principal amount.

**PARTICIPATION IN POOLS OF RESIDENTIAL MORTGAGES**  Participations in pools of residential mortgages may be either (1) issued or guaranteed by an agency of the U.S. Government or (2) issued by private entities with no government guarantee.

(1) *Government-guaranteed certificates of participation in pools of residential mortgages:*

Included are:

(a) Participation certificates guaranteed by the Government National Mortgage Association (GNMA), but issued by a financial institution, in pools of FHA, FmHA, or VA mortgages (so-called GNMA pass-throughs);

(b) Participation certificates issued and guaranteed by the Federal National Mortgage Association (FNMA) or the Federal Home Loan Mortgage Corporation (FHLMC). FNMA and FHLMC issue guaranteed participation certificates in pools of residential mortgages, including those exchanged for mortgage loans in so-called "mortgage swap" arrangements. The swap arrangements involve an exchange by the swapping institution, at par, of mortgages it owns for a participation certificate guaranteed by FNMA or FHLMC.

FNMA and FHLMC certificates may carry a stated interest rate different from that of the underlying mortgages reflecting the guarantee fee deducted by FNMA or FHLMC and any servicing fees.

(2) *Privately-issued certificates of participation in pools of residential mortgages:*  Privately issued certificates take a variety of forms. For example, they may involve private insurance arrangements, the issuance of different classes of participation certificates, or standby letters of credit.

**PASSBOOK**  A record of deposits and withdrawals. Passbooks generally are kept in the possession of the depositor and entries are made by the bank at the time of transaction. Entries may include date, amount of transaction, new balance, interest payments, teller's initials, and account number.

**PASS-THROUGH RESERVE BALANCES**  Under the Monetary Control Act of 1980, and as reflected in Federal Reserve Regulation D, depository institutions that are members of the Federal Reserve System must maintain their required reserves (in excess of vault cash) directly with a Federal Reserve Bank. However, nonmember depository institutions may maintain their required reserves (in excess of vault cash) in one of two ways, either directly with a Federal Reserve Bank or indirectly in an account with a correspondent institution which, in turn, is required to pass the reserves through to a Federal Reserve Bank. This second type of account is called a "pass-through" account and a depository institution passing its reserves to the Federal Reserve through a correspondent is referred to as a "respondent." This pass-through reserve relationship is legally and for supervisory purposes considered to constitute an asset/debt relationship between the respondent and the correspondent, and an asset/debt relationship between the correspondent and the Federal Reserve. Since the respondent will not know from its own books the amount that the correspondent has actually passed through to the Federal Reserve for the respondent's account, the respondent bank must obtain a statement of this amount from its correspondent.

**PAY**  The exchange of a check for cash, or to charge a check against a customer's account.

**PAYING BANK**   The institution upon which a check is drawn.

**PAYMENT**   The transfer of funds in any form between two parties. Generally, the installment of principal or interest, or principal and interest which is due at a prearranged time.

**PAYMENTS MECHANISM**   Any system that can transfer funds, including checks, credit cards, cash, automated teller machines, point-of-sale terminals, or electronic funds transfer devices. The Federal Reserve plays a major role in the nation's payments mechanism through its distribution of currency and coin, check processing, wire transfers, and automatic clearinghouses.

**PAYOFF**   The total amount due, including principal and interest, as of a certain date, which is required to retire a debt in full.

**PERCENT PER MONTH**   A method of calculating interest when the interest is specified as a monthly percentage of the outstanding balance, such as "one percent per month on the unpaid balance."

**PERFECTED LIEN**   A lien is perfected when the security interest is properly documented and filed or recorded with the appropriate legal authority.

**PERMANENT CURRENT ASSETS**   The base level of current assets that the company maintains at all times. The level of cash, accounts receivable, and inventory that the company requires regardless of seasonal requirements.

**PERMANENT FINANCING**   Generally, a long term mortgage used to pay off or "take out" an interim, short term loan.

**PERSONAL IDENTIFICATION NUMBER (PIN)**   A secret code, usually numeric, and either customer-selected or randomly assigned to a bank card holder for purposes of confidential identification of the customer in order to permit an automated transaction such as a withdrawal, transfer, deposit or inquiry initiated by use of the card. It is intended to prevent unauthorized use of the card.

**PESETA**   Monetary unit of Spain.

**PESO**   Monetary unit of Argentina, Chile, Colombia, Cuba, Dominican Republic, Mexico, Republic of the Philippines, and Uruguay.

**PLACEMENTS AND TAKINGS**   Deposits between a foreign office of one bank and a foreign office of another bank. For reporting purposes, they are to be treated as "due from" or "due to" depository institutions.

**PLEDGED ASSETS**   The securities owned by a bank which must be pledged as collateral security for funds deposited by the U.S. government, or by state or municipal governments. Pledged assets are generally U.S. government bonds and obligations.

**POINT**   A measurement of percentage, as in "one percentage point" or "50 basis points."

**POINT OF SALE**   A system that allows a bank customer to electronically debit a deposit account for the purchase of goods or services at the time and location where the goods or services are sold. A point of sale terminal is a communication and data capture device installed at a merchant's location and electronically connected to the bank. It is designed to authorize, record and forward electronic data on each sale as it occurs.

**POOLED INVESTMENTS, MORTGAGES**   SEE PARTICIPATION IN POOLS OF RESIDENTIAL MORTGAGES.

**PORTFOLIO**   Generally, the bank's total loans by category, or total deposits by category, e.g., "the consumer loan portfolio," or the "money market portfolio."

**POSITIVE AMORTIZATION**   That which occurs when all installment payments, as scheduled, completely retire the principal and interest. SEE ALSO NEGATIVE AMORTIZATION.

**POSITIVE GAP**   The excess of interest sensitive assets over interest sensitive liabilities.

**POUND**   Monetary unit of Cyprus, Egypt, Ireland, Lebanon, Sudan, Syria, United Kingdom.

**PREAUTHORIZED PAYMENTS**   Payments which are automatically debited from a demand deposit account by prior authorization of the depositor. For example, an arrangement whereby the account holder authorizes an insurance company to debit the account holder's account for monthly premiums on a certain day of each month.

**PREFERRED STOCK**   A form of ownership interest in a bank or other company which entitles its holders to some preference or priority over the owners of common stock, usually with respect to dividends or asset distributions in a liquidation. *Limited life preferred stock* is preferred stock that has a stated maturity date or that can be redeemed at the option of the holder. It excludes those issues of preferred stock that automatically convert into perpetual preferred stock or common stock at a stated date. *Perpetual preferred stock* is preferred stock that does not have a stated maturity date or that cannot be redeemed at the option of the holder. It includes those issues of preferred stock that automatically convert into common stock at a stated date.

**PRELIMINARY TITLE REPORT**   The results of a title search conducted and reported by a title company prior to issuing a policy of title insurance.

**PREMIUMS AND DISCOUNTS**   A *premium* arises when a bank purchases a security, loan, or other asset at a price in excess of its par or face value, typically because the current level of interest rates for such assets is less than its contract or stated rate of interest. The difference between the purchase price and par or face value represents the premium which all banks are required to amortize.

A *discount* arises when a bank purchases a security, loan, or other asset at a price below its par or face value, typically because the current level of interest rates for such assets is greater than its contract or stated rate of interest. A discount is also present on instruments which do not have a stated rate of interest such as U.S. Treasury bills and commercial paper. The difference between par or face value and the purchase price represents the discount which all banks are required to accrete. Premiums and discounts are accounted for as adjustments to the yield on an asset over the life of the asset. A premium must be amortized and a discount must be accreted from the date of purchase to maturity, not to call or put date. The preferable method for amortizing premiums and accreting discounts involves the use of the interest method for accruing income on the asset. The objective of the interest method is to produce a constant yield or rate of return on the carrying value of the asset (par or face value plus unamortized premium or less unaccreted discount) at the beginning of each amortization period over the asset's remaining life. The difference between the periodic interest income that is accrued on the asset and interest at the stated rate is the periodic amortization or accretion. However, a straight-line method of amortization or accretion is acceptable if the results are not materially different from the interest method.

A premium or discount may also arise when the reporting bank, acting either as a lender or a borrower, is involved in an exchange of a note for assets other than cash and the interest rate is either below the market rate or not stated, or the face amount of the note is materially different from the fair value of the noncash assets exchanged. The noncash assets and the related note shall be recorded at either the fair value of the noncash assets or the market value of the note, whichever is more clearly determinable. The market value of the note would be its present value as determined by discounting all future payments on the note using an appropriate interest rate, i.e., a rate comparable to that on new loans of similar risk. The difference between the face amount and the recorded value of the note is a premium or discount. This discount or premium shall be accounted for as an adjustment of the interest income or expense over the life of the note using the interest method described above. SEE ALSO DISCOUNTS.

**PREPAYMENT**   Payment prior to maturity.

**PREPAYMENT PENALTY**   A monetary penalty imposed for payment prior to maturity.

**PRESENTING BANK**   The bank that forwards a negotiable instrument to another bank for payment.

**PRESENTMENT**   Delivery of a negotiable instrument by the holder for acceptance or payment by the drawee or maker.

**PRETERMITTED**   Unintentionally omitted. For example, a pretermitted heir or pretermitted child is one to whom no share in an estate is left and there is no affirmative provision in the will showing an intention to omit.

**PREVIOUS BALANCE METHOD**   A method of calculating finance charges by subtracting payments and credits posted during the billing period from the most recent previous balance.

**PRIME RATE**   The interest rate charged by a bank to its most creditworthy commercial customers and, generally, represents the lowest rate charged. Usually, the prevailing prime rate is set by East Coast money-center banks, followed by banks throughout the United States. The prime rate will fluctuate ("move") as the cost of funds periodically changes or other market conditions prevail.

**PRINCIPAL**   The net proceeds of a deposit or loan upon which interest is earned or charged. Interest is charged or earned on the principal amount.

**PRIOR LIEN**   The senior mortgage or a superior lien.

**PRO FORMA STATEMENT**   A projection based upon certain assumptions about future economic events.

**PROBATE**   The legal process of proving the authenticity of a last will and testament showing that the document is in fact the last will of the decedent.

**PROCEEDS**   The actual sum given to the borrower.

**PROFIT**   That remaining after deducting all costs and expenses from gross sales or revenue.

**PROFIT AND LOSS STATEMENT (P&L)**   Income and expense statement. The total revenues and expenses during a defined time period.

**PROFIT PLAN**   A projected or pro forma income statement detailing revenues and expenses that are expected for some future period.

**PROFIT SHARING**   An arrangement where employees share in the profit of the company according to a definitive plan.

**PROHIBITED BASIS**   The Equal Credit Opportunity Act (Regulation B) prohibits discrimination in any aspect of a credit transaction on the basis of race, color, religion, national origin, sex, marital status, age (provided that the applicant has the capacity to enter into a binding contract), receipt of income from public assistance programs, and the good faith exercise of any right under the Consumer Credit Protection Act. Those factors are referred to throughout the regulation as prohibited basis. In addition, discrimination is unlawful if an application is declined because of race, color, religion, national origin, sex, marital status or age of an applicant's business associates, or of the persons who will be related to the extension of credit, e.g., those residing in the neighborhood where collateral is located. Illegal discrimination means treating an applicant or a group of applicants less favorably than another group because of a prohibited basis.

**PROMISOR**   The maker or primary obligor.

**PROMISSORY NOTE**   A written promise to pay a sum.

**PROOF**   A system for testing the accuracy of another system or operation. The proof department of a bank sorts, distributes and proofs all transactions arising in the bank and creates accurate records of all transactions.

**PROPRIETORSHIP**   A business solely owned by an individual.

**PUBLIC FUNDS**   Deposit accounts held by government agencies or political subdivisions.

# *Q*

**QUALIFIED ENDORSEMENT**   An endorsement containing the words "without recourse" or similar language intended to limit the endorser's liability if the instrument is not honored.

**QUALIFIED PENSION PLAN**   A pension, profit-sharing, or other employee benefit plan that meets the requirements of section 401(a) of the Internal Revenue Code of 1954, which, among other things, must be written, permanent, for the exclusive benefit of employees or their beneficiaries, and not discriminatory in favor of officers, stockholders, supervisors, or other higher paid employees.

**QUASI-CONTRACT**   An obligation between parties which arises out of their relationship or by the voluntary act of one or more of the parties.

**QUEUE**   A waiting line such as that for teller service or for implementation of a task.

**QUICK ASSETS**   Those assets of a company that can be converted to cash in a period of less than one year.

**QUICK RATIO**   Current assets divided by current liabilities; an indication of a company's ability to pay off its liabilities rapidly with available funds. SEE ALSO CURRENT ASSETS AND CURRENT LIABILITIES.

**QUITCLAIM DEED**   A deed that transfers only such right, title and interest in real estate as the grantor may have at the time the conveyance is executed.

# R

**RAND**   Monetary unit of South Africa.

**RATE OF INTEREST**   A percentage expressing the interest to be charged or paid.

**RATIO ANALYSIS**   Evaluation of the relationship of items in financial statements. Some commonly used ratios are:

- CURRENT RATIO: Total current assets divided by total current liabilities. An indication of a firm's ability to service its current obligations.
- QUICK RATIO: Cash and equivalents plus trade receivables divided by total current liabilities. A refinement of the Current Ratio also known as the "Acid Test" ratio; a more conservative measure of liquidity.
- SALES TO RECEIVABLES: Net sales divided by trade receivables, this ratio measures the number of times trade receivables turn over during the year. The higher the turnover, the shorter the time between sales and cash collection.
- DAYS' RECEIVABLES: 365 divided by the Sales to Receivables Ratio expresses the average time in days that receivables are outstanding.
- COST OF SALES TO INVENTORY RATIO: The cost of sales divided by the value of inventory measures the number of times inventory is turned over during the year. High inventory turnover can be a measurement of better liquidity.
- DAYS' INVENTORY: The Cost of Sales to Inventory Ratio divided into 365 indicates the average length of time units are in inventory.
- COST OF SALES TO TRADE PAYABLES RATIO: Cost of sales divided by trade payables indicates the number of times trade payables turn over during the year. The higher the turnover, the shorter the time between purchase and payment, indicating good liquidity.

- SALES TO WORKING CAPITAL RATIO: Net sales divided by the difference between current assets and current liabilities (working capital).
- FIXED ASSETS TO NET WORTH RATIO: Fixed assets (net of accumulated depreciation) divided by tangible net worth measures the extent to which owner's equity has been invested in fixed assets.
- DEBT TO WORTH RATIO: Total liabilities divided by tangible net worth expresses the relationship between capital contributed by creditors and that contributed by owners.
- SALES TO NET FIXED ASSETS RATIO: Net sales divided by net fixed assets is a measure of the productive use of a firm's fixed assets.
- NET SALES TO TOTAL ASSETS RATIO: Net sales divided by total assets is a general measure of a firm's ability to generate sales in relation to total assets.

**READILY MARKETABLE COLLATERAL** Insured deposits, financial instruments, and bullion in which the lender has a perfected interest. Financial instruments and bullion must be salable under ordinary circumstances with reasonable promptness at a fair market value determined by quotations based on actual transactions, on an auction or similarly available daily bid and ask price market. Readily marketable collateral should be appropriately discounted by the lender consistent with the lender's usual practices for making loans secured by such collateral.

**REAL ESTATE MORTGAGE** A pledge of real property to secure a debt.

**REAL ESTATE MORTGAGE INVESTMENT CONDUIT (REMIC)** An investment vehicle comprised of security interests in pooled commercial and residential mortgages held in trust. A REMIC is exempt from federal taxes and can be established as a trust, corporation, partnership, or association.

**REAL ESTATE-RELATED FINANCIAL TRANSACTION** Any transaction involving: the sale, lease, purchase, investment in or exchange of real property, including interests in property, or the financing thereof; the refinancing of real property or interests in real property; or the use of real property or interests in property as security for a loan or investment, including mortgage backed securities.

**REAL ESTATE SETTLEMENT AND PROCEDURES ACT (RESPA)** The 1974 Act, commonly known as RESPA, was significantly amended on June 30, 1976, to provide borrowers with pertinent and timely disclosures regarding the nature and costs of the real estate settlement process. The act also protects borrowers against certain abusive practices, such as kickbacks, and places limitations on the use of escrow accounts. RESPA is implemented by Regulation X of the Department of Housing and Urban Development (HUD) and is applicable to all federally related mortgage loans.

**RECEIVABLES** The accounts receivable of a firm.

**RECONVEYANCE** The act of conveying title back to the former owner.

**RECOURSE** The right of a holder in due course of a negotiable instrument to force a prior endorser or other party to pay the amount of the instrument if it is dishonored.

**REDEMPTION** The right to repurchase or repossess pledged, sold, or mortgaged property, within a specific time and according to statutory or contractual conditions.

The *redemption period* is the time during which a mortgagor, by paying the amount owed on a foreclosed mortgage (or other agreed upon amount), may buy back the property. SEE ALSO RIGHT OF REDEMPTION.

**REDISCOUNT**  To discount a negotiable instrument a subsequent time.

**REDLINING**  A prohibited practice in which a lender discriminates against certain geographic areas of a community on the basis of income, race, or other unjustifiable reason.

**REFINANCE**  To retire an existing loan through the proceeds of a new loan.

**REGIONAL CHECK CENTERS**  Depository institutions in the United States may deposit checks for processing at Federal Reserve Bank regional check centers just as they do at Reserve Banks or branches. Depository institutions include member and nonmember commercial banks, savings banks, savings and loan associations, credit unions, and certain foreign bank agencies. The type of institution eligible to deposit checks for collection at Reserve Bank regional centers, Reserve Banks or branches was broadened by the International Banking Act of 1978 and the Monetary Control Act of 1980. The MCA mandated Reserve Banks to charge institutions, at explicit prices, for certain services, including check-related operations. Today, virtually any institution may deposit checks for processing at any Federal Reserve office by paying for the items in the deposit. The Reserve Bank regional centers were proposed in 1971 to help improve the nation's payments mechanism. In 1972, the first regional center, the Baltimore-Washington unit of the Richmond Fed. became fully operational after a one-year test.

The regional offices receive deposits of checks from customers around the country and present them to institutions in the area the office serves. The procedure is the same as that followed at the Reserve Banks and branches. The regional offices occasionally serve depository institutions in areas that may cross Federal Reserve district or state lines. Since the function of the regional offices is to accelerate nationwide check collection, boundaries for the centers are determined by check flows.

Regional offices routinely receive checks from other Reserve Bank regional offices, Federal Reserve Banks and their branches, and "direct-sending" depository institutions. A direct-sending depository institution sends checks drawn on banks in other Reserve districts to the appropriate Reserve Bank, branch or regional office. For example, some large New York City banks send checks drawn on Chicago banks directly to the Chicago Fed. The direct-sending bank gets credit for those checks in its reserve or clearing account at its Reserve Bank. The primary objective of a regional check center is to process overnight checks drawn on financial institutions outside a city with a Federal Reserve office. To accomplish this, the centers sort, clear and deliver checks rapidly.

Personal and corporate checks comprise the bulk of items deposited at Reserve Bank regional centers. These checks are generally delivered to the regional office by private carriers hired by the depository institutions. Other items deposited at Reserve Bank regional centers include checks drawn on the Treasury and postal money orders. However, regional offices do not handle cash or securities. In addition to providing speedy clearance, the processing of checks at regional centers results in quicker identification of fraudulent and other invalid items.

**REGULATION A**  Governs borrowing by depository institutions at the Federal Reserve discount window. The Federal Reserve discount window is open to any depository institution that maintains transaction accounts or nonpersonal time deposits. The regulation provides for lending under two basic programs. First "adjustment credit" is advanced for brief periods to help borrowers meet short-term needs for funds when their usual sources are not reasonably available. Second, "extended credit" is designed to assist depository institutions meet longer-term needs for funds. This category includes seasonal credit to smaller depository institutions lacking access to market funds; assistance to an individual depository institution that experiences special difficulties arising from exceptional circumstances; and assistance to address liquidity strains affecting a broad range of depository institutions. "Emergency credit" may also be advanced to entities other than depository institutions where failure to obtain credit would adversely affect the economy.

**REGULATION AA**  Establishes consumer complaint procedures. Under the regulation, any consumer complaint about an alleged unfair or deceptive act or practice by a state member bank, or an alleged violation of law or regulation, will be investigated. Complaints should be in writing, and submitted to the director of the Division of Consumer Affairs at the Board of Governors of the Federal Reserve System, Washington, D.C. 20551, or to the Reserve Bank for the district in which the institution is located. The complaint should describe the practice or action objected to and should give the names and addresses of the bank concerned and the person complaining. The Board will attempt to give a substantive reply with 15 business days, or, if that is not possible, will acknowledge the complaint within 15 business days and set a reasonable time for a substantive reply. The Board will also receive complaints regarding institutions other than state member banks, and refer them to the appropriate federal agencies. A person filing a complaint does not have to be a customer of the institution in question, and the acts or practices complained of do not have to be subject to federal regulation. Consumers may complain about acts or practices that may, in fact, be expressly authorized, or not prohibited, by current federal or state law or regulation.

**REGULATION B**  Prohibits creditors from discriminating against credit applicants, establishes guidelines for gathering and evaluating credit information, and requires written notification when credit is denied. The regulation prohibits creditors from discriminating against applicants on the basis of age, race, color, religion, national origin, sex, marital status, or receipt of income from public assistance programs. As a general rule, creditors may not ask (on applications) the race, color, religion, national origin, or sex of applicants. In addition, if the application is for individual, unsecured credit, the creditor may not ask the applicant's marital status. Exceptions apply in the case of residential mortgage applications. Creditors also may not discriminate against applicants who exercise their rights under the Federal consumer credit laws.

Model credit application forms are provided in the regulation to facilitate compliance. By properly using these forms, creditors can be assured of being in compliance with the application requirements of the regulation. Creditors may use credit-scoring systems that allocate points or weights to key applicant characteristics. Creditors also may rely on their own judgment of an applicant's creditworthiness.

The regulation also requires creditors to give applicants written notification of rejection of an application, a statement of the applicant's rights under the Equal Credit Opportunity Act, and a statement either of the reasons for the rejection or of the applicant's right to request the reasons. Creditors who furnish credit information, when reporting information on married borrowers, must report information in the name of each spouse.

The regulation establishes a special residential mortgage credit monitoring system for regulatory agencies by requiring that lenders ask residential mortgage applicants their race, national origin, sex, marital status, and age.

**REGULATION BB**   Implements the Community Reinvestment Act (CRA) and is designed to encourage banks to help meet the credit needs of their communities. Under Regulation BB, each bank office must make available a statement for public inspection indicating, on a map, the communities served by that office and the type of credit the bank is prepared to extend within the communities served. The regulation requires each bank to maintain a file of public comments relating to its CRA statement. The regulatory authorities, when examining a bank, must assess its record in meeting the credit needs of the entire community, including low and moderate income neighborhoods, and must take account of the record in considering certain bank applications.

**REGULATION C**   Requires depository institutions making federally related mortgage loans to make annual public disclosure of the locations of certain residential loans. The regulation carries out the Home Mortgage Disclosure Act of 1975 (HMDA), providing citizens and public officials with enough information to determine whether depository institutions are meeting the housing credit needs of their local communities.

The regulation applies to commercial banks, savings banks, savings and loan institutions and credit unions that make federally related mortgage loans, with the exception of institutions with assets of $10 million or less and institutions that do not have an office in a Metropolitan Statistical Area or a Primary Metropolitan Statistical Area. Institutions covered by the regulation must disclose annually, in central locations within their communities and at certain of their own offices, the number and total dollar amount of residential mortgage loans originated or purchased during the most recent calendar year, itemized by census tract in which the property is located.

**REGULATION CC**   Implements the Expedited Funds Availability Act of 1987, setting endorsement standards on checks collected by depository institutions. The endorsement standard is designed to facilitate the identification of the endorsing bank and prompt return of unpaid checks. The regulation specifies funds availability schedules that banks must comply with, and procedures for returning dishonored checks.

**REGULATION D**   Imposes uniform reserve requirements on all depository institutions with transaction accounts or nonpersonal time deposits, defines such deposits and requires reports to the Federal Reserve, and sets phase-in schedules for reserve requirements.

Regulation D sets uniform reserve requirements on all depository institutions that have transaction accounts or nonpersonal time deposits. Transaction accounts are defined to include checking accounts, NOW accounts, share draft accounts, savings accounts that allow automatic transfers or third party payments by automated teller machines, and accounts that permit more than a limited number of telephone or preauthorized payments or transfers each month. Reserves are maintained in the form of vault cash or noninterest-bearing balances held with a Federal Reserve Bank on a direct or indirect basis.

**REGULATION E** Establishes the rights, liabilities and responsibilities of parties in electronic fund transfers (EFT) and protects consumers using EFT systems. Regulation E prescribes the rules for the solicitation and issuance of EFT cards, governs consumers' liability for unauthorized electronic fund transfers (resulting, for example, from lost or stolen cards), requires institutions to disclose certain terms and conditions of EFT services, provides for documentation of electronic transfers (on periodic statements, for example), sets up a resolution procedure for errors on EFT accounts, and covers notice of crediting and stoppage or preauthorized payments to and from a customer's account.

**REGULATION F** Requires certain state-chartered member banks to register and file financial statements with the Board of Governors. The regulation applies to state-chartered member banks that have 500 or more stockholders and at least $1 million in assets, or whose securities are registered on a national securities exchange. Generally, it does not apply to banks whose shares are owned by holding companies since these usually have fewer than 500 stockholders.

In general, these State-chartered member banks must file registration statements, periodic financial statements, proxy statements, statements of election contests, and various other disclosures of interest to investors. Officers, directors, and principal stockholders also must file reports on their holdings in the bank.

The regulation also prohibits tender offers for the stock of a bank subject to the regulation unless certain information is filed with the Board at the same time. Regulations issued by the Board of Governors in this area are substantially similar to those issued by the Securities and Exchange Commission. Information filed under the provisions of Regulation F is available to the public at the offices of the Board of Governors in Washington, D.C., and at the Federal Reserve bank in the district where the registrant is located.

**REGULATION G** Governs credit secured by margin securities extended or arranged by parties other than banks, brokers, and dealers. This regulation applies to lenders, other than broker-dealers and banks, who are required to register with the Board of Governors. Registration is required within 30 days after the end of the quarter during which credit (secured, directly or indirectly by margin stock) is extended in an amount of $200,000 or more or which exceeds $500,000 in total. Once a lender is required to be registered, the regulation applies to all loans which are secured, directly or indirectly by margin stock; if the loan is also for the purpose of purchasing or carrying margin stock, the margin requirements of the regulation apply. An exception to the general rule applies to lenders who extend credit via an eligible employee stock option plan which will be used to purchase margin stock of the employer.

Margin stock includes any equity security listed on or having unlisted trading privileges on a national stock exchange, any debt security convertible into such a security, most mutual funds, and any security included on the Board's List of OTC margin stocks (published three times annually and available at the Board or from any Federal Reserve bank). SEE ALSO REGULATION T, U AND X.

**REGULATION H**  Defines the membership requirements for state-chartered banks, describes membership privileges and conditions imposed on these banks, explains financial reporting requirements, and sets out procedures for requesting approval to establish branches and for requesting voluntary withdrawal from membership. The regulation sets forth the procedures for state-chartered banks to become members of the Federal Reserve System, as well as the privileges and requirements of membership. State-chartered member banks are prohibited from engaging in practices that are unsafe or unsound or that result in violation of law, rule, or regulation. The regulation imposes specific restrictions on the conduct of some banking practices, including issuance of letters of credit, acceptances, and lending on the security of improved real estate or mobile homes located in flood hazard areas. The regulation also requires state-chartered member banks, acting as securities transfer agents, to register with the Federal Reserve Board and imposes requirements on registered State-member bank transfer agents or clearing agencies.

**REGULATION I**  Requires each bank joining the Federal Reserve System to subscribe to the stock of its District Reserve Bank in an amount equal to 6 percent of the member bank's capital and surplus. Half the total must be paid on approval. The remainder is subject to call by the Board of Governors. A 6 percent dividend is paid on paid-in portions of Reserve Bank stock. The stock is not transferable and cannot be used as collateral. Whenever a member bank increases or decreases its permanent capitalization, it must adjust its ownership of Reserve Bank stock to maintain the same ratio of stock to capital. Payment for additional shares of Reserve Bank stock, cancellation of shares, as well as semi-annual dividend payments, are made through the member bank's reserve account. A member bank's ownership of Federal Reserve stock is subject to cancellation on discontinuance of operations, insolvency, or voluntary liquidation, conversion to nonmember status through merger or acquisition, or voluntary or involuntary termination of membership.

**REGULATION J**  Establishes procedures, duties and responsibilities among Federal Reserve Banks, the senders and payers of checks and other cash items and noncash items, and the originators and recipients of transfers of funds. Regulation J provides a legal framework for depository institutions to collect checks and other cash items, and to settle balances through the Federal Reserve System. It specifies terms and conditions under which Reserve Banks will receive items for collection from depository institutions and present items to depository institutions and establishes rules under which depository institutions return unpaid items. The regulation also specifies terms and conditions under which Reserve Banks will receive and deliver transfers of funds from and to depository institutions. The regulation is supplemented by operating circulars issued by the Reserve Banks and detailing more specific terms and conditions under which they will handle checks and other cash items, and transfers of funds.

**REGULATION K**  Governs the international banking operations of banking organizations and of foreign banks in the United States. Corporations organized to engage in international banking or other financial operations are chartered by the

Board of Governors under Section 25(a) of the Federal Reserve Act. This section of the act was introduced as an amendment in 1919 by Senator Walter E. Edge of New Jersey. Thus, these corporations are known as "Edge Corporations." The regulation permits Edge Corporations to engage in a broad range of international banking and financial activities, subject to supervision, while limiting transactions within the U.S. to those clearly international in character. It also imposes reserve requirements, as specified in Regulation D, on certain deposits of these corporations and specifies prudential limits on their operations. The regulation further authorizes, and sets forth the rules governing, Edge Corporation and bank holding company investment in de novo or existing export trading companies. As to foreign bank operations, the regulation reflects limitations on interstate banking and specific exemptions from nonbanking prohibitions. With respect to loans by domestic banking organizations to foreign borrowers, the regulation provides for the establishment of special reserves against certain international assets which have been impaired and provides rules for accounting for fees on international loans.

**REGULATION L** Restricts the interlocking relationships that a management official may have with depository organizations to avoid restraints on competition among depository organizations. The regulation prohibits a management official of a state member bank or bank holding company from serving simultaneously as a management official of another depository organization if both organizations are not affiliated, or are very large, or are located in the same local area.

**REGULATION M** Implements the consumer leasing provisions of the Truth-in-Lending Act. Regulation M applies to leases of personal property for more than 4 months for personal, family, or household use. It requires leasing companies to disclose in writing the cost of a lease, including security deposit, monthly payments, license, registration, taxes and maintenance fees, and, in the case of an open end lease, whether a "balloon payment" may be applied. It also requires written disclosure of the terms of a lease, including insurance, guarantees, responsibility for servicing the property, standards for wear and tear, and any option to buy.

**REGULATION N** Governs relationships and transactions among Reserve Banks and foreign banks, bankers, and governments, and describes the role of the Board of Governors in these relationships and transactions. This regulation is internal to the Federal Reserve System and gives the Board the responsibility for approving in advance negotiations or agreements by Reserve Banks with any foreign banks, bankers or governments. Reserve Banks must keep the board fully advised of all foreign relationships, transactions, and agreements. Under direction of the Federal Open Market Committee, a Reserve Bank maintaining accounts with a foreign bank may undertake negotiations, agreements, or contracts to facilitate open market transactions. Reserve Banks must report to the Board at least quarterly on accounts they maintain with foreign banks.

**REGULATION O** Prohibits member banks from extending credit to their own executive officers, and insured banks that maintain correspondent relationships with other banks from extending credit to one another's executive officers, on preferential terms. Regulation O also limits the amount of credit that may be extended by a member bank to its executive officers. Each executive officer and principal shareholder of an insured bank is to report annually, to the bank's board of directors, the amount of his or her own indebtedness, and that of "related interests," to each of the insured bank's correspondent banks outstanding 10 days before the report is filed. The range of interest rates on such loans and other terms and conditions of the loans must also be reported. A "related interest" is a company controlled by political or campaign committees controlled by or benefiting bank officials and shareholders. Each insured bank is required to include with its quarterly report of condition the aggregate extensions of credit by the bank to its executive officers and principal shareholders, together with the number of these individuals whose extensions of credit from the bank are 5 percent or more of their bank's equity capital or $500,000, whichever is less. The regulation also requires each insured bank to disclose publicly, upon request, the names of its executive officers and principal shareholders who had extensions of credit outstanding to them or their related interests from their own or correspondent bank(s) of 5 percent or more of the reporting bank's equity capital or $500,000, whichever is less.

**REGULATION P** Sets minimum standards for security devices and procedures state-chartered member banks must establish to discourage robberies, burglaries, and larcenies and to assist in identifying and apprehending persons who commit such acts. A member bank must appoint a security officer to develop and administer a security program at least equal to the requirements of the regulation. The program must be in writing and approved by the bank's directors.

**REGULATION Q** Describes the maximum rates of interest that may be paid by member banks on time and savings deposits. Under the Depository Institutions Deregulation and Monetary Control Act of 1980, limitations on maximum rates of interest that may be paid on time and savings deposits were to be phased out gradually and eliminated by 1986. In addition, Regulation Q includes rules governing the advertising of interest on deposits by member banks.

**REGULATION R** Aims at avoiding interlocking relationships between securities dealers and member banks, and thus any potential conflict of interest, collusion, or undue influence on member bank investment policies or investment advice to customers.

**REGULATION S** Establishes the rates and conditions for reimbursement to financial institutions for providing records to a government authority. Regulation S implements that section of the Right to Financial Privacy Act of 1978 requiring government authorities to pay a reasonable fee to financial institutions for providing financial records of individuals and small partnerships to federal agencies. Costs for searching for, reproducing or transporting books, papers, records, or other data requested are covered, with exceptions for such information as records furnished in connection with government loan programs or Internal Revenue summons.

**REGULATION T** Governs credit extensions by securities brokers and dealers, including all members of national securities exchanges. The regulation applies to broker-dealers and all national securities exchange members. In general, such entities may not extend credit to their customers unless the loan is secured by margin securities nor may they arrange for credit to be extended by others on terms better than they themselves are permitted to extend. The term margin securities includes any equity security listed on or having unlisted trading privileges on a national securities exchange, most mutual funds, OTC margin bonds, meeting criteria specified by the Board, any OTC stock designated by the Securities and Exchange Commission as qualified for trading in the national market system, and any security included on the Federal Reserve Board's List of OTC Margin Stocks, published four times annually and available from any Federal Reserve Bank. Generally, a broker-dealer may not extend credit on margin securities used as collateral in excess of the percentage of current market value permitted by the Board. The Board also prescribes rules governing cash transactions among brokers, dealers, their customers, and other brokers and dealers. It also limits the sources from which borrowing brokers and dealers may secure funds in the ordinary course of their business. The regulation permits any registered self-regulatory organization or registered broker-dealer to establish more stringent rules than those required by the regulation. SEE ALSO REGULATION G, U AND X.

**REGULATION U** Governs extension of credit by banks for purchasing and carrying margin securities. The regulation applies to banks which extend credit secured, directly or indirectly, by margin stock. Any time a loan is made in which a margin stock serves as collateral, the bank must have the customer execute a purpose statement regardless of the use of the loan. The margin requirements imposed by the regulation apply if the loan is both margin stock secured and is for the purpose of purchasing or carrying margin securities. Certain exceptions exist for specified special purpose loans to brokers-dealers, for loans to qualified employee stock option plans, for loans to plan lenders, or for emergencies. For the purposes of this regulation, the definition of margin stock is the same as for Regulation T. SEE ALSO REGULATION G, T, AND X.

**REGULATION V** Facilitates and expedites the financing of contractors, subcontractors and others involved in national defense work. The Defense Production Act of 1950 and Executive Order 10480, as amended, authorize several federal departments and agencies to guarantee loans by private financing institutions to contractors, subcontractors, and others involved in national defense work. Regulation V spells out the authority granted to Reserve Banks, as fiscal agents of the United States, to assist federal department and agencies in making and administering these loan guarantees and sets maximum rates of interest, guarantee fees, and commitment fees.

**REGULATION W** Revoked in 1952, Regulation W prescribed minimum downpayments, maximum maturities, and other terms applicable to extensions of consumer credit. Such action was authorized by Executive Order during World War II, and by congressional legislation in 1947-48 and again during the Korean conflict. With repeal of authorizing legislation in 1952, Regulation W was revoked.

**REGULATION X** Extends the provisions of Regulations G, T and U (governing extensions of credit for purchasing or carrying securities in the United States) to certain borrowers and to certain types of credit extensions not specifically covered by those regulations. The regulation applies to persons who obtain credit outside the United States to purchase or carry United States securities, or within the United States to purchase or carry any securities. In general, whenever the regulation applies, the borrower is responsible for ensuring that the credit conforms to one of the three margin regulations. The determination as to which one applies is dependent

upon the nature of the lender and is specified in the regulation. SEE ALSO REGULA-
TIONS G, T AND U.

**REGULATION Y**   Relates to the bank and nonbank expansion of bank holding
companies and to the divestiture of impermissible nonbank interests. Under the
Bank Holding Company Act of 1956, as amended, a bank holding company is a
company which directly or indirectly owns or controls a bank. The regulation contains presumptions and procedures the Federal Reserve Board uses to determine
whether a company controls a bank. The regulation also explains the procedures for
obtaining Board approval to become a bank holding company and procedures to
be followed by bank holding companies acquiring voting shares in banks or nonbank companies. The Board has specified in the regulation those nonbank activities
that are closely related to banking and therefore permissible for bank holding companies.

**REGULATION Z**   Prescribes uniform methods of computing the cost of credit,
disclosure of credit terms, and procedures for resolving billing errors on certain
credit accounts. The credit provisions of the regulation apply to all persons who extend credit more than 25 times a year or, in the case of real estate, more than 5 times
a year. Consumer credit is generally defined as credit offered or extended to individuals for personal, family or household purposes, where the credit is repayable
in more than four installments or for which a finance charge is imposed.

The major provisions of the regulation require lenders to provide borrowers
with meaningful, written information on essential credit terms, including the cost
of credit expressed as a finance charge and an annual percentage rate; respond to
consumer complaints of billing errors on certain credit accounts within a specific
period; identify credit transactions on periodic statements of open end credit accounts; provide certain rights regarding credit cards; inform customers of the right
to rescind certain residential mortgage transactions within a specified period; and
comply with special requirements when advertising credit.

**REJECT ITEMS**   Checks, drafts, or electronic payment that cannot be processed
when presented for payment due to unreadable microencoding, miscoding of the
dollar amount or account number, an incorrect routing or transit mumber, stale or
post dating, insufficient funds or other such reason. Reject items require special
handling which usually results in the imposition of a fee or special handling charge.

**REMIC**   SEE REAL ESTATE MORTGAGE INVESTMENT CONDUIT.

**REMITTANCE**   Generally refers to proceeds or payments. For example, remittance means the proceeds from a check submitted to another bank for collection
while it can also refer to the payment toward satisfaction of a debt. Payment can
be either cash or cash equivalents, such as checks, drafts and other negotiable instruments.

**REMITTER**   The party who is the source of funds to the receiver.

**REMOTE SERVICE UNIT**   A free standing automated teller machine or cash dis-
penser. The term originated when the Federal Home Loan Bank Board, during the
1970s, began approving applications from savings and loan associations to establish
self-service automated teller machines at locations distant from branch offices.

**RENEWAL**  Extending the maturity of an existing loan obligation. Renewals are generally accomplished through the substitution of a new promissory note for a matured or maturing one and the cancellation of the old note.

**REPO**  SEE REPURCHASE AGREEMENT.

**REPORT OF CONDITION**  SEE CALL REPORT.

**REPOSSESSION**  When other attempts to persuade the borrower to make payments that are past due are ineffective, the lender may seize, or take possession of, the collateral securing the loan.

**REPUDIATION**  The intentional refusal to pay.

**REPURCHASE AGREEMENT (REPO)**  An arrangement by which the borrower of debt securities may borrow money by selling the securities to a buyer while at the same time promising to repurchase them at a fixed price. Also known as a buyback agreement. Repurchase agreements involving the Federal Reserve usually have maturities of 7 days or less but are most frequently overnight transactions for the purchase of Treasury securities.

**RESERVABLE DEPOSITS**  Deposits subject to the reserve requirements under Federal Regulation D such as transaction accounts, savings accounts, and nonpersonal time deposits. SEE ALSO REGULATION D.

**RESERVE FOR BAD DEBTS**  A reserve account to which bad debt losses are charged.

**RESERVE REQUIREMENTS**  The balances that must be maintained by depository institutions with the appropriate Federal Reserve Bank, in cash, or at a correspondent bank as funds set aside in the form of reserves. The reserve requirement ratio determines the growth of deposits that can be supported by each additional dollar of reserves. The Federal Reserve, in addition, has the right to impose special supplementary reserves of up to 4% in cases where the Fed believes it is necessary to increase reserves to carry out monetary policy. The Board of Governors may also, after consulting with Congress, impose a reserve of any ratio on any bank liability in periods of extraordinary circumstances for up to 180 days. SEE ALSO REGULATION D.

**RESIDENTIAL MORTGAGE**  A purchase money or other loan secured by real property generally consisting of a 1 to 4 family dwelling.

**RESIDENTIAL PROPERTY**  Real property improved by single family homes, dwellings for from two to four families, and individual units of condominiums and cooperatives, and used or intended to be used for residential purposes.

**RESOLUTION TRUST CORPORATION (RTC)**  A corporation established by the Financial Institutions Reform, Recovery and Enforcement Act of 1989 (FIRREA) to transfer assets of insolvent savings and loan associations to financially sound institutions and to liquidate troubled real estate and other assets. The RTC is managed by the Federal Deposit Insurance Corporation (FDIC) and has responsibility for managing the assets and liabilities of S&Ls that became insolvent between 1989 and August 1992. The RTC derives a portion of its funds from the Resolution Funding Corporation (RFC), a corporation also established by FIRREA to raise funds for use in liquidating insolvent savings and loan associations. Also called Refcorp., the RFC is authorized to borrow through the issuance of long term bonds (such as 30 year zero coupon securities). Interest on the RFC bonds is to be paid by the RTC, the savings and loan industry, and from U.S. Treasury funds. The Resolution Trust Corporation's authorization as a receiver of insolvent thrifts expires in 1996.

**RESPA**   SEE REAL ESTATE SETTLEMENT PROCEDURES ACT.

**RESPONSE TIME**   The time needed, measured in seconds, to electronically approve or deny an authorization request made by terminal inquiry.

**RESTRICTED ASSETS**   Assets such as cash or other resources, the use of which is restricted by legal or contractual procedures providing limited right of access or withdrawal.

**RETAIL BANKING**   Banking services offered to the general public. May also be referred to as consumer banking and consists of a group of banking services such as installment loans, mortgage loans, credit card services, personal time deposits, and IRAs in contrast to corporate banking or business banking.

**RETAINED EARNINGS**   Accumulated and undistributed earnings which have not been paid out to stockholders or transferred to a surplus account. Part of a bank's capital or net worth.

**RETURN ITEMS**   Negotiable instruments such as checks, drafts or notes that have been sent by an originating bank to a drawee bank for collection and payment and are returned unpaid so as to avoid a loss or to provide the originator to correct any errors or irregularities on the instrument and then present the items a second time for collection.

**RETURN ON ASSETS (ROA)**   A key profitability ratio which divides net income by total assets to indicate how efficiently those assets are utilized.

**RETURN ON EQUITY (ROE)**   A key profitability ratio which divides net income by net worth to determine how effectively equity capital is invested.

**RETURN ON INVESTMENT (ROI)**   A key profitability ratio which divides net profit by total assets.

**REVENUE**   Gross inflow of cash resulting from the sale of goods or services.

**REVERSE MORTGAGE**   A mortgage loan in which the borrower, under a formula based upon the accumulated equity in the property affected, receives periodic payments from the lender. Designed for retirees and other fixed-income homeowners who owe little or nothing against their residences, it typically permits them to use some or all of the equity in the home as supplemental income while retaining ownership. The ultimate source of repayment is the borrower's estate. Reverse mortgages may be structured as rising debt loans with periodic (i.e., monthly) advances to the borrower, or disbursed in a lump sum payment. There is no standard method for underwriting the loans or distributing the proceeds.

**REVOLVING CREDIT**   A commercial or consumer credit facility which does not have a fixed payment schedule calculated to amortize the outstanding balance over a predetermined period of time. Examples of revolving credit include a business line of credit (under which the borrowing entity may draw down the line at any time or repay it in full without penalty), a credit card, an overdraft protection facility which gives consumers the option of borrowing against a pre-approved line of credit, or a home equity line of credit.

**REVOLVING LETTER OF CREDIT** A letter of credit issued for a specific amount and automatically renewed for the same amount at the end of a pre-set period.

**RIAL** Monetary unit of Iran, Oman and Yemen.

**RIEL** National currency of Cambodia and Kampuchea.

**RIGHT OF OFFSET** Sometimes also referred to as right of set-off, a clause in a loan agreement which allows the lender to use the balances in any account held on deposit in the name of the borrower as full or partial payment for the loan in the case of default.

**RIGHT OF REDEMPTION** The right of a defaulted borrower to cure the default by paying the loan current plus the fees associated with the filing of foreclosure, and redeem the mortgaged property. SEE ALSO REDEMPTION.

**RIGHT OF RESCISSION** A provision in the Truth-in-Lending Act, as implemented by federal Regulation Z, which gives the borrower a "cooling off period" of three days during which he may cancel a transaction which is to be secured by real estate. During this rescission period, no interest, fees or other charges may accrue. SEE ALSO REGULATION Z.

**RISK BASED CAPITAL** A bank's risk based capital ratio is determined by dividing its qualifying capital by its weighted risk assets. Capital regulations adopted by all regulatory agencies, designed to encourage banks to keep a sufficient cushion of equity capital to support balance sheet assets, and to include off-balance sheet items in the computation of capital adequacy.

The risk based capital formula increases the mandatory capital from 5.5% of assets to 8% (4% of which must be in Tier 1 capital which is common stock plus noncumulative preferred stock and 4% in other types of capital which includes loan loss reserves, perpetual preferred stock, hybrid capital instruments and subordinated debt). The risk based capital guidelines are a fundamental change in calculation of bank capital from previous measures of calculating capital adequacy. Capital determination is shifted from the liability side of the balance sheet to the asset side, using a formula that assigns specific risk weights to different groups of assets. Assets given a 100% risk rating, such as commercial loans and consumer installment loans, require an institution to maintain total equity capital (the total of Tier 1 and Tier 2 capital) equal to 8% of the asset's book value. On the other end of the spectrum, assets having a risk rating of zero, such as cash and U.S. government securities, require no capital to be held in reserve.

**RIYAL** Monetary unit of Saudi Arabia.

**ROA** SEE RETURN ON ASSETS.

**ROE** SEE RETURN ON EQUITY.

**ROI** SEE RETURN ON INVESTMENT.

**ROLLOVER** To extend the maturity of, or to renew, a loan or other obligation, or to reinvest a maturing certificate of deposit. A rollover mortgage is one in which the finance charge is periodically adjusted, such as a "Canadian Rollover" mortgage, where the loan is renegotiated at a new rate every five years.

**RTC** SEE RESOLUTION TRUST CORPORATION.

**RUBLE** Monetary unit of Russia.

**RULE OF 78ths** Also known as the "sum of the digits" method, the Rule of 78ths is a mathematical formula used in consumer loans to compute the interest to be rebated when a borrower pays early a loan in which the finance charges were determined by using the "add-on" or "discounted interest" methods. 78 is the sum of the digits 1 through 12. Therefore, for example, in the first month of a 12 month loan, the borrower had use of the entire amount borrowed and the finance charge is 12/78 of the total interest. In the second month it is 11/78, in the third month 10/78, and so on.

**RUPEE** The national currency of India, the Maldives, Mauritius, Nepal, Pakistan, the Seychelles, and Sri Lanka.

**RUPIAH** The monetary unit of Indonesia.

# S

**SAFE DEPOSIT BOX** A numbered or otherwise identifiable storage container of various sizes maintained in the vault area of a bank and rented to customers for the storage and safekeeping of personal property. Each container is kept in a corresponding compartment, access to which can be made only by the customer and a designated employee of the bank.

**SAFEKEEPING** A service by which securities and valuables of all types, particularly those too large to be kept in safe deposit boxes, are kept in the vault of a bank.

**SAFETY AND SOUNDNESS** Regulatory objective of federal and state chartered banks.

**SAIF** SEE SAVINGS ASSOCIATION INSURANCE FUND.

**SALE AND LEASEBACK** Sale of an asset and an agreement to lease it back from the purchaser on a long term basis. Common in real estate and luxury items such as private aircraft and yachts, and generally motivated by potential balance sheet or income tax benefits.

**SAME DAY FUNDS** Funds which are available for withdrawal or transfer on the same day as deposited or presented, subject to the net settlement of accounts between involved banks.

**SAVINGS ACCOUNT** An interest bearing deposit account, usually in the form of either a passbook account or a money market deposit account.

**SAVINGS AND LOAN ASSOCIATION**   A federally or state chartered financial institution which, by law, is required to make a certain percentage of all loans as home mortgages. Savings and loan associations may also make consumer loans, issue credit cards, offer some commercial loans to the extent permitted by law. Mutual savings and loans are, in theory, owned by the depositors; however, many savings and loans are owned by stockholders through either direct ownership or holding companies.

**SAVINGS ASSOCIATION INSURANCE FUND (SAIF)**   The successor to the Federal Savings and Loan Insurance Corporation. It is operated by the Federal Deposit Insurance Corporation along with its counterpart, the Bank Insurance Fund. Insurance premiums paid by SAIF-insured savings and loans are set by the FDIC; financial institutions offering SAIF-insured deposits display the insurance logo stating, "backed by the full faith and credit of the United States Government."

**SAVINGS BOND**   SEE U.S. SAVINGS BOND.

**SBA**   SEE SMALL BUSINESS ADMINISTRATION.

**SCHILLING**   National currency of Austria.

**SCRIP**   Any temporary document that entitles the holder or bearer to receive stock or a fractional share of stock in a corporation, cash, or some other article of value upon demand.

**SEASONED LOAN**   A loan that has been on the books for over a year and reflects a satisfactory payment record.

**SECOND MORTGAGE**   A mortgage that is subordinate to the first mortgage but senior to other liens and generally characterized by a shorter amortization.

**SECONDARY MARKET**   A supplier of additional liquidity to mortgage lenders who sell mortgage loans to a national market where pools are assembled and sold to investors. Mortgage originators have access to pools of capital managed by pension funds, insurance companies, and other institutional buyers of mortgage backed bonds.

**SECURITY AGREEMENT**   That loan document which gives the lender a security interest in the collateral pledged. The agreement describes the collateral in detail and is signed and dated by the borrower. A security agreement may cover non-possessory liens in intangibles such as accounts receivable, or possessory liens in which the lender holds the collateral, such as stock certificates. The agreement generally gives the lender control over the collateral in the case of default in order that the collateral be used in partial or total satisfaction of the loan amount outstanding.

**SELF-DIRECTED IRA**   An individual retirement account that gives the depositor/investor control over the form of investments and the option to change investments. SEE ALSO INDIVIDUAL RETIREMENT ACCOUNT.

**SEPARATE TRADING OF REGISTERED INTEREST AND PRINCIPAL (STRIPS)**
A U.S. Treasury security in zero-coupon form that accrues interest during the life of the bond and pays interest in a lump sum at maturity.

**SERVICE CHARGE**   Bank fees for maintaining or servicing accounts, for handling and processing returned items, or charges imposed when collected deposit balances fall below prescribed limits.

**SERVICING AGREEMENT**   A contract between a bank and an institutional buyer of a loan sold to the secondary market, covering, in general, the duties, fees, and auditing requirements of the seller and the buyer's right to conduct periodic inspections of the seller's records.

**SET-OFF**   Lenders generally have the right to seize deposits of a borrower to satisfy all or part of an obligation in default. The Truth-in-Lending Act, however, prohibits the right of set-off in consumer credit transactions.

**SETTLEMENT**   Part of the accounting process of the check system, settlement is that point at which funds are available for withdrawal. It is reached when the respective debit and credit positions of the banks involved in a transfer of funds have been completed. Settlement is provisional in the case of checks, automated clearing house transfers, and other payments between banks because of the possibility of insufficient funds in the initiating account to cover the payment.

**SHARED NETWORK**   An automated teller network which is shared by many financial institutions and open to customers of each member, as contrasted with a "proprietary network."

**SHEKEL**   National currency of Israel.

**SHILLING**   National currency of Kenya, Somalia, Tanzania, and Uganda.

**SHORT TERM FINANCING**   A loan or line of credit with a term of one year or less.

**SILVER CERTIFICATE**   Replaced by federal reserve notes in 1967, silver certificates were U.S. paper currency issued by the Treasury Department.

**SIMPLE INTEREST**   When interest is computed on the principal balance only, without compounding, it is referred to as simple interest. For example, simple interest at the rate of 9.25% for a year on a loan of $1,000 is $92.50.

**SMALL BUSINESS ADMINISTRATION (SBA)**   Established in 1953, the SBA is an independent federal agency chartered to provide financial assistance to small businesses by making loans to borrowers who are unable to obtain conventional financing. A guarantor of loans made by banks and other financial institutions, the SBA also provides disaster assistance to individuals and small businesses. The Small Business Administration also licenses small business investment companies which provide equity capital and long term loans to small businesses.

**SMALL SAVER CERTIFICATE**   A time deposit with no minimum balance at a fixed interest rate and a term of 18 months. These were established in 1980 to allow banks and savings and loan institutions to compete with money market funds for small consumer deposits, generally under $10,000. When interest rate ceilings on bank and savings and loan time deposits with maturities in excess of 31 days were removed in 1983, the Small Saver Certificates were no longer in demand.

**SMART CARD**   A bank card with an internal memory supplied by a computer chip, giving it the capability of storing pertinent information and performing certain calculations. Some capabilities may include verification of the cardholder's personal identification number, retail purchase authorization, account balance verification, and storage of personal data such as account relationships with the cardholder's financial institution.

**SMURF** A money launderer. Drug traffickers, in response to the $10,000 limitation for financial transaction reporting imposed by the Bank Secrecy Act, might break their deposits of currency into multiples of less than $10,000 each and hire couriers ("smurfs") to travel around the United States purchasing cashier's checks or negotiable certificates of deposit in amounts of less than $10,000 each. Once delivered back to the individual source, these negotiable instruments would be transferred outside the United States for either local offshore deposit or investment, or to be wired back into the country as "clean" money.

**SOL** National currency of Peru.

**SOLE PROPRIETOR** The owner of a business which is unincorporated and controlled by one person and may be operating under a fictitious name in lieu of the name of the sole proprietor. Sole proprietor accounts are treated by the banks as individual accounts, and unlike corporations, may open and maintain interest bearing transaction accounts.

**SPLIT BORROWING** The practice of borrowing money from more than one bank, usually frowned upon and discouraged by lenders.

**SPREAD** The net difference between the interest earned on all interest earning assets and the bank's cost of funds or interest paid on all interest bearing liabilities.

**SPREADSHEET** A paper or electronic accounting worksheet consisting of rows and columns allowing for the representation of debits and credits in an organized and analytical manner. Computer programs offering electronic spreadsheets have become invaluable in financial forecasting due to their speed, accuracy, and ability to provide "what-if" hypotheses.

**STALE DATED** A negotiable instrument which is dated more than six months prior to date of presentment need not be honored under the terms of the Uniform Commercial Code.

**STANDBY COMMITMENT** The promise by a bank to lend money to a borrower upon the occurrence of an agreed upon condition. Once that condition is satisfied, the standby commitment is converted to a credit facility such as a line of credit.

**STANDBY LETTER OF CREDIT** A liability of the issuing bank contingent upon the bank customer's inability to perform under the customer's agreement with a third party, who becomes the beneficiary of the standby letter of credit.

**STATE BANK** A bank which is chartered and supervised by the state banking department of the chartering state. State chartered banks may be members of the Federal Reserve System and are required by the Federal Deposit Insurance Corporation to follow Federal Reserve Board regulations even if they are not Federal Reserve member banks. State banks differ from national banks which are chartered and supervised by the Office of the Comptroller of the Currency.

**STATE CERTIFIED APPRAISER**  Any individual who has satisfied the requirements for certification in a state or territory whose criteria for certification as a real estate appraiser meet the minimum criteria for certification issued by the Appraiser Qualifications Board of the Appraisal Foundation. No individual shall be a state certified appraiser unless such individual has achieved a passing grade upon a suitable examination administered by a state or territory that is consistent with and equivalent to the Uniform State Certification Examination issued or endorsed by the Appraiser Qualifications Board of the Appraisal Foundation. In addition, the Appraisal Subcommittee must not have issued a finding that the policies, or procedures of the state or territory are inconsistent with Title XI of FIRREA. Bank regulatory agencies may, from time to time, impose additional qualification criteria for certified appraisers performing appraisals in connection with federally related transactions within their jurisdiction.

**STATE LICENSED APPRAISER**  Any individual who has satisfied the requirements for licensing in a state or territory where the licensing procedures comply with Title XI of FIRREA and where the Appraisal Subcommittee has not issued a finding that the policies, practices, or procedures of the state or territory are inconsistent with Title XI. As with State Certified Appraisers, bank regulators may impose additional qualification criteria for licensed appraisers performing appraisals in connection with federally related transactions with their jurisdiction.

**STATEMENT**  A detailed record, prepared by a bank for a depositor, listing all checks cleared and deposits posted, transfers between accounts, service charges and any other transaction which affected the depositor's account during the reported statement cycle. A reported statement cycle is usually the preceding calendar month.

**STOP PAYMENT**  An order by a depositor to a bank directing the bank not to honor a specific check or a group of checks.

**STRIP**  A security created by separating the bond principal from the interest payment coupons. There are two types of strip securities, generic STRIPs (SEE SEPARATE TRADING OF REGISTERED INTEREST AND PRINCIPAL) and those zero-coupons issued by brokerage houses, such as Certificates of Accrual on Treasury Securities (CATS) and Treasury Income Growth Receipts (TIGR). SEE ALSO ZERO COUPON SECURITIES.

**SUBCHAPTER S**  A corporation with 35 or fewer shareholders may elect to be taxed as a partnership. A small business corporation qualifies for the privilege of electing to be taxed as a partnership or sole proprietorship if it meets certain tests set forth in 28 USCS 1371(a) and (c). These tests are strictly applied, and the failure to meet all of them will defeat the right to make the election:
    (1) the corporation must be a domestic corporation;
    (2) none of the shareholders may be nonresident aliens;
    (3) there must be only one class of outstanding shares with equal rights;
    (4) all the shareholders must be individuals or estates; none of the shareholders may be corporations, partnerships, trusts or the like;
    (5) the corporation must not be a group of affiliated corporations.
    To be effective for a particular taxable year, an election by a corporation to be treated as an "S corporation" must be made in the first month of the taxable year

involved or in the last month of the preceding taxable year. A small business that elects to be treated as an S corporation is generally exempt from all federal income taxes on its earnings and profits. Instead, the shareholders must include in their income their proportionate share of the corporation's undistributed taxable income, regardless of whether the corporation actually makes any distributions. The principal tax advantages in a corporation's election to be treated as an S corporation may be summarized as follows:

(1) avoidance of double tax;

(2) pass through of capital gains;

(3) pass through operating losses; and

(4) avoidance of accumulated earnings tax.

The election of a small business corporation to be treated as an S corporation may be terminated, directly and voluntarily, by revocation of the election by unanimous consent of all persons who are shareholders on the day of revocation.

**SUBORDINATION AGREEMENT** An agreement in which another interested party grants the bank a priority claim or preference to the assets of the borrower.

**SUCRE** National currency of Ecuador.

**SUPER NOW ACCOUNT** Depositors who are eligible to hold Negotiable Order of Withdrawal (NOW) accounts are also eligible for Super Now accounts which were authorized in January 1983 and have no interest rate ceilings, unlimited deposit and withdrawal capability, and a minimum balance of $2,500 thus combining the features of NOW accounts and Money Market Deposit Accounts (MMDA).

**SWING LOAN** Short term financing generally used to cover a home buyer's financing costs when selling one residence and purchasing another to provide funds needed to purchase the new home before they are available from the sale of the former residence. Also called a "bridge loan."

# T

**TAKA** National currency of Bangladesh.

**TAKE OUT** Usually the replacement of a temporary loan with a permanent loan. For example, a construction loan granted for a 1-year term is due and payable at the end of the year. The construction project, a single family residence, is now complete and the borrower/builder desires to pay off ("take out") the construction loan with a 30-year mortgage. A *take out commitment*, the promise to make the 30-year mortgage, is obtained from a *take out lender*, usually a savings and loan association or federal savings bank, to make the *take out loan*, a 30 year conforming first mortgage loan, to pay off the temporary construction loan.

**TALA** Currency unit of Western Samoa.

**TANGIBLE ASSET** Material capable of being appraised at an actual or approximate value. Tangible assets include real property, furniture, fixtures, machinery, vehicles, equipment, and so on, as compared to intangible assets such as goodwill, copyrights and trademarks.

**TANGIBLE NET WORTH**  Equity measured by common stock, cash, and investments, less intangible assets (e.g., good will or franchise rights).

**TAX EQUITY AND FISCAL RESPONSIBILITY ACT OF 1982 (TEFRA)**  Federal legislation designed to ensure that both business and individual taxpayers pay their fair share of the total tax burden. Aside from the fundamental objective of increasing government tax revenues, TEFRA was intended to curtail perceived abuses and unintended benefits in the tax system, ensure better compliance with the existing tax laws, and impose increased excise taxes on selected products and services.

**TAX REFORM ACT OF 1986**  Perhaps the most important change in the United States tax structure in over 50 years, the act:
* Established a new corporate alternative minimum tax on depreciable expenses, such as accelerated depreciation on capital equipment;
* Imposed, effective in 1988, a 5% income tax surcharge for some taxpayers;
* Restructured the allowance for loan and lease losses (loan loss reserves) for large banks (above $500 million in assets) allowing a deduction for losses only when loans are written off;
* Reduced to $7,000 a year from $30,000 a year the limit on individual contributions to 401(k) plans;
* Eliminated from equipment lessors the previously allowed 15% investment tax credit;
* Restricted the application of passive tax shelters to gains or losses from investment portfolios only, rather than from the taxpayer's gross income;
* Changed the deductibility of Individual Retirement Account contributions by allowing total deductibility only by those taxpayers who (1) were not covered by a qualified plan or (2) whose joint gross income was less than $40,000 or single income was less than $25,000;
* Incorporated a 5-year phase out of consumer interest deductions resulting in zero allowance for interest charges effective in 1991;
* Allowed for a 3-year carry back and 15-year carry forward of net operating losses;
* Imposed a corporate alternative minimum tax of 20% on nonessential municipal bonds issued after August 7, 1986;
* Limited foreign tax credits on non–U.S. investments, including financial services income, passive investments, and dividends from foreign corporations in which a U.S. corporation holds a minority interest;
* Authorized the sale of mortgage backed securities through Real Estate Mortgage Investment Conduits (REMICs);
* Eliminated the 100% deduction of interest attributed to municipal bonds acquired after August 7, 1986;
* Prohibited the use of cash-basis accounting by banks;
* Increased to 27½ years from 19 years the recovery period for residential real estate for depreciation purposes and provided for straight line depreciation;
* Increased to 31½ years from 19 years the recovery period for commercial real estate for depreciation purposes and provided for straight line depreciation;

- Taxed Clifford Trusts to the trust grantor and imposed a calendar year accounting period for tax purposes;
- Eliminated the use of the installment method for sales made under revolving credit plans.

**TEFRA** SEE TAX EQUITY AND FISCAL RESPONSIBILITY ACT OF 1982.

**TELEPHONE BILL PAYMENT** A service offered by financial institutions to consumers providing for the payment of certain recurring bills by automatic debit triggered through the use of a touch-tone telephone and thus eliminating the requirement to write and mail a personal check.

**TELEPHONE TRANSFER** The transfer of funds between accounts triggered through the telephonic order of the account holder as contrasted with the written order.

**TELLER** A bank employee who handles transactions for customers such as cashing checks, accepting deposits, and other banking services generally conducted from behind a counter usually referred to as a "teller line." Tellers may have specific areas of responsibility as denoted by additional titles such as "paying and receiving teller," "full service teller," "merchant teller," and "vault teller."

**TENANCY** The holding of real property by one of several estates. Some examples are:
- JOINT TENANCY is an estate in fee-simple, fee-tail, for life, for years, or at will, arising by purchase or grant to two or more persons. Joint tenants have one and the same interest, accruing by one and the same conveyance, commencing at one and the same time, and held by one and the same undivided possession.
- SEVERAL TENANCY is a tenancy which is separate, and not held jointly with another person;
- TENANCY BY THE ENTIRETY is created by a conveyance to a husband and wife, whereupon each becomes seized and possessed of the entire estate and after the death of one, the survivor takes the whole.
- TENANCY IN COMMON is the holding of an estate in land by different persons under different titles, but there must be a unity of possession and each must have the right to occupy the whole in common with his co-tenants.

**TENANT** Generally, one who holds or possesses real property belonging to another who is usually referred to as a landlord. The duration of the tenancy is usually fixed by an instrument referred to as a lease.

**TERM** The maturity period, usually expressed in months but frequently in years. Applies to loans or deposits and the phrase "long term," applicable to both, refers to a period in excess of one year. Term is also used to refer to the components of how a loan or deposit is structured. For example, loan terms include finance charge, annual percentage rate, fees, number of payments, and so forth. Term loan generally refers to a required and scheduled repayment of principal during the course of the loan.

**TERM LOAN** SEE TERM.

**TERMINATION** When either party pursuant to a power created by agreement or law puts an end to the contract otherwise than for its breach. On termination, all obligations which are still executory on both sides are discharged but any right based on prior breach or performance survives.

**TERMINATION STATEMENT**   A financing statement that records the termination of a lender's security interest upon satisfaction of the loan obligation. The termination statement (UCC-3) is required under the Uniform Commercial Code to be filed to release a lender's claim or security interest in a borrower's assets if a recorded lien (UCC-1) was previously filed by the lender with the secretary of state.

**TESTAMENTARY TRUST**   A trust established by the terms of a will, becoming irrevocable upon the death of the maker, or testator. SEE ALSO TRUST.

**THIRD PARTY CHECK**   A check made payable to a party other than the holder or the maker. Transferred by an endorsement such as "pay to the order of," the subsequent holder (endorsee) has all of the rights of the original endorser with respect to negotiation or subsequent endorsement.

**THIRD PARTY TRANSFER**   A deposit or withdrawal to or from an account belonging to someone other than the person who initiates the transaction.

**THRIFT INSTITUTION**   A general term often used for mutual savings banks, savings and loan associations, and credit unions as these institutions served to encourage personal savings.

**THRIFT INSTITUTIONS ADVISORY COUNCIL**   Representatives of savings banks, savings and loan associations, and credit unions who provide information and views on the special needs and problems of thrifts. The Council was established subsequent to the passage of the Monetary Control Act of 1980.

**TILA**   SEE TRUTH-IN-LENDING ACT.

**TIME DEPOSIT ACCOUNTS**   Deposit accounts which either limit or prohibit third-party transfers and, depending on the type of account, involves a reserve requirement smaller than that required for transaction accounts or no reserve requirement at all. Time deposit accounts include savings accounts, money market deposit accounts (MMDAs), and special time-deposit accounts that require a minimum seven-day maturity period and the imposition of limited early withdrawal penalties. Nonpersonal time deposits are defined as time deposits, including MMDAs, or any other savings deposit that represents funds in which any beneficial interest is held by a depositor that is not a natural person or funds that are deposited to the credit of a depositor that is not a natural person, other than a deposit to the credit of a trustee or other fiduciary if the entire beneficial interest in the deposit is held by one or more natural persons. Early withdrawal penalties are designed to help maintain distinctions between nonpersonal time deposits of different maturities for reserve requirement purposes. Any deposit accounts failing to meet the definition of either a time deposit or a savings deposit are considered transaction accounts subject to reserve requirements.

**TITLE DEFECT**   Any imperfection in the recording of ownership of real property, or an involuntary lien placed on the property by a creditor of the owner, or the failure to remove junior liens when required.

**TITLE INSURANCE**   Insurance that protects the buyer against losses resulting from liens or other claims which are not identified by the title search or claims not specifically listed as exemptions to the title insurance policy.

**TITLE SEARCH** The process by which the ownership of real property is verified by searching public records for successive transfers in the chain of ownership.

**TOTTEN TRUST** A trust created by the deposit of one's own funds into an account controlled by the depositor in his or her own name as trustee for another, who is named beneficiary. The trust is revocable during the lifetime of the trustee and is taxed to his estate upon death, although the balance is transferred to the beneficiary.

**TRACT DEVELOPMENT** A real estate development project of five units or more that is constructed or is to be constructed as a single development.

**TRANSACTION ACCOUNT** A deposit account such as a demand deposit, NOW account, Super NOW account, or other accounts which are accessible by negotiable instrument, in person withdrawals, telephone transfers, or electronic transfer and subject to reserve requirements as defined by the Monetary Control Act of 1980.

**TRANSACTION VALUE** For loans or extensions of credit, the amount of the loan or extension of credit. For sales, leases, purchases, and investments in or exchanges or real property, the market value of the real property interest involved. For the pooling of loans or interests in real property for resale or purchase, the amount of the loan or market value of the real property calculated with respect to each such loan or interest in real property.

**TRANSACTION VELOCITY** SEE VELOCITY OF MONEY.

**TRANSIT** The collective term used for negotiable items drawn on banks other than the collecting bank itself. The term may include clearing house items and local regional check processing center items, depending on bank preference. Transit items are generally separated from on-us items (checks written by a bank's own customers) and are submitted to the drawee bank either by direct presentment, through a local clearing house, or through a federal reserve bank or regional check processing center, and are accompanied by a transit letter which lists the number and total dollar amount of checks being sent.

**TREASURY BILL** A bill issued by the U.S. Treasury with a maturity of one year or less, yielding no interim coupon payments, only a lump sum final payment. A $10,000 one-year Treasury bill sold at a 5 percent discount, that is for $9,500 can be redeemed for $10,000 at maturity. The yield, 5.26%, is the discount ($500) divided by the purchase price ($9,500). Treasury bills are issued in minimum denominations of $10,000 and usually are issued for maturities of 13, 26 or 52 weeks. SEE ALSO TREASURY BOND.

**TREASURY BOND** Long term securities, usually with initial maturities of ten years or more, issued in minimum denominations of $1,000. Treasury bonds pay interest semiannually with principal at maturity. SEE ALSO TREASURY BILL.

**TREASURY INVESTMENT GROWTH RECEIPTS (TIGR)** SEE STRIP.

**TREASURY NOTE** Treasury securities that are coupon bearing and issued in denominations of $1,000 or more with maturities of less than ten years. They pay interest semiannually with principal at maturity.

**TRUNCATION**   The process of holding customers' checks by the customers' bank as opposed to returning the canceled checks with the account statement. Also known as "check safekeeping," this service is offered by many banks to customers who are permitted to request photocopies of individual checks when necessary, thus eliminating the need for bulky check storage. Banks which promote this service are generally motivated by the potential savings in mailing costs of monthly account statements without the added weight of canceled checks.

**TRUST**   A fiduciary relationship in which a person or corporation (the trustee) holds the legal title to property (the trust assets or corpusor estate) placed in trust by the trustor (or settler) subject to an obligation (such as a trust agreement) to keep or use the property for the benefit of another person (the beneficiary). Different common types of trusts include a BLIND TRUST, which is generally created to avoid the appearance of conflict of interest by a person whose profession or employment involves a conflict with investing and knowledge of the investment portfolio (corpus) may compromise the integrity or independence of his performance. A CHARITABLE TRUST is created for a beneficiary who is a legal charity for educational, scientific or other charitable purposes. A CLIFFORD TRUST is a short term trust with a minimum period of ten years plus one day, commonly used by a parent trustor to set aside funds for the education of his or her child beneficiary. The trust assets were thereafter returned to the trustor. During the life of the trust, and prior to the elimination of tax benefits by the Tax Reform Act of 1986, trust income tax liability was transferred to the beneficiary who was generally in a lower tax bracket than the trustor. INTER VIVOS TRUSTS are also called "living trusts" and are created during the life of the trustor. An IRREVOCABLE TRUST cannot be revoked by the trustor unless he has express approval of the beneficiary. A PASSIVE TRUST, also referred to as a "naked trust," is one in which the trustee has no active duties to perform. A REVOCABLE TRUST is one in which the trust agreement can be altered or revoked by the trustor and a REVOCABLE TRUST WITH CONSENT OR APPROVAL allows termination of the trust and reclamation of the trust assets by the trustor but only with the express consent of one or more other people. A TESTAMENTARY TRUST, or "trust under will," is established by a valid will and becomes operative only upon the death of the trustor, at which point it also becomes irrevocable.

**TRUST COMPANY**   A corporation chartered and licensed to engage in the trust business to serve both individuals and businesses in activities such as accepting and executing trusts and acting as trustee under wills as executor or guardian. Trust companies may serve as fiscal agents for corporations, state and local governments.

Trust companies may also be chartered with banking powers allowing them to accept deposits, make loans and perform other banking services. State chartered trust companies may become members of the Federal Reserve and qualify to be insured by the Federal Deposit Insurance Corporation. National banks, on the other hand, may engage, with regulatory approval, in trust activities.

**TRUST DEED**   A deed that conveys title to a third party trustee who holds title for the benefit of a lender, the beneficiary of the trust. Used in some states in lieu of a mortgage, the trustee holds legal title to the property until the underlying loan is paid in full, at which time title passes to the borrower. The trustee is entitled by law to sell the property under a "trustee's sale" in case of default by the borrower, in attempt to satisfy the debt owed to the lender beneficiary.

**TRUST DEPOSIT**   Money or property deposited and to be kept intact, not co-mingled with other funds or property and to be returned in kind to the depositor.

**TRUST FUND**   A fund which is devoted to a particular purpose and cannot be diverted, held by the trustee for a specific purpose usually defined in the terms of the trust agreement.

**TRUSTEE**   A person appointed, or otherwise required by law, to execute a trust by a power vested, under express or implied agreement, to administer the trust for the benefit of the trust beneficiary. One who holds the legal title to property for the benefit of another.

**TRUSTEE IN BANKRUPTCY**   A person in whom the property of a bankrupt is vested in trust for creditors.

**TRUTH-IN-LENDING ACT (TILA)**   An act passed by the U.S. Congress in 1969 requiring lenders to clearly disclose key terms in loan documents such as the method of computing finance charges, the conditions under which a finance charge may be imposed, and the finance charge expressed as an annual percentage rate. The purpose of the Truth-in-Lending Act (TILA) is to assure meaningful disclosure of credit terms so that consumers will be able to compare more readily the various terms available and avoid the uninformed use of credit. It is also designed to protect the consumer against inaccurate and unfair credit billing and credit card practices. SEE REGULATION Z.

The Truth-in-Lending Simplification and Reform Act was enacted on March 31, 1980, as Title VI of the Depository Institutions Deregulatory and Monetary Control Act of 1980. That legislation added new administrative enforcement provisions to the TILA and subsequently amended other provisions. The amendments were originally scheduled to take effect on April 1, 1982, but subsequent legislation changed the effective date to October 1, 1982. A completely revised Regulation Z implemented the amendments contained in the Truth-in-Lending Simplification and Reform Act. Compliance with the revised regulation became mandatory on October 1, 1982.

All consumer leasing provisions were deleted from the revised Regulation Z and transferred to Regulation M (12 CFR 213). In addition to disclosure requirements, Regulation Z imposes certain restrictions on banks by regulating (1) the form and content of advertisements for consumer credit, (2) resolution procedures for billing errors on open-end credit accounts, (3) issuance of credit cards, and (4) consumers' liability for the unauthorized use of credit cards. The regulation also provides certain rights to consumers by permitting the consumer to (1) revoke a credit transaction, with some exceptions, if the credit involves a security interest in the consumer's principal dwelling, and (2) assert against the bank as a credit card issuer claims and defenses arising out of a credit card purchase if the consumer fails to resolve a dispute satisfactorily with the person or merchant who honored the credit card. SEE ALSO CONSUMER CREDIT PROTECTION ACT AND REGULATION Z.

# *U*

**UCC-1 STATEMENT**   Also called a "financing statement," a document prescribed by the Uniform Commercial Code which, when recorded by the lender with the appropriate secretary of state or other public official, perfects a lien on certain specified non real property assets of the borrower. SEE ALSO TERMINATION STATEMENT.

**UNAUTHORIZED TRANSFER OR USE**   The use of a credit card or ATM access device by a person other than the cardholder who does not have the authority, either actual, implied or apparent, to use the card. Generally, the term "unauthorized transfer" applies to the use of a debit card (such as an ATM access device) while "unauthorized use" refers to the use of a credit card. In either case, the consumer's liability for unauthorized transfer or use is generally limited to $50, although exceptions apply.

**UNCOLLECTED FUNDS**   Negotiable instruments accepted for deposit and credited to a customer's account but not yet paid by the drawee bank and collected. The bank may impose a withdrawal restriction called a "hold" until the checks deposited have cleared. The holds that some banks place on funds deposited into their customers' accounts before the funds may be withdrawn has been a subject of growing concern in the U.S. Congress for several years. Consumers have argued that the holds placed by many banks were unnecessarily long and that depositors had a right to a prompter access to their funds. Banks responded that their availability schedules accurately reflect the time needed for the collection and return of checks dishonored by the paying bank and provide a measure of protection against the risk that the bank could not recover funds from the depositor if those funds had already been withdrawn from the depositor's account. Congress concluded that federal legislation was required to address delayed availability practices and passed the Expedited Funds Availability Act (Title VI of the Competitive Equality Banking Act enacted on August 10, 1987). The act seeks to ensure prompt availability of funds and to expedite the return of checks. The Federal Reserve Board was directed to issue regulations to implement the act, which became effective as Regulation CC on September 1, 1988. SEE ALSO REGULATION CC.

**UNCONFIRMED LETTER OF CREDIT**   A letter of credit for which credit has been established but the correspondent (advising) bank does not guarantee payment of drafts against it.

**UNEARNED DISCOUNT**   Interest received in advance of the use of funds becoming "earned" with the passage of time and seasoning of the loan.

**UNIFORM COMMERCIAL CODE**   A coordinated code of laws governing the legal aspects of business and financial transactions in the United States. It regulates such aspects as the sale of goods, commercial paper, bank deposits and collections, letters of credit, bulk transfers, and documents of title in nine separate sections called articles. The Code was drafted by the National Conference of State Law Commissioners and was adopted during the 1950s by most states and the District of Columbia. The most recent addition to the Uniform Commercial Code is Article 4A dealing with electronic payments such as wire transfers and automated clearing house credit transfers. SEE ALSO UCC-I STATEMENT.

**UNIFORM GIFTS TO MINORS ACT**   Provides for the transfer of property to minors by a designated custodian who has the legal right to act on a minor's behalf without the necessity of a guardianship. During minority, the beneficiary can be provided care and education through invasion of the principal. Upon reaching majority, the principal is vested in the beneficiary and the trust terminates.

**UNINSURED DEPOSITS**   Transaction or time accounts which exceed the maximum insured limit of $100,000 per account as established by the Federal Deposit Insurance Corporation.

**U.S. SAVINGS BOND**   A security issued by the U.S. Treasury Department which is nonnegotiable and is bought from, or sold back to, the federal government for a set price. Its principal attraction is its relative lack of risk from price changes as it is not subject to market fluctuations. Series EE, introduced at the start of 1980, replaced the highly popular Series E bonds and are sold at one half of face value in denominations of $50, $75, and up to $10,000. Series HH bonds are bought at face value, pay interest semiannually and mature in 10 years.

**UNPAID BALANCE**   The amount of a loan which is yet to be repaid.

**UNPERFECTED SECURITY INTEREST**   The failure to take the steps necessary to achieve a security interest in real or personal property. For example, a deed of trust or financing statement does not create a valid security interest until properly recorded.

**UNSECURED CREDITOR**   A claimant of unsecured money owed by a debtor who has filed a petition in bankruptcy.

**UNSECURED DEBT**   A debt instrument not backed by the pledging of assets by the issuer. Unsecured bonds are called debentures.

**UNSECURED LOAN**   Funds loaned with no pledge of collateral or with collateral which is worth less than the amount loaned. Also, a loan for which a lender does not physically control the security for the full term of the loan.

**UNSOLICITED CREDIT CARDS AND ACCESS DEVICES**   The Electronic Funds Transfer Act, as implemented by Federal Regulation E, governs the issuance of ATM access devices, including those connected with preexisting overdraft accounts. The Truth-in-Lending Act, as implemented by Federal Regulation Z, governs the issuance of combined access device credit cards. Banks may issue credit and access cards to a consumer only upon written or oral request or as a renewal or in substitution for an existing accepted card or access device. A bank may issue an unsolicited access device only when it is (1) not validated and cannot be used alone to initiate an electronic funds transfer, (2) validated only upon oral or written request from the consumer and after a verification of the consumer's identity by some reasonable means, (3) accompanied by the explanation that it is not validated and the method for disposal if the consumer does not wish to keep it, and (4) accompanied by a complete disclosure of the rights and liabilities which will apply if the access device is validated. These conditions are intended to reduce the potential for unauthorized use if the access device is lost or stolen en route to the consumer. They also ensure that the consumer is informed of account terms and conditions before deciding whether to accept the responsibilities of having an access device.

**USURY** A higher rate of interest than that allowed by the laws which stipulate the maximum rates of interest to be charged. An illegal contract for a loan or forbearance of money or goods, by which illegal interest is reserved, or agreed to be reserved, or taken. A profit greater than the lawful rate of interest, intentionally exacted as a bonus, for the forbearance of an existing indebtedness or a loan of money.

# *V*

**VALID DATE** A date before and after which a bank card is not valid. The valid date generally appears on the face of the card in embossed characters and in the magnetic stripe.

**VALUATION ALLOWANCE** An account established against a specific asset category or to recognize a specific liability, with the intent of absorbing some element of estimated loss. Such allowances are created by charges to expense in the Report of Income section of the Report of Condition (Call Report), and are netted from the asset accounts to which they relate for presentation in the Report of Condition. Provisions establishing or augmenting such allowances are to be reported as "other noninterest expense" except for the provision for loan and lease losses and the provision for allocated transfer risk for which separate, specifically designated income statement items have been established on Schedule RI, and except for the net unrealized loss on marketable equity securities for which a direct adjustment to the bank's total equity capital is made.

**VALUE** An opinion or estimate, set forth in an appraisal or evaluation, whichever may be appropriate, of the market value of real property, prepared in accordance with the agency's appraisal regulations and guidance. For loans to purchase an existing property, the term "value" means the lesser of the actual acquisition cost or the estimate of value.

**VARIABLE RATE CERTIFICATE** A savings certificate on which the interest rate varies, in consonance with the variance of some stated index, market rate, or condition.

**VARIABLE RATE MORTGAGE** A type of mortgage which permits the interest charges on the loan to rise and fall automatically in accordance with a predetermined index. Also referred to as Adjustable Rate Mortgages (ARMs), they include consumer protection against rapid escalation in borrowing costs, such as an annual cap or a lifetime cap on the interest rate.

**VAULT** The armored storage facility where bank cash is stored and safety deposit boxes are located. The vault must meet the minimum security standards set forth in Federal Reserve Regulation P.

**VAULT CASH** The cash kept in the vault to meet the day to day requirements of the bank's needs, including check cashing requirements of its customers.

**VEBA**   SEE VOLUNTARY EMPLOYEES' BENEFICIARY ASSOCIATION.

**VELOCITY OF MONEY**   The rate at which money circulates, measured by the number of times money balances turn over in the economy. Velocity measures include "transactions velocity" which refers to spending, and "income velocity" which refers to income, and is usually expressed as the ratio of gross national product to the amount of money available for spending.

**VENDOR SINGLE INTEREST INSURANCE (VSI)**   Insurance which protects the lender's security interest in a vehicle used as collateral for an installment loan. The policy is written naming the lender as the loss payee and the policy premium is generally added to the outstanding balance of the loan at the time the policy is placed.

**VERIFICATION**   An auditing process during which the auditor contacts a bank customer directly to confirm the bank's records regarding a loan or deposit balance.

**VOLUNTARY EMPLOYEES' BENEFICIARY ASSOCIATION (VEBA)**   Under section 501(c)(9), a VEBA is a tax-free trust or non-profit association which provides for payment of life, sick, accident or other benefits for members of the association or their dependents or designated beneficiaries, provided no assets (other than through payment of such benefits) inures to the benefit of a private shareholder or individual.

**VOTING TRUST**   An arrangement whereby voting stockholders assign their voting rights to a group called voting trustees.

**VOUCHER**   Any written form proving that money has been paid or received. Vouchers include canceled checks, petty cash receipts, and receipted bills.

**VOUCHER SYSTEM**   A system which involves the preparation of vouchers for transactions involving payments and the recording of those vouchers, in order of payment approval, in a voucher register.

**VSI**   SEE VENDORS SINGLE INTEREST INSURANCE.

# W

**WAGE EARNER PLAN**   The popular name for Chapter 13 of the Federal Bankruptcy Act whereby the bankrupt debtor pays over a predetermined portion of his wages to a trustee who in turn pays an agreed amount to creditors. The wage earner does not have to liquidate personal assets under such a plan and is protected from further collection activities of creditors. Creditors, on the other hand, are more reasonably assured of collecting all or a substantial portion of the debt owed.

**WAREHOUSE FINANCING**   A form of inventory financing where inventory is held in trust as collateral for the loan. As a portion of the inventory is sold, the trustee releases it to the purchaser and transmits the sale proceeds to the bank to repay the loan. The two basic types of warehouse financing are "Public Warehouse Financing" and "Field Warehouse Financing." In public warehouse financing, the goods financed are placed in a warehouse located away from the borrower's premises and are under the control of an independent third party. In field warehouse financing, a third party controls the goods in a location physically on the borrower's property.

**WAREHOUSING**   The borrowing of short term funds by a mortgage banker who collateralizes the borrowings with permanent mortgage loans until they are sold to the secondary market.

**WARRANT**   An interest bearing short term note generally issued by municipalities to pay debts and repayable from a defined source such as tax revenue.

**WILL**   The legal expression or declaration of a person's mind or wishes as to the disposition of his property, to be performed or to take effect after his death. A revocable instrument by which a person makes disposition of his property, a will is a legally enforceable declaration of a person's wishes in writing about matters to be attended to after his death. It is amendable by codicil, or revocable, up to the time of death.

**WITHDRAWAL**   The removal of funds on deposit.

**WORKING CAPITAL**   The capital available for the current operations of a business as measured by the excess of current assets over current liabilities. Often, working capital is measured as a ratio of current assets divided by current liabilities, to determine liquidity.

**WORKOUT**   A loan to accommodate the impaired cash flow or repayment capability of a distressed borrower.

**WORLD BANK**   The International Bank for Reconstruction and Development originally formed to provide long term capital to rebuild countries of Europe after World War II, the World Bank now focuses attention on impoverished Third World countries. The World Bank raises capital for lending through the sale of bonds in the capital markets of member countries and from direct contributions of member governments.

**WRAPAROUND**   A financing device that permits an existing loan to be refinanced and new money to be advanced at an interest rate between the rate charged on the old loan and the current market interest rate. The creditor combines or "wraps" the remainder of the old loan with the new loan at the intermediate rate.

**WRONGFUL DISHONOR**   The improper refusal to negotiate a check. A drawee bank has a duty to pay its customers' checks that are drawn against sufficient funds. If the bank fails to pay a properly payable check, it becomes liable to its customer for the damages caused by its wrongful dishonor. Under the Uniform Commercial Code, when a wrongful dishonor of a check occurs through a mistake, the payor bank is liable to its customer only for those damages actually sustained and clearly resulting from the wrongful dishonor. Generally, claims for speculative damages, such as embarrassment and humiliation, cannot be recovered as they cannot be measured in actual dollars.

# Y

**YANKEE CERTIFICATES OF DEPOSIT**    Negotiable certificates of deposit issued and payable in dollars to bearers in the United States (more specifically in New York) by the branch offices of major foreign banks. They are sometimes referred to as foreign-domestic CDs. The foreign issuers of Yankee CDs are well-known international banks headquartered primarily in Western Europe, England, and Japan. Investors in Yankee CDs look to the creditworthiness of the parent organization in assessing their risk, since the obligation of a branch of a foreign bank is in actuality an obligation of the parent bank. The Yankee CD market is primarily a shorter-term market; most newly issued instruments have maturities of 3 months or less.

**YEN**    The monetary unit of Japan.

**YIELD**    The annual rate of return from an investment, such as the bank's loan portfolio, expressed as a percentage. Generally, yield refers to income produced by an investment, stated as a percentage of the investment. For example, "nominal yield" is calculated from the amount invested multiplied by the interest rate paid and the maturity. "Dividend yield" equals the annual dividend per share of stock divided by the market price per share. "Yield leverage" is the return on an investment when it is sold at a price higher than that originally paid.

**YIELD CURVE**    A relationship that shows the rate of return currently available to investors in the market on debt obligations of varying maturities. Information to plot the yield curve on government securities is published every day in the *Wall Street Journal*. The yield curve for U. S. Treasury securities, comparing securities from 3 months to 30 years in maturity, is the benchmark for comparing yields of other fixed income investments. Corporate bonds, mortgage backed bonds, and asset backed bonds are described as having a yield spread, measured in basis points, over Treasury securities.

**YIELD TO MATURITY**    The rate of return calculated by dividing the total income received from an investment, plus the increments through appreciation minus the loss through amortization, by the original cost of the investment. The yield to maturity is the rate of return that the buyer of a security can expect if the security is held to full term, assuming that all interest payments are made on time and in full. The yield to maturity changes whenever the market price of the security changes.

**YUAN**    Monetary unit of the Republic of China.

# Z

**ZAIRE**    Monetary unit of Zaire.

**ZERO BALANCE ACCOUNT**   A corporate demand deposit account kept, by agreement, at a zero balance. Checks are generally paid against the account creating an overdraft which is then covered by deposit or loan funds to bring the balance in the account back to zero. The account may be a "zero balance collection account" in which collected balances are collected at the end of the business day and transferred to a "concentration account."

**ZERO COUPON SECURITIES (ZEROs)**   Interest coupons that are removed from the body of a note or bond and treated as separate securities. Each coupon calls for payment of a certain dollar amount on a specific date, while the body of the security calls for repayment of the principal amount at maturity.

The body of the stripped securities and the separate coupons are known as "zero coupons" because there are no periodic interest payments on each instrument. After stripping, each piece trades at a discount from face value. An owner benefits only from the difference between the purchase price and the payment received.

In the late 1970s some U.S. government securities were traded without one or more coupons. Sometimes the detached coupons were bought and sold separately. When a 1982 law tightened the Internal Revenue Code treatment of stripped securities, the Treasury withdrew earlier objections to coupon stripping. With the withdrawal of Treasury objections, several securities dealers created a new product to offer their customers, incorporating receipts for stripped debt securities.

In 1985, the Treasury took a more active role introducing its own coupon stripping program called STRIPS: "Separate Trading of Registered Interest and Principal of Securities." The Treasury's STRIPS program had several objectives. One was to reduce the cost of financing the public debt "by facilitating competitive private market initiatives."

Coupon stripping was historically associated with Treasury issues because of their abundant supply, absence of default risk and because there were fewer cases of securities being "called," or paid off, by the issuer before the final maturity date. By the time the Treasury began its active participation in stripping, about $45 billion of U.S. Treasury securities had been turned into zero coupon products. In addition, the market created zero coupons from other types of securities.

The value of zero coupons at any given time is determined by the market. The parts generally are sold at a deep discount from the face value on the body and from the interest payment specified on the coupons. Their value generally increases as their payment date gets closer. Since their increase in value usually is taxable in the year it occurs, zeros have become most popular for investments on which taxes can be deferred, such as Individual Retirement Accounts and for pension plans or for non-taxable accounts. However, they can be tailored to meet a wide range of portfolio objectives because of their known cash value at specific future dates.

For example, a 20 year bond with a face value of $20,000 and a 10 percent interest rate could be stripped into 41 negotiable zero coupon instruments. The main body, or principal, and each of the 40 semi-annual interest coupons becomes one zero coupon instrument. The body, of course, would be worth $20,000 face value upon maturity. The other zeros created from the semi-annual interest coupons would each be worth $1,000, or one-half the annual interest of $2,000 (10% of $20,000) on the specified payment date. Each of the 41 zero coupon instruments could be traded until its due date.

When physical securities (those in engraved certificate form) are stripped, the investor may receive one or more actual coupons or that part of the security specifying payment of the principal — depending upon the terms of his purchase.

Although the first stripped Treasury coupons appeared in the marketplace in the late 1970s, the market for securities such as these did not blossom until the 1982 tightening of the Internal Revenue Code treatment of striped securites. In August 1982, one major bond dealer began marketing receipts that evidenced ownership of Treasury zeros held by a custodian. The first of these "receipt products" were named Treasury Investment Growth Receipts, or TIGRs. Other firms entered the market with similar products, given names such as Certificates of Accrual on Treasury Securities (CATS) and Treasury Receipts (TRs).

Zeros have broadened the appeal of U.S. Government securities, the Treasury believes. And the book entry or computer record-only feature of STRIPS provides a more efficient means of transferring ownership, thus enhancing the trading of zero coupon instruments. SEE ALSO STRIP.

**ZEROs**   SEE ZERO COUPON SECURITIES.

**ZLOTY**   National currency of Poland.